T0294201

BLUEBIRD HEAVEN

BLUEBIRD HEAVEN

CARDIFF CITY'S
TEN YEARS OF UPS AND DOWNS
AND A RETURN TO THE PROMISED LAND

JAMIE KEMBLE

First published by Pitch Publishing, 2018

Pitch Publishing
A2 Yeoman Gate
Yeoman Way
Worthing
Sussex
BN13 3QZ
www.pitchpublishing.co.uk
info@pitchpublishing.co.uk

A CIP catalogue record is available for this book
from the British Library.

ISBN 978-1-78531-457-5

Typesetting and origination by Pitch Publishing

Printed and bound in GB by TJ International Ltd, Padstow, Cornwall

Contents

Acknowledgements

FIRST OF all, I have to thank Paul and Jane Camillin at Pitch Publishing for allowing me to peruse this project. They've given me a tremendous opportunity. And they've done that by taking a chance on me with this being my first book. I also have to say a big thank you to Duncan Olner who produced a brilliant front cover, Derek Hammond and everyone else at Pitch Publishing who has played a part in this book making it to the shelves.

I'd like to say a big thank you to Dominic Booth, who was kind enough to write the foreword. He also helped by providing his insight, which you will come across later in the book. Dom is brilliant at what he does, and I've had the pleasure of working alongside him for what has become a very special season. We don't work for the same publication, but we're part of the small – soon to become much bigger – number of people who cover Cardiff City week-in, week-out.

Ian Mitchelmore is another who has shared in the drama of the last 12 months and I'd also like to say thank you to Ian. He is another very talented writer who has been kind enough to lend a hand to this book.

So many people have been kind enough to lend their time to help this project by answering questions and providing insight. I'd like to say thank you to Keith Morgan, Laurence Mora, Vince Alm, Ben Price, Jordan Jones, Joshua Slack, Kevin Ellis, Callum Ellis, Thomas Griffiths and Jon Candy. I'd also like to thank Leanne Bennett and all the anonymous supporters who helped with the 'Trouble at the bridge' chapter.

A number of former players were also kind enough to offer their time and my thanks go to Andy Campbell, Gavin Rae and Steven Thompson.

I also have to extend my thanks to the media team at Cardiff City Football Club and particularly to Mark Denham, Jamie DeCruz and Sam Roberts. They've been so accommodating over the last 18 months or so, and they've made it a pleasure to cover the club. It was also great to see these people, and indeed everyone at the club, celebrating promotion in May. There have been some very testing times over the years, as you will discover over the course of this book. And the people who continued their work at the football club through such times deserve to be working in the Premier League again.

I would like to thank my family for their continued support, to my partner for putting up with the endless hours on the laptop, not only through a non-stop season, but through the process of writing this book on the back of it. To my mother, Theresa, a special thanks also, for taking the time to proof read my work.

With all the thanks aside, I'd like to express how much of a privilege it has been to cover Cardiff City, especially during the most recent promotion season. The manager, Neil Warnock, has been so brilliant to deal with, so open and honest in press conferences and at games. He's given the football club a gift of a lifetime in promotion. He has also reinstalled core values that had gone missing over the course of a previous turbulent decade.

His players, including the likes of Sol Bamba, Sean Morrison, Joe Ralls, Joe Bennett, Lee Peltier and so many more have been a pleasure to talk to during a memorable season and it was a delight to see them achieve such a happy ending to a long, hard campaign.

It's a happy ending that enabled me to write this book, adding a fitting end to a crazy decade at the football club. It's been a roller coaster; an endless stream of ups and downs, and I hope you enjoy reliving it all in this book.

Foreword

CARDIFF CITY is an infectious club with an endearing set of fans who have always demanded a hard-working team and a charismatic manager, which of course they now have. They are a hardy bunch who in the summer of 2018 basked in the most unlikely glory.

But it hasn't always been this way. The last ten years have been a roller-coaster ride for the club and its supporters. From the dark depths of a divisive colour change and the disquiet towards controversial owner Vincent Tan to the heady days under Neil Warnock. Throw in Dave Jones, Malky Mackay, cup finals, play-off heartbreak. They've seen it all down here.

I arrived in the city of Cardiff as a university student in September 2011 with the Mackay era just getting revved up. I started covering the Bluebirds as a journalist for Media Wales in September 2016 as the Warnock era was about to set sail. In between I'd always had a passing interest in the club (as a wannabe sports journalist) but it was covering the 2017/18 season that I was truly captivated by Cardiff City and of course by Warnock, the architect of this sensational return to the Premier League.

I met the author of this book, Jamie Kemble, at weekly press conferences and matches. And we rode the wave together in many ways, lapping up the media-friendly soundbites that Warnock would offer at the Vale Hotel on a Friday morning and then waiting patiently in the bowels of Cardiff City Stadium with a cup of tea and a pie as the 3pm Saturday kick-off approached. What unfolded before our eyes that season was not just the culmination of Warnock's incredible work in the dressing room, nor the masterful coaching of Kevin Blackwell and Ronnie Jepson on the training ground. It was not just the personality of Sol Bamba, the resilience of Sean Morrison, the pace of Nathaniel Mendez-Laing, the trickery of Junior Hoilett.

It was an entire fanbase reawakening. A promotion clad in their true blue colours secured by a figure, in Warnock, so universally loved and admired that it felt like those awful intervening years had never happened. It marked the end of an astonishing decade at Cardiff City, which this book superbly chronicles.

Jamie combines the fine eye for detail of a journalist who has been at the heart of the matter, with the passion and knowledge of a lifelong Cardiff supporter. The result is this compelling read, which is a must for any 21st-century Bluebird.

Dominic Booth, WalesOnline digital sports writer

The start of something new

WE BEGIN our journey a decade ago, as the light finally begins to shine on the turbulent yet seldom dull life of Cardiff City following years of mediocrity and disappointment in the lower leagues. It's the Bluebirds' fifth season in the Championship following a stunning hometown play-off final win at the Millennium Stadium in 2003. Andy Campbell's extra-time winner may have felt like a giant springboard for the club at the time, but four difficult mid-table-at-best seasons have already dampened any hopes of putting together a surge through the English football pyramid.

However, this season would be the next springboard for Cardiff City and an ambitious manager in Dave Jones would discover that his work at the club could inspire a whole city to rediscover the optimism and ambition which had deserted them once again following dormant seasons in the second tier. It's not as if Cardiff fans were standing up and protesting about the lack of success in the Championship – there was no need – this was almost a treat given the years in the lower divisions that had preceded, and a decent season prior to the upcoming 2007/08 campaign kept supporters feeling content.

The 2006/07 season started incredibly, with Cardiff winning nine of their first 12 and striker Michael Chopra becoming the name on everyone's lips. But a wretched December would send hopes crashing, not for the first time in this tale, and another mid-table finish ensued. That opening few months was important, though, because you could say it whet Dave Jones's appetite.

The former Wolves boss is heading into his third season in charge for the 2007/08 campaign, and having been successful in the past with Wolves and Southampton, one can only imagine how difficult it must have been to rock up in the Welsh capital in the falling-down stadium that was Ninian Park and then being instructed to work on, well I would say a budget, but I'm not sure there was one. Still, undeterred, that small vision of success born of the shrewd signing of Chopra the previous season perhaps made him realise that he could achieve more with the club than many realised, even without a budget to support his vision.

Chopra enjoyed a good pre-season after scoring 22 league goals during the campaign before, but he would say goodbye to Cardiff for now as he returned to the north-east to sign for Sunderland for a whopping £5m – a big figure in those days, believe it or not, especially for a player leaving a Championship club.

Chopra supported Newcastle United as a boy and even graduated from the Magpies' academy. But with newly promoted rivals Sunderland, he was given another crack at the Premier League and as an ambitious young striker, it's not something he, nor Cardiff – who desperately needed the money – were about to turn down.

Why did Cardiff need the money? Well the Bluebirds rarely enjoyed the financial limelight following years in the lower leagues, but when the club appointed former Leeds United chairman Peter Ridsdale following Sam Hammam's stepping down, the club was reportedly £35m in debt and losing a further £10m each year; troubled waters indeed. Not least as Hammam-owned Langston, a major financial backer of the club, announced just after the first game that they would begin legal proceedings against the club over a £30m loan that hadn't been repaid.

We'll come back to the finances, but the short story was that Jones didn't have a pot to pee in as far as his budget for the 2007/08 season was concerned. The sale of Chopra helped things, because he could now reinvest some of that money, especially as the Langston court news hadn't arisen by the time he began scouring the market in pre-season.

And this is where Jones thrived: his decision making in the transfer market often left others in admiration and very few could understand how on earth he convinced players to sign for a club like Cardiff, who were seemingly going nowhere.

That confusion was to be even greater when former superstars of the game began to rain down on Ninian Park during pre-season in 2007/08. Former Liverpool striker Robbie Fowler joined the Bluebirds on a free transfer in July and the signing of the famed English goalscorer immediately gave the whole of the city a lift as media attention doubled, while the season-ticket sales must have, too.

And if that shock deal wasn't enough, former Chelsea star Jimmy Floyd Hasselbaink signed up in the August on another free and suddenly Cardiff possessed strikers who shared a mind-blowing 383 league goals between them from throughout their career. Yes, they were in their later years, but do you think the fans, who had grown used to seeing bottom-half Championship and League 1 players, with the exception of Chopra, really cared about their creaky knees? Absolutely not!

There was still magic in those old boots and the excitement around Ninian Park ahead of the season was something many hadn't experienced for years. It was fantastic to see the spotlight being shone on the club once again. Even former Manchester City winger Trevor Sinclair was added to the list of signings, and the Bluebirds' faithful began to lick their lips once more. There was an incredible air of excitement around the club and for the first time in a long while, there was a genuine feeling that something was lifting off, that City was going somewhere.

Yes, there were whispers of promotion during the good start to the previous season, and yes, there was excitement, but it didn't feel all that sustainable, and fans quickly saw first-hand that it wasn't. Why was this different? It's only signing a few high-profile players after all, isn't it? Well not quite, as the club had already announced the building of a brand-new stadium by this point, just across the road on the old Leckwith athletics ground, and that signified the building of the future of Cardiff City in many ways. In 2017 it doesn't feel like that big of a thing, perhaps because almost every Championship and Premier League club has a stadium they can be proud of.

The stadiums built in the last 25 years, or radically improved in that time frame, largely outnumber the old grounds like Brentford's Griffin Park, for example, but back in 2007, a new stadium was huge, especially for Cardiff, whose finances were all over the shop.

City fans loved Ninian Park like you wouldn't believe, it simply can't be put into words how special the atmosphere was at that old cathedral, but even back in 2007, it was widely recognised that if Cardiff wanted to keep up with their rivals they had to dream a little bigger, and a new stadium would symbolise that. While no one could quite understand how the stadium was being paid for at the time, the finances behind the new signings were a little easier to understand.

Dave Jones received £5m for his star striker during the pre-season and he opted not to spend a penny of it on transfer fees for the whole of the upcoming campaign. Instead, it would be put into wages to sign experienced players who had larger wages compared to the players already at the club.

It was bold and injuries were a concern, especially for Fowler and Sinclair, two players who had spent their fair share of time in the treatment room, but Jones had a tendency to take these risks and to be fair to him, when they backfired, he also dealt with it very well. Not everyone appreciated Jones, but his ambition for the club to achieve a little more than mid-table obscurity would set the tone for a football club and indeed a city whose passion wasn't matched by their local club's achievements on the football field.

Bluebirds flying high

IN TRUE Cardiff City fashion, the optimism surrounding the league season died out as quickly as it had grown. Two wins in the opening nine games already gave Cardiff a lot to do and form didn't get a lot better. The Bluebirds were painfully inconsistent; in fact, they didn't put successive wins together until December, and that tells a tale in itself. So it didn't go to plan in the league, not as Dave Jones, who had assembled an mini army of star veterans, had hoped.

But a silver lining was cast Cardiff's way in the form of the FA Cup. The competition the Bluebirds won in 1927 – those four numbers are probably the combination to most supporters' credit cards to this day too. They're still immensely proud of winning the famous competition, even though 99 per cent of them weren't alive to see it. It's a competition special to every football fan in the English leagues, or at least it should be. It provides, at the very least, a welcome distraction to league football. A competition where anything can happen and indeed, anything does happen, as City would find out.

Saturday 5 January is where it all started, in the FA Cup third round with a trip to Chasetown, who were playing in the eighth tier of English football at the time, and some occasion it was. The Bluebirds ran out 3-1 winners with young Aaron Ramsey scoring his first senior goal in front of just under 2,500 spectators. An expected result, but it was much more than that, with Cardiff City fans forging a friendship with their lower league opponents which would continue for many years to come and that, perhaps, is the true magic of the FA Cup.

With the third round out of the way, City received another favourable draw for the fourth – they were pitched against League 2 club Hereford United. A short trip across the border to a side who would end the season with promotion to League 1, but who would end this day with defeat to their Championship superiors. It finished 2-1 and produced a rare goal for Kevin McNaughton, a club legend defender who would only ever score two City goals, and this fine long-distance strike was the most memorable.

However, the main story was that Cardiff were in the hat again, this time for the fifth round, and belief started to take over when fellow Championship club Wolves came out of the hat for a clash at Ninian Park. The draw was kind and Cardiff didn't waste their opportunity. Jimmy Floyd Hasselbaink curled in an iconic strike to put them ahead and Peter Whittingham made sure his team progressed once more. Very quickly, the Bluebirds found themselves in the quarter-final.

The cup run seemed to take hold so quickly at the time, it was rather strange. Former Bluebirds midfielder Gavin Rae recalls, 'We got off to a terrible start away to Chasetown when Kev [McNaughton] scored an own goal – then Whitts [Whittingham] and Rambo [Ramsey] got us through. Then it just sort of snowballed and we hit good form in the cup games. We got a good draw with Barnsley having put out Liverpool and Chelsea, then we got them out. It worked out well.'

The draw certainly helped, of course, but the belief was high among supporters after the win over Wolves. As a football fan, that sense of something special arrives and it's difficult to describe or indeed shake off. Sometimes you just know – and the City faithful seemed to know. They were right, too, as they travelled in their thousands to Premier League Middlesbrough in anticipation of securing a spot at Wembley.

The new Wembley stadium saw a change in format in the FA Cup and this was the first season that it would come into force. Semi-finals were now going to be played at the final venue, unlike previous years when the likes of Hillsborough or Villa Park hosted the penultimate stages. The decision from the FA sparked lots of opposition, but you wouldn't have found many complaints in South Wales.

The change meant the Bluebirds were just one win away from an appearance at the shiny new Wembley, completed less than a year earlier, and they believed they could do it, even against top-flight opposition managed by Gareth Southgate, who would become England boss a decade later.

There were over 32,000 in attendance to see this one but it was the away fans who were sent into pandemonium instead of the expectant Teessiders. Whittingham lit up the Riverside by tiptoeing his way through a crowd of bodies in the box before curling a fine strike into the top corner of the red-and-white striped net. And it got even better when defender Roger Johnson found the net with a diving header to all but seal Cardiff's place in the national stadium.

It was a historic win, and it felt like one throughout South Wales. Middlesbrough were a solid Premier League team at the time and they had won the League Cup in 2004. They had a nice new ground, it was full, and they felt like a massive club compared to Cardiff, and yet, still, Dave Jones and his men seemed to make relatively easy work of them in their now symbolic black kit. This was a day that would become etched in the memory of City fans, a giantkilling of sorts, but it was the special atmosphere created by thousands of fans who had made the mammoth trek to Teesside to back their team. The players celebrated on the pitch and the fans in the stand followed suit. 'We're going to Wembley', the flags and T-shirts read, and that, in itself, would take some getting over. This was a miracle.

The black kit became something of a lucky charm, just like the black cat, Trixie, during the Bluebirds' FA Cup win in 1927. The team wore black at Boro despite being able to wear blue, and it was quickly adopted as the lucky kit. They even wore it in the semi-final but before that even came around, while fans were jumping up and down in the away end at the Riverside, those at home were already plotting their travels to Wembley and pondering how they could get their hands on a precious ticket.

Cardiff received another favourable draw for the last four in the form of fellow Championship club Barnsley, although the Tykes had managed to beat Liverpool and Chelsea on their route to the semi and they too were pleased to avoid Premier League club Portsmouth and Championship leaders West Brom in the penultimate stage.

Having said that, they were still up against it. Barnsley were battling relegation and Cardiff were still fancying themselves for a late run towards the play-offs. But the FA Cup was now the very clear objective for both teams who sensed they possessed a once-in-a-lifetime opportunity, just like the supporters did, and that's what created such a huge clamour for tickets in South Wales.

People who hadn't even been to a game all season were in the market, sensing their chance to get to Wembley and rivalling others, who had supported the club for so long, and that's just the way it is in such games. Season ticket holders got theirs but that left many more without. Season ticket holders weren't quite so common back then. Cardiff certainly didn't have the 14,000 or so they have in the modern day, and walk-ups or ticket collections were relied upon more to bump up attendances. So for those without season tickets, it was a case of attending a midweek league game against Hull City. You had to possess a ticket stub from that night to be in with a chance and predictably there was a spike in the attendance as more than 17,000 turned up to see a 1-0 win thanks to Steve McPhail's stunning strike from outside the box.

However, many actually missed the goal. The demand for tickets was unprecedented for a midweek game and many were left queuing outside to collect their tickets while listening to the roar from inside the ground – it was the only goal of the game, too! But it wasn't about the game on this occasion, just like it wasn't really about the league competition for Cardiff anymore. It was about the FA Cup run for the players, the fans and probably even the manager.

The excitement surrounding the semi-final was huge in South Wales and it was intensified because not only did the club take around 33,000 fans to London, but each one of them believed that they would be returning for the final in a month's time. That belief remained and again it was helped by the draw. The Bluebirds' faithful weren't over confident, as Barnsley had earned even more credit for getting to this stage after their tricky run of ties while still managing to pull through. But Cardiff were the better team on paper, despite drawing 1-1 with Barnsley in the league.

And so it proved to be. There were 82,752 in attendance to watch the all-Championship FA Cup semi-final and to appreciate the magic of the FA Cup, which could be strongly felt with the draw guaranteeing at least one second-tier team in the final. In fact, three of the four semi-finalists were from the Championship. That's not something you see often.

Wembley was painted blue, with supporters from South Wales outweighing those from South Yorkshire, and it took just nine minutes for the Welsh side to send their fans wild. A trademark long throw into the box from Tony Capaldi found its way to Joe Ledley, and the born-and-bred Cardiff boy found the top corner with a stunning volley, despite having to lift his leg as high as his head to make contact, and he drifted off towards the corner doing his trademark celebration with his palms pointing simultaneously out to his side. A special moment for all connected with Cardiff City, and one that will go down in folklore, for sure. A strange occurrence, too. In 2008, Cardiff hadn't won the FA Cup for 81 years, and the goal arrived with 81 minutes remaining. Each one of those minutes passed by slowly, too.

The Bluebirds controlled things well, with the exception of the 67th minute. Kayode Odejayi was sent clean through and the stadium went silent. Everyone present, even the Barnsley fans, couldn't bear to even squeak as they watched on in expectation of a goal. Even Cardiff's supporters were resigned to an equaliser as their defenders hopelessly chased back. Perhaps it was the pressure, or even the lucky black kit, but somehow, the striker slotted it wide and on to the side-netting. A cruel blow for Barnsley, who knew there and then that they had missed their big chance and that it wasn't going to be their day. By contrast, Cardiff, at that moment, probably knew luck was on their side and it became a day of joy, one of celebration.

There's a fantastic clip of a section of Cardiff fans in Wembley all doing the famous 'Ayatollah', smiling, in celebratory mood as a 'do the Ayatollah everyone' chant echoed around the impressive stadium. This was City's moment in the limelight after years of struggle and everyone wanted to make the most of it. The celebrations continued until the final whistle and way beyond. The players celebrated on the pitch afterwards, waving flags. Match-winner Ledley raced around the pitch with a Welsh flag draped over his shoulders and the players created a special image, sliding towards the supporters while linking hands. It was iconic and it was a moment the city and the football club deserved. One they knew they would treasure forever, long after the final, whatever happened there, and long after it all died down. But it wasn't going to die down yet.

The Bluebirds had upset the odds to reach the final, but it wasn't all by chance or by luck. They possessed this tremendous team spirit and anyone in football will tell you that having a good dressing room is half or even two thirds of the battle. Gavin Rae says of that special team spirit and how it helped the Bluebirds to achieve something special, 'We had a great team atmosphere in that season, the cup run certainly helped that too. The camaraderie and characters we had made for a great team spirit and I loved that season, my first outside Scotland.'

Another player who was a huge part of the dressing room was striker Steven Thompson, whose iconic words ahead of the final are now brandished in the club shop. The Scotsman played a big part in the camaraderie around the club and he also remembers a special atmosphere among the players during the cup run. He reveals, 'The changing room was brilliant that year. We had big characters and superstar players like Robbie Fowler, Jimmy Floyd Hasselbaink and Trevor Sinclair. It was almost surreal. We all enjoyed a night out as well so we became good friends. I remember coming back from Wembley after the semi and we stopped the bus to get a carry out, and after a few beers, Roger Johnson decided to see if he could fit in the overhead luggage on the bus. He managed it as he's so skinny, but then was stuck!'

Back to the football, with another clamour for tickets ensuing, and this time it was even more difficult for supporters. The task this time was to buy a season ticket. That saw hundreds and even thousands of fans, even just neutrals, buying them to get their hands on a final ticket, but many couldn't afford the luxury. These weren't easy times financially around Wales and over £300 was a lot of money to lay out.

Thousands of Cardiff supporters were left without tickets and it left a bitterness in their mouth with so many neutrals seizing the opportunity through having the luxury of being able to buy a season ticket. Still, some were lucky enough to get their hands on some through other avenues. There was a general sale window but tickets flew off the shelf quicker than milk on a snow day in the UK. Everyone from South Wales and around the country knew this was probably a once-in-a-lifetime opportunity to watch Cardiff City at Wembley in the FA Cup Final and that it was something special. It hadn't happened since 1927, and that tells you that you're not likely to see it again for as long as you'll live. This was a Championship team with an average attendance of 13,900 reaching the final of a country-wide competition which includes the likes of Manchester United, Liverpool and Chelsea, and you had to see it to believe it.

Portsmouth were the opponents, the second Premier League club Cardiff would meet during their run, and they would provide a stern test, too. They had secured a top-eight finish under Harry Redknapp, at his peak, and it was the side many associate him directly with to this day. The likes of Hermann Hreidarsson, David James, Lassana Diarra, Glen Johnson, David Nugent, Sulley Muntari, Niko Kranjcar, Sol Campbell, Pedro Mendes and Nwankwo Kanu. England international Jermain Defoe had signed during the season, too, but Cardiff thanked their lucky stars that he was cup-tied.

Nevertheless, this was going to be a big test for the Bluebirds, who had just finished mid-table in the Championship following a disappointing league season, but it didn't dampen their spirit. That's what the FA Cup is all about, after all, the underdog believing in themselves, and in this case, they had reason to. They had got to the final just as Portsmouth had and in 90 minutes in a one-off game, anything can happen.

The supporters, even had two songs for the final. One was by Cardiff fan and singer James Fox, who wrote a catchy 'Bluebirds Flying High' track. And there was a much lighter effort from fans called 'Do the Ayatollah', which took the comedy approach. Though, they were both fine efforts in their own respects and it just encapsulated the excitement surrounding the club at the time. Even striker Steven Thompson had a go with his guitar during the player awards two weeks before the final.

The spotlight was firmly on once again and Dave Jones probably didn't enjoy that as much as other managers would. He'd had a hard time in the past with journalists and he wasn't too kind to them; he wasn't even a fan of the local media in South Wales. He liked to stay out of the public eye and he liked his players to do the same, but his relaxed approach with his players would catch up with him later on.

When the players arrived at their hotel in London, the approach they took to avoid the media was clear. Each one stepped off the bus on a phone call, or pretending to be on one, which is a standard trick in trying to avoid being asked questions. Fans got their opportunity to meet the players but while the television cameras filmed their arrival, it was a case of avoiding conversation with them at all costs for the team. Their attention had to be on the game, and there was no room for distractions. Supporters, funnily enough, took the same approach – no distractions. Work didn't matter, nothing mattered but the cup final in the lead-up to it and that, beyond anything, encapsulates what the FA Cup is all about. It may be lost on big clubs, it may become just another trophy, but not for others and certainly not for Cardiff City in 2008.

Wembley was a sea of blue, mixed with the free black and yellow flags given to supporters on 17 May 2008. You had to see it to believe it as Cardiff City and Portsmouth filled the stands with a record crowd for the new stadium of 89,874, which remains at the time of writing in 2018 the highest attendance for a football match there.

Cardiff volunteered to play in their 'lucky' black, allowing Portsmouth to play in their traditional blue, but the majority of the Welsh supporters wore the traditional colours too, so it made for an unbelievable sight. It was quite the occasion and many from South Wales were reduced to tears as the Welsh national anthem sounded around Wembley. Welsh singer Katherine Jenkins sung it, battling with the yet-to-be-perfected Wembley PA system, and she also did a duet of the traditional FA Cup song 'Abide With Me' with Lesley Garrett, who had sung the English national anthem.

It was a proud moment for Cardiff City, a sight they thought they'd never see, and there was a real sense of that inside the stadium. Whether Cardiff, who hadn't won it since 1927, or Portsmouth, who hadn't won it since 1939, went home with the trophy, no one could deprive either side of the pride they felt in their team during the moments leading up to kick-off. Hearing 'Abide With Me', which was introduced for the first time the year Cardiff won the competition, and then the Welsh anthem, which invoked that sense of pride in being Welsh, of being a people who are always willing to upset the odds, to punch above their weight, was emotional.

The game itself wasn't one for the neutrals; an incredibly tight affair which was ultimately decided by a goal from veteran striker Nwanku Kanu eight minutes before half-time. Cardiff keeper Peter Enckelman parried a low cross into the Nigerian's path and he made no mistake.

There was some controversy when Glenn Loovens was denied a goal having found the net. The ball hit his armpit and a handball decision was given. It was one you could argue either way but Cardiff fans, of course, felt a little hard done by. Portsmouth ground out the win and the afternoon ended in disappointment for Cardiff, who had come so close to making history, but perhaps they had anyway. They missed out on the £1m prize money, they missed out on European qualification but beyond all that, the supporters were still immensely proud of their team and it was clear even after the defeat that the feeling of pride remained.

Lifelong Bluebirds fan Kevin Ellis says, 'Personally I enjoyed the semi-final more as it was my first time at the new Wembley having previously visited the grand old ground for an England v Wales game in the late '70s in what was known as the Home Nations tournament. What stood out for me in the final was the tremendous party atmosphere generated by both sets of fans, and in particular the colours, painted faces, banners, flags, hats and scarves and of course the walk down Wembley Way.

'It was very surreal seeing the team you've supported since 1970 playing in the FA Cup Final when one remembers all the great teams to have graced these occasions. Thoughts went back to the old Fourth and Third Division days when we struggled and our attendances were very poor, but you only truly appreciate the good times when you have experienced the bad. It was something that the true fans of the clubs involved will never forget and it was a memorable day.'

It was a missed opportunity and you always feel that after losing in the final, but this team had no right to be in a final with

Portsmouth. Not given the size of the club, the size of the budget or the level of the team. However, they had proved everyone wrong to become the talking point of the nation. It would put City back on the map and whet the appetite for more success.

Not that supporters were able to see that amid the depths of disappointment felt after the final and among the raw emotions you feel after such a setback. Striker Steven Thompson reflects on the final after coming on as a substitute. He adds, 'I still can't believe I've played in an FA Cup Final. We had belief after the Middlesbrough game and got a decent draw in the semi. I was convinced we'd win the final but it wasn't to be. The Pompey team, on paper, was frightening. It's definitely one of the best moments of my career and something I'm proud to have been part of.'

Gavin Rae also played in the final and, similarly, he reflects on the occasion with nothing but pride. He says, 'The final itself was a massive occasion and probably only one of a handful of games that I got a little nervous about before the game. Just understanding the magnitude of it really. It was awesome to play at Wembley in the semi and final of course. I had all my family down and the reception afterwards was a good night – although a little bittersweet as we never managed to win the cup. But for my family to be mixing it with Jimmy Floyd and Robbie Fowler etc. – They are good memories.'

The Bluebirds' faithful have been hardened by failure, they are used to disappointment like so many other football fans of teams outside the top four in the Premier League, and it would serve them well on this day as well as days to come in the next few years.

After the final, Dave Jones revealed his disappointment: 'You've got to let us wallow in our self-pity. I've just lost a cup final. Being a Championship club doesn't soften the blow. I wanted to win.'

That probably summed up the feeling among fans, too. Yes, Cardiff were the underdogs, but they also believed they could do it and how close they pushed Portsmouth shows you that on another day, they might have. But there was to be no FA Cup gold, and that would create regret given the opportunity of being in the final, although progress had to be made from this pivotal moment in time.

Youngster Aaron Ramsey signified that, in many ways. His presence suggested that there was a future beyond the cup final and after that initial feeling of disappointment, it was quickly realised by those in the club, as well as the fans, that this achievement of reaching the final had to be built upon. Going backwards from here simply wasn't an option.

Back to reality

THE 2008/09 season was to be Cardiff's final one at Ninian Park, a special stadium that the Bluebirds called home for 99 years before its gates were closed for good in 2009. This meant that regardless of what the club achieved, it was going to be a tough season for supporters, and it proved to be just that.

Cardiff were busy in the summer after their FA Cup heartbreak and in a sense their activity was forced, with Aaron Ramsey, the brightest talent to come through the club's academy for years, leaving for Premier League giants Arsenal for just under £5m. Popular defender Glenn Loovens was also snapped up by Celtic for £2.5m. Players like Jimmy Floyd Hasselbaink and Trevor Sinclair retired and Robbie Fowler also moved on, freeing up some funds for Dave Jones to reinvest.

And invest he did, in wages at least. Jones again saw the money from the transfer fees plunged into keeping the club afloat and he was left with very little. That didn't stop him from working wonders, though. Jay Bothroyd, who would have a big say in years to come, arrived for just over £300,000 from Wolves, Gabor Gyepes signed for £200,000 from Northampton Town and Ross McCormack, a player who would go on to cost Aston Villa £12m in the future, was snapped up from Motherwell for just £120,000. There were a few other free signings, too, with experienced defender Mark Kennedy coming in, as well as Tom Heaton and Eddie Johnson on loan.

The signs were good for Cardiff. Things seemed a bit more relaxed after the whirlwind that was the FA Cup Final, and the pre-season went well. The Bluebirds emerged victorious in the Algarve Cup, which saw them beat Vitoria and Scottish champions Celtic.

Pre-season usually means very little but the outlook was positive and fans were happy. Quite frankly, they couldn't be anything else having seen their team reach the FA Cup Final, and there was a hope, particularly in this season that the club would achieve something in the league. The cup dreams had been fulfilled – albeit the run didn't end with glory – and after a disappointing league campaign in the year previous, there was a sense that it was now time to knuckle down in the league. And anything else was a distraction, especially as fans wanted a good send-off for Ninian Park.

The opening day came around as quickly as it always does and it offered up a home clash with Southampton in the worst conditions imaginable for an August fixture. It absolutely belted down with rain from the first minute to the 90th, and suddenly a fully enclosed stadium didn't sound so bad. Fans were kept warm when Cardiff shook off the disappointment of conceding an equaliser by scoring a winner in the final knockings of the game – Roger Johnson with the dramatic goal, followed by a bizarre penguin celebration. It was a fine start to the season, even if a severe strain was placed upon the towel industry in South Wales that day.

Cardiff then went on an unbeaten run but drew their next four games, and after a win and another draw, they tasted their first league defeat of the season when Birmingham left Ninian Park with a 2-1 success. Quincy Owusu-Abeyie scored the winner, and he would actually end the season on loan with the Bluebirds.

But before that defeat came a bitter moment for Bluebirds fans. Swansea City had returned to the second tier ahead of this season after finally navigating their way out of League 1, but like the proverbial London bus, after such a long wait, two South Wales derbies arrived at once with the two teams being drawn together in the League Cup third round. It was a big spectacle at the Liberty Stadium, broadcast on television, but it didn't really live up to the billing and was a poor game by all accounts until Jordi Gomez scored with a deflected free kick to claim the first bragging rights of the season. And as that ball hit the back of the net, thousands of Bluebird hearts hit the floor. Swansea, the inferior rivals for so many years, had claimed a scalp over Cardiff in their first season back in the division and knocked the Bluebirds out of the cup. It felt like a disaster.

Cardiff would have to live with it, though, at least until the two teams met in the league. And they coped well by going on an unbeaten run of over a month after that Birmingham defeat. Then, after three losses in four games, they put together their best run of the season, not losing in 13 matches from the end of November to the end of February. That sequence included an entertaining 2-2 league draw at the Liberty Stadium against Swansea. The bragging rights hadn't been reclaimed but at least it wasn't another defeat and it was the league derby that really mattered, claimed Cardiff fans, of course.

The fantastic run either side of the derby was aided by some winter signings and the most exciting of the bunch for the Bluebirds faithful was the return of Michael Chopra, who joined on loan just one year after his big-money move to Sunderland. Chopra initially signed for a short-term move but he would extend his move until the end of the season. Scotsman Chris Burke, who was previously a hit with Rangers fans, also joined on a free transfer and he would have a big say in years to come, too. Everything started to look up and a play-off spot, with the acquisition of these players, seemed inevitable, especially with the fantastic run the Bluebirds were now on.

One gut-wrenching result must be mentioned; the Boxing Day visit to Reading, because it's, perhaps, the most Cardiff City-like game of football you'll ever see or hear about. It was a very tight affair, and expectedly so with Reading targeting promotion, but Cardiff took the lead in front of a huge away following thanks to Chopra's goal just one minute from time.

Only Cardiff could blow it away from here – and they did, in the most ridiculous way possible. Eight minutes into stoppage time, Reading goalkeeper Adam Federici – usually their number two – went up for a corner and miraculously, the ball landed at his feet. The Australian absolutely smashed it home from close range and Reading equalised. There are many moments that may have impacted how this season would end for Cardiff but that, given the circumstances, had to be one.

With the Madejski madness in the rear-view mirror, Cardiff got back on the bike and continued to pedal towards the play-offs, and in April came another obstacle. It was time for another mouth-watering South Wales derby, the third of the season. It was the last at Ninian Park and that made it even more special and poignant for supporters who had witnessed so many down the years. It also made it a must-not-lose, especially with Cardiff looking good for a play-off spot and Swansea heading into it knowing it was their last chance to put a run together to have any chance of reaching the top six, though even then it seemed a little unlikely.

It was a feisty affair with a packed-out ground, a superb atmosphere and nice weather just to top things off. And, not only was it to be the final derby at Ninian Park, it was also the last in an 'old' ground of any sort with Swansea in the new Liberty Stadium having moved out of the Vetch Field a few years previous.

Over 20,000 watched on as Swansea took a surprise lead through Nathan Dyer, and that's how the score stayed until nine minutes after the break when Chopra turned home Bothroyd's cross to cue a deafening roar.

Swansea then took the lead on the 88th minute through teenager Joe Allen – some player he would turn out to be – leaving the stadium stunned before referee Mike Dean, who was earlier hit in the head by a coin that was probably thrown by Cardiff fans, awarded a penalty to the hosts in controversial circumstances. Ashley Williams gently nudged Ross McCormack to win the ball but the Scotsman's dramatic fall to the ground was enough to convince Dean to give a spot kick. It was an opportunity to snatch something from the jaws of defeat and McCormack obliged, blazing the penalty down the middle to spark scenes of delirium at Ninian Park for the final time in a South Wales derby. It wasn't going to be a win, but Cardiff would have the final say at their beloved stadium, and that was a fitting tribute in the final derby day edition at the ground.

Speaking of McCormack, it would be an injustice if he wasn't talked about in a little more detail. He provided Cardiff fans with real hope during the 2008/09 season and he was the first real quality forward – who wasn't a veteran – to play for the club since the departure of Michael Chopra. He brought pace, strength and a wonderful technique every time he played. And he provided more than a few special moments across the course of the season. In fact, he managed an impressive 21 goals in his first year in English football, only Wolves star Sylvan Ebanks-Blake eclipsing him with 25. Many of McCormack's goals were penalties, but he scored a fair few from open play, too, and his ability to dispatch free kicks lit up Ninian Park. He was quite the signing, 21 goals for just over £100,000. It wouldn't be going too far to say he made the difference in what could have been another average season for the Bluebirds and for that, he gets a special mention.

After the Swansea draw, Cardiff did manage to put together a solid run of form which left them in a position where they only needed two points from their last four games to secure a play-off spot. First up were Preston, and Cardiff began their quest to earn the necessary points in the worst possible fashion, losing 6-0 at Deepdale, a scoreline that would cost them dearly. The Bluebirds then managed a 2-2 draw at Charlton before being thrashed by Ipswich Town in the final game at Ninian Park.

That defeat was to provide a sad end for the stadium, at least in terms of its last fixture, which many believed it wouldn't be with the prospect of there being a play-off semi-final still to host. Fan Jon Candy recalls, 'The actual final game at Ninian Park against Ipswich was never going to be our final game, as of course we had the play-offs to look forward to, so the final game had gone before I knew it.'

The defeat against Ipswich meant Cardiff went into the last game of the season, away to Sheffield Wednesday, knowing they needed a point, but weighed down by the dip in form that could potentially cost them a top-six spot. The Owls didn't make it easy at Hillsborough, showing scores from the other games to put pressure on Cardiff – something many fans will never forgive – and it paid off for the home side. Jermaine Johnson scored the killer goal after 71 minutes and Cardiff couldn't find a reply.

Preston won their final match 2-1, and it left them and Cardiff on exactly the same points and exactly the same goal difference, but the Welsh side would miss out by a hair with the Lilywhites having scored one more goal. Now how costly that 6-0 defeat to Preston was, or perhaps not holding out at Reading. But there were so many other moments that ended up defining the season, perhaps even a refereeing disaster from Paul Taylor which saw Cardiff have two men sent off at home to Sheffield United. If you ask Cardiff fans, they would probably tell you that the moment they look back on as the biggest turning point was McCormack's missed penalty at Preston, but the player certainly couldn't be blamed given all the goals he'd given his team across the season. He was perhaps the biggest reason why Cardiff were even in that lofty position.

Dave Jones provided his assessment on why the Bluebirds missed out following that final-day defeat, telling BBC Sport, 'Ability-wise, running, strength, pace, it's all there, but maybe we just lacked that mental strength to see it through. I thought the team was good enough. It proved it wasn't. We'll all look at ourselves, but I thought this squad was good enough to go up, not in the play-offs but automatically. But the table doesn't lie. We had a fantastic record until four games ago and we'll all take responsibility.'

The finger of blame was pointed here, there and everywhere but the fact was that Cardiff did miss out on the top six and indeed in cruel fashion, just one goal. But it was enough, and such is football, it moves on and you have to accept it. But it was difficult for supporters. Two seasons in a row their hopes had been built up through the hope of achieving something special, and twice they were left heartbroken.

Football can be a cruel mistress and Cardiff fans knew that more than most, but they would have to get used to it. And the disappointment, getting over it and learning to move on, would serve them well in years to come.

This sounds like something from a soap opera or a love drama, but this is Cardiff City, this is just how it is. Only they could make a mess of this, needing so little to make the play-offs and still coming up short. It was a sad end to the Ninian Park era and there lingered a real sense of not doing the venue justice in its final season. Of all the years to disappoint, this shouldn't have been one of them, but it was, and only time could heal the wound that failure to reach the play-offs had caused.

Farewell Ninian Park – the end of an era

THEY SAY time is a great healer, but even time can't fill the void that remains in many a Cardiff City fan's heart left by Ninian Park. Most weren't alive to see the day when City moved into the Sloper Road-based venue in 1910, after Lord Ninian Crichton-Stuart provided the financial support needed for the club to land their first real stadium. Around 7,000 people watched the opening game at Ninian Park in 1910 when the First Division champions, Aston Villa, defeated the Bluebirds 2-1. And those supporters must have felt as disheartened as the crowd at the final game on the hallowed turf which saw Ipswich Town win 3-0. However, between the first and last games, a countless number of special memories were created – 99 years' worth.

Every fan is brought up with an education of the special days at Ninian Park, like when Brian Clark scored to defeat Real Madrid in 1971. But for many of the generation that had to say a tearful goodbye to their beloved stadium, that wasn't the home they had the pleasure of knowing. For an older generation it was, perhaps, even tougher leaving for the very last time after a lifetime of memories, ones like that Clark goal, when the stadium held more than 50,000. For the majority, though, they knew a ground that held just over 21,000 – but that didn't affect the atmosphere.

In the 1980s and '90s, even the early 2000s to a degree, it was one of the most intimidating grounds to visit for away teams and their supporters. That was partly down to the hooligan culture, but the atmosphere in the ground itself always made it difficult for visiting teams. Opposition players weren't always used to getting into a dated dressing room, then walking down the narrow tunnel and out into a cauldron of noise and, at times, animosity. Players in the modern day may never know the feeling that former favourites like Andy Campbell, scorer of the Bluebirds' play-off final-winning goal in 2003, experienced. He recalls, 'Playing at Ninian Park was always special and that was due to atmosphere, as fans made it an intimidating place for opponents to come and play. It gave us that advantage over other sides.'

It's difficult to describe the atmosphere in one of these old grounds and it's something that will always be sorely missed by supporters who got to experience not only Ninian Park, but any of the old-fashioned venues which were replaced by modern-day designs in the last ten or 20 years.

Campbell continues, 'Ninian Park was special to me as the fans were so close to the pitch and it had that hostile atmosphere. I came from Middlesbrough and it reminded me so much of Ayresome Park where I watched loads of games as a child growing up. Stadiums nowadays don't seem to have any atmosphere, but Ninian Park had that in abundance and it made it easy to play for the fans. They got behind us no matter what, and as long as we ran through a brick wall for them, they backed us!'

'Quite simply it was home,' says City fan Jon Candy, who reveals how he managed to say a very special goodbye to the famous stadium. 'It wasn't the biggest stadium or the best stadium, but it was OUR stadium. The people, the atmosphere, the proximity to the pitch, it was a special place. In the weeks leading up to the final game I began to really take in every moment, realising that this was all going to be gone shortly and I'd never be able to experience it again. In the following months, seeing the ground slowly disappear as I walked past over the summer and into the autumn was like watching a slow death, and I ended up wishing it would just vanish. I got to say my final farewell when the grandstand roof was pulled down, having tail-gated a TV cameraman into the ground and mingled with the journalists, that day I spent a good few hours sitting on the Bob Bank for the last time on my own and said my final goodbyes.'

It was a special atmosphere at Ninian Park and there's no doubt that it helped shape the club's history. The club wasn't so successful in the modern day and make no mistake, there were some dire evenings at the ground when you could hear a pin drop. However, they were far outweighed by monumental occasions like when Nathan Blake scored a stunner to defeat Manchester City against all odds, and when the Bluebirds toppled Premier League club Leeds United in the FA Cup in 2002.

They were moments forged in the club's history and as a supporter, when you walked up Sloper Road and through the rusty turnstiles with that unique smell oozing from inside, there was an undeniable sense of belonging. You didn't always appreciate that when it was hammering with rain on the Bob Bank terrace, but the day the stadium closed its gates, you wanted nothing more than to be soaked to your skin just one last time. It was difficult for every supporter, and it still is for many who make the same walk down Sloper Road, only to now turn right instead of left and head into the Cardiff City Stadium, which now stands opposite the old site. The old ground has since been replaced by a housing estate which continued the name, Ninian Park.

The move to the new ground was inevitable as Ninian Park was falling to pieces and the terracing had to go to comply with Football League rules. Many actually looked forward to the new stadium, and there's no denying that it was a mouth-watering prospect for fans to get a new £38m home which would set the club up for long-term success. However, when it came to saying goodbye, the shiny new venue across the road was no consolation; in fact, it made many detest the sight of it for a while. People wanted the roughness and the intimidation back. They wanted the cambered playing surface and loose, striped nets. But that's just part of the grieving process and for a football fan, nothing can be likened to leaving an old stadium behind, not moving office nor moving home. It's a unique feeling to say goodbye to a place that held so many happy memories.

It was made no easier by that end-of-season collapse but a 3-0 defeat against Ipswich almost felt like a 'Cardiff City way' to say goodbye to the old ground which, as well as special moments, had played host to so many failures. People took with them seats, pieces of turf and even the advertising hoardings. Everyone wanted a piece to keep, something that represented the years in time they had spent at the ground, where they experienced elation, defeat, tears of joy and tears of sorrow. That's why it will always leave a hole in every Bluebird's heart and that's why it's so important that – and not only at Cardiff City – the older generation must continue to share stories of yesteryear when it wasn't all super clubs and all-seated works of art.

The new stadium itself is rather impressive, apart from the name which could have been a little more imaginative. The Cardiff City Stadium, which resembles a Lego structure from the outside, was welcomed as a design with the glass front. It also has plenty of space around it, unlike its predecessor. The inside is spacious, with a gap around the top which is there to allow possible extensions to each of the three one-tier stands – one of which was later completed – and fans are relatively close to the pitch, which you don't always get in these new designs.

Supporters didn't like the fact they had to sit down, but they were never going to after moving from a partly-terraced ground, and it took the fans and the club some time to strike up some sort of agreement on that front. However, for the most part, they were always happy with the new facilities. And while it wasn't going to feel like home for some time, for a 'typical bowl' it wasn't such a bad new home, and Jon Candy concurs; 'The Cardiff City Stadium has grown on me, initially I guess I was homesick but as with all transitions these things happen in time, today I am happy in the CCS, but if I could turn back time would I? You bet I would.'

Memories are what makes a place home, after all, and only time can offer the opportunity to make such memories, something supporters, to their credit, were always rather understanding about after moving from such a loved ground as Ninian Park. It was heartbreaking and tearful, but a new era beckoned, and the only choice in such a situation, is to embrace it. After all, it was never going to take long to build up a bank of memories at the Cardiff City Stadium. This is Cardiff City.

It's the hope that kills you

A NEW chapter beckoned for Cardiff City after the disappointment of the previous season, which was topped off by the heartbreak of leaving Ninian Park. It was time for a fresh start and as the new season approached in 2009, it truly felt like one. There was a shiny new home, creatively named the Cardiff City Stadium, and there was even a new kit manufacturer, with the Bluebirds linking back up with Puma, who had created some iconic shirts of recent history. One that stands out was a shiny effort in 2005, upon which Puma coupled a giant collar with so much silk that it put opponents in danger of a serious static shock. This new one was a lot better, though, with a nice yellow patch under the arm, white shorts and white socks.

It was, however, like the new stadium, missing a sponsor, and the stomach area would remain blank until September, when, after agreeing one deal with a company whose logo was probably the ugliest creation of all time, was removed due to a loss of licence. The new kit finally brandished a sponsor that was there to stay until the end of the season when the club teamed up with SBOBET, who also featured on West Ham's kit that season.

Beyond a new kit and a new stadium, there were a few new players, but none as exciting as the permanent signing of fans'-favourite striker Michael Chopra, who returned for a club-record deal of £3m. Two iconic figures of the future also joined during the summer of 2009 in Mark Hudson – who was quickly made captain – and goalkeeper David Marshall. Steven Gerrard's cousin, Anthony

Gerrard, also joined, along with Paul Quinn and Solomon Taiwo – don't ask about the latter.

There weren't too many more signings from Dave Jones ahead of the new season, nor did there need to be. After all, the Bluebirds had been one goal away from the play-offs, and with the top six still their aim it felt there weren't too many tweaks that needed to be made ahead of the new season. That belief was proved to be right when Cardiff picked up four wins from their first seven games and things looked promising from the off, despite an early-season defeat at home to Newcastle United, who would go on to win the league at a canter after their surprise relegation to the second tier the season before.

The Bluebirds then went unbeaten in October with Jones and Peter Whittingham picking up the Manager and Player of the Month awards respectively. And things were relatively plain sailing, or as least as much as they can be in one of the most unpredictable leagues in the world. Having said that, November was a tricky month for everyone connected to the club, partly through defeat away to rivals Swansea City, but that felt like small fry when later in the month midfielder Stephen McPhail was diagnosed with a rare form of cancer. Thankfully he would pull through, but news of his diagnosis was certainly felt by supporters and team-mates alike. McPhail was and still is a much-loved figure in South Wales, and he wasn't short of well-wishers through a difficult time in his life and indeed career.

Back to matters on the pitch and it was yet another rocky Christmas for Cardiff City, who were teased with the 'bottlers' tag – *a person or team with little mental strength or resilience* – again after going winless through the festivities. That feeling was inevitably made worse by an afternoon in Peterborough that the Cardiff faithful will seldom forget. The Bluebirds lead 4-0 going in at half-time at London Road, only for the home side to drag the game back in the second half, scoring an injury-time fourth to make it 4-4.

And that unforgettable day of football was just one game in a very poor run for the Bluebirds. A 6-0 home win over Severnside rivals Bristol City – famed for Chopra's 'hot boot' celebration – softened the blow but a 5-1 defeat at Newcastle and a 3-0 loss to

Preston gave the impression that Cardiff were capitulating again. Four wins in 14 left things a little precarious, but Jones and his team would manage to steer the ship on to softer seas.

Though not on to a softer pitch. The turf of the Cardiff City Stadium was a lush green ahead of the new season, but come the last couple of months, it more closely resembled the Barry beach. There was no grass to be seen, instead heaps of sands mixed with dirt, and it certainly didn't help anyone's cause. It was to be expected, with the Desso Grassmaster surface, which is partly made up of plastic, usually taking a year to settle in.

However, Jones did employ a direct style of football with a straightforward 4-4-2 formation, so neat passing through the lines wasn't often on the cards anyway, despite possessing Peter Whittingham and Stephen McPhail, genius passers of the ball. Despite the sand, Cardiff picked up form towards the end of the season, and a huge 2-1 home win over Leicester City put them back en route for the play-offs, even if it did take a Gabor Gyepes sending-off through a rugby tackle that saved his team from an equaliser. It was one of the more comical red cards you'll see, but it epitomised the fighting spirit that had returned towards the end of the season, and Gabor, as much as anyone, was a player who would die for the cause.

After that Leicester win, it was time for the next edition of the South Wales derby, and this one was bigger than most with Swansea still harbouring an outside hope of making the top six, while Cardiff were looking to consolidate their spot in the play-offs; a giant occasion, and the first derby in the new stadium, which was quickly nicknamed 'Legoland' by Swans fans due to the block-like nature of the design.

More than 25,000 packed out the capital's newest sporting venue and it was a game that will live long in the memory for Cardiff fans, although it didn't feel like it would when Andrea Orlandi scored direct from a corner after 28 minutes. However, a superb stab into the top corner from Chopra before half-time got the home fans back in the mood. Bothroyd and Chopra enjoyed some great times together up front, despite not always getting on off the field, and if you need a reminder as to why they linked up so well then this goal was it. The typical big-man-little-man combination.

A tense second half ensued and with the game in the balance, Swansea thought they had won it when substitute Shefki Kuqi turned a free kick towards the far post with a header, but David Marshall, much criticised during the season, pulled off a marvellous save with his outstretched leg to keep his team level.

At this point, Cardiff fans were on the ropes. Neither team had ever managed a league double over the other in a South Wales derby, and it felt like Swansea could well manage just that as Kuqi glanced that header goalwards. Cardiff responded well, but it seemed to be too late when the ball rolled out of play level with the Swansea box on the far side. But two minutes into stoppage time there was still time for one last launch into the box from youngster Adam Matthews. The ball was cleared, then headed back into the box by teenager Aaron Wildig with his first touch of the ball, and it fell to Chopra down the right-hand side, just outside the six-yard box.

Time stops for a moment and this is where we hand you over to a piece of iconic Sky Sports commentary as Chopra takes a touch on his chest, allows the ball to bounce and adjusts his body accordingly, 'Chance for Chopra to win it … HE HAS!'

Chopra strikes the ball low and hard across the keeper and into the left-hand corner of the goal, sending the home support into pandemonium. It's what every football fan dreams of, a stoppage-time winner against your biggest rivals. Even Chopra, a serial goalscorer, doesn't know how to celebrate. He runs towards the corner and ends up just doing a pointless-looking roll on a sheet of advertising before climbing to his feet and embracing his team-mates. The scenes inside the Cardiff City Stadium are indescribable, youngsters these days would call them 'limbs' – *the scene of football fans celebrating a goal wildly with arms flying everywhere* – and the sort many hadn't seen before.

It was the first real memory for this grand new venue, and that in itself is so important. They talk about atmosphere and the rest of it, but much of a stadium and the love for it is made up of memories and this was the first in a long list in years to come. It was also a win that would further cement Cardiff's spot in the play-offs, and a top-six position was officially wrapped up with a win at QPR just three games later, allowing Jones and his 'Barmy Army' time to prepare with two games remaining.

Play-off semi-final day eventually arrived with the Bluebirds travelling to Leicester for the first leg on what was a beautiful day. The fans travelled in their numbers, and it felt like it was a long time in the making after the devastation of missing out the season before. The first leg was a cagey affair, as they so often are, but Cardiff left with a one-goal advantage thanks to an iconic free kick from Peter Whittingham, scoring from a position from which he had no right to score from.

Those Cardiff fans in attendance will tell you that when they recall the day, they can still hear the sound the post made when the ball crashed against the inside of it before diverting into the back of the net. The Walkers Stadium, as it was then known, fell silent as Whittingham stepped up to take the free kick and the roar from the away end was quite something. It was a stunning goal to win it and it meant Cardiff would take a one-goal advantage home for the return leg.

However, the second leg, just three days later, was a much more nervy affair. Over 26,000 watched on inside the stadium fearing the worst – that typical Cardiff City attitude – as they waved their blue flags, given to each supporter on the night. Those nerves were eased when Michael Chopra stroked home a lovely finish from the edge of the box to double the advantage and the Bluebirds were on their way – or were they?

Things took a turn for the worse when Matty Fryatt's effort proved too much for David Marshall to keep out just four minutes later and before half-time, a free kick deflected off the head of Mark Hudson before finding its way into the Cardiff net. The nervousness descended once more upon the Cardiff City Stadium.

It got worse, too. Wales international Andy King headed Leicester in front just four minutes after the restart and it looked as if Cardiff had blown it. That was until Chopra – who was actually offside – burst through before being tripped in the box and referee Howard Webb pointed to the spot. The ever-reliable Whittingham stepped up and made no mistake. There was no winner during the remaining 21 minutes and extra time beckoned, which Cardiff dominated, but the woodwork would stand in the way, sending the game into penalties. This was it, it had to be. Cardiff City, known for blowing things at the last minute going to penalties, they had to lose, didn't they?

Three perfectly taken Cardiff penalties by Joe Ledley, Ross McCormack and Chopra were all matched by Leicester's first three spot kicks. The score was level at 3-3, the tension was unbearable, next up was Leicester striker Yann Kermorgant and what happened next had to be seen to be believed. The Frenchman stepped up and amid all the pressure he found an inner confidence to chip the ball down the middle. Marshall fell as he started his dive but with barely any pace on the ball, he was able to stop and stick a hand up to claw it away. 'Of all the times to do that,' said the Sky Sports commentator, and that about summed it up, as does a song on YouTube from Leicester fan and comedian Dave Henson, who created 'The Yann Kermorgant Song' – it's impressive.

The experienced Mark Kennedy then put the Bluebirds in front with a calm penalty, followed by a fist pump that told the supporters 'you have nothing to worry about'. This was Cardiff's game to win and Leicester then had to score. Youngster Martyn Waghorn stepped up to take the Foxes' final penalty and to his credit, he put it as close to the post as he could have wished to, but Marshall flew across the goal, trailed his left arm in the air and pulled off a world-class save to send the Bluebirds to Wembley for the play-off final. The home fans raised the roof with a huge roar before many stormed the pitch, and yet another fantastic memory was etched in the Cardiff City Stadium's young history during its first year.

Just ten days after those dramatic scenes it was down to London for the final against unlikely opponents in Blackpool, who had steered their way past Nottingham Forest in the semi-final. The build-up, as ever, was huge, and while there was nothing cocky or over the top, there was an undeniable confidence that the final was Cardiff's to win.

In truth, many Blackpool fans must have felt that, too. Cardiff had the better team, they'd had a better season, and with many more supporters inside Wembley on the big day, it was bound to be the Bluebirds' turn to reach the promised land.

The day itself saw sweltering temperatures – highs of 41°C were recorded at ground level – around London and indeed Wembley, and made for a fabulous pre-match atmosphere. Nerves were ever-present, and you can bet that applied to the players, the fans, and right into the board room, especially with £90m on offer, an amount that could change the fortunes of both of these cash-strapped clubs. Wembley looked as breathtakingly beautiful as ever as the players walked out on to the pitch to a sea of blue, met by the unmistakable orange of Blackpool, and it was the blue half who were celebrating first.

Chopra struck after just nine minutes to hand the Bluebirds the lead, sliding the ball into the far bottom corner, but within four minutes, Charlie Adam levelled with an inch-perfect long range free kick, finding the very top corner of Marshall's net. Ledley eased fears of an upset eight minutes before the break, racing on to a through ball before scoring from an angle, but still Cardiff managed to fall behind before half-time.

The Bluebirds capitulated and it would cost them dearly. First, Gary Taylor-Fletcher headed home to ensure they conceded within four minutes of scoring for the second time in the game, and then more shambolic defending allowed veteran Brett Ormerod to stab home before the break.

Guardian football correspondent David Hytner remembers watching on in disbelief. 'It was possible for neutrals to revel in the Disneyland defending on show. All that the centre-halves were missing were the over-sized shoes and giant ears, but it made for a thrilling playground-style shoot-out.'

From there, it was Blackpool's to lose and lose it they didn't. Cardiff lost one of their key players, Jay Bothroyd, in the first half, and they missed his presence. The timing of that injury still hurts Bothroyd to this day, too. He reveals, 'At Cardiff, it really burns me that I got injured in the final of the play-offs. Had I been on the pitch, I really thought we would have got promoted to the Premier League that year, that always hurts at my time at Cardiff.'

Jones's men seemed to have nothing to offer up front in the second half and with plenty of smoke but no fire despite hitting the post through Chopra, they were condemned to defeat, falling at the final hurdle when nobody saw it coming. Manager Jones conceded, 'Well done to my mate Ollie and Blackpool. We just weren't good enough.'

Little old Blackpool had snuck into the play-offs and upset the Championship's big boys to storm into the Premier League and in that moment, it felt as though Cardiff would never get there. From missing out on the top six by one goal to missing out on the Premier League at the last hurdle, the football club was left on its knees, financially as well as mentally.

'It was the most heartbreaking day of my football life,' said captain Mark Hudson, a comment that reflected the mood of most, including team-mate Bothroyd. He said, 'Losing the play-off final hurts more than any other defeat in my career. I would love to have gone up with Cardiff. Back in the dressing room, everybody was low. We were dejected because losing in the play-off final is the worst feeling. But it made me determined to come back the following season a stronger player.'

Another season drew to a close and once again, despite all those unforgettable highs during the season, City fans were left feeling nothing but low. Supporter Kevin Ellis says, 'Put simply it was definitely one of over optimism! Blackpool fans came for their day out while City supporters came with only the Premiership in mind. The game against Blackpool and the game against Sheffield Wednesday the season before are stand-out low points in nearly 50 years of following the City.

'My two sons, who are also season ticket holders, were gutted after both games, and after the Blackpool game I recall having to walk back through all the Blackpool fans. I also recall where my son and I were listening to the Sheffield Wednesday game on the radio and being devastated at the final whistle. To be nailed on for the play-offs and miss out by one goal is still hard to take among our fans and the final was just as bad. In reality we were over confident but did not make the same mistakes again.'

The Bluebirds were becoming 'the bottlers' of the division and they knew it. This time, it just felt too much to take, especially losing to Blackpool, who, on paper, didn't have the players or the infrastructure. All credit to the Tangerines, though, they showed more desire than the Bluebirds on the day and they deserved it, but it really was an upset and that's what hurt the supporters. They felt this was the golden opportunity, the likes of which would never come again for what seemed like a golden generation of players.

Trouble at the bridge

DURING THE 2009/10 season, Cardiff City were drawn to play Chelsea at Stamford Bridge in the FA Cup fifth round, but there's a reason that day wasn't mentioned in the previous chapter. That's because it was not the football played on 13 February 2010 that made the news.

The events that unfolded in the areas surrounding Stamford Bridge on that day caused the longest investigation into football violence in English football history and saw 96 people charged. Around 45 Cardiff fans were handed prison sentences, and notorious Chelsea hooligans of yesteryear, such as Jason Marriner and Andy 'The Nightmare' Frain, were also put back in prison for their role in the violence.

The day itself was a treat for Bluebirds fans, a chance to visit one of the Premier League's biggest clubs and a rare opportunity to see their team pit their wits against one of Europe's elite. More than 4,000 made the trip and they had the joy of seeing their team score an equaliser through Michael Chopra, but that was as good as it got with Chelsea winning 4-1. As fans left the stadium, spirits were relatively high given the experience of visiting Stamford Bridge. Then it all turned sour and became one of the biggest nightmares in many a supporter's life. The events would change people's lives forever.

Tension began to build as supporters left the away end and headed towards the main gate, then out on to the main road. Even from the back of the long queue of people, it was clear that the situation was going to be uneasy. Visiting followers found themselves walking out into a sea of the home side's faithful, and while that's not necessarily uncommon, it certainly felt wrong given the 'old rivalry' between the two sets of supporters. And beyond that, the compact nature of Stamford Bridge and the surrounding neighbourhood made it more intimidating than many of the other grounds in English football.

Chants began to surface, from both sets of fans, and the atmosphere quickly began to sour. David, a Bluebird, recalls, 'I remember walking out of the stadium and I could hear the chants "We are evil" from a small number of Cardiff fans. You could just feel the atmosphere was about to turn dark. As I got to the main road, you could see large groups of fans goading each other.

'Objects were being thrown, even at me, and it all seemed a bit strange at the time. It almost felt as if the police had set the whole thing up. You had Cardiff fans one side, Chelsea fans the other and police in the middle, but they just let them all carry on while filming everything.

'You see trouble at games now and again, but this just felt different, with a lot of the fans being older blokes rather than youngsters. At the time, I just remember thinking they must all be crazy because the police were just watching and filming all the drama. Even heading back to the coaches there was an uneasy feeling, with people running around shouting, as if something big was going to happen.'

And something did happen. Both sets of fans emerged on King's Road where the bulk of the trouble occurred, and many who were not from a hooligan background got caught up in it. As police watched on, filming the incidents, many innocent supporters were left to protect each other. Unprotected by the authorities, thanks to their actions in attempting to help others, to help themselves, their lives would never be the same again.

Many faced prison sentences, despite not, thanks to involved in such incidents before, and many would also receive bans from watching football. They had had travelled to London with no intention of causing any trouble, but it was a day which would become a route to them losing their livelihoods.

Of course, there were plenty of supporters with opposing intentions, who had the desire to cause trouble and make it their business to strike fear into the hearts of football fans. They have notorious reputations, both with the Chelsea 'Headhunters' and Cardiff's 'Soul Crew'. For so long, both clubs had been desperately trying to rid themselves of these perceptions.

Most supporters were not interested in all the trouble, but still, these men, many of them in their 40s and 50s, still travelled to games in the hope of causing a riot, in the hope of hurting other supporters. Det Supt Lyle confirmed, 'A high number were in their 30s, 40s and even their 50s. The oldest one was 55. A lot of them went because they knew there was a high possibility of violence.'

Why? Well that may just be another book in itself. But if you don't understand why then you're probably a real, honest football fan, or at least you may have a level of decency far beyond what these yobs possess.

Leanne Bennett, a Cardiff supporter who attended with her family, tells of the fear she felt on that day, 'Most of the violence I saw was just as we left the stadium. I also missed the King's Road part of it but what I saw was bad enough. I was with my dad and two brothers, we'd travelled on the supporters' bus from Cardiff and parked somewhere past the cemetery [which we had to walk through to get to the stadium]. Sad to say I saw some unsavoury behaviour from our own fans inside the tunnel to get out of the Shed End, people pulling ceiling tiles down and smashing things up, I even saw one man put his child on his shoulders and tell him to pull the ceiling tiles down. Utterly shameful!

'As we got outside, there were a few police horses and then we were confronted by the Chelsea fans who were let out to the same time as us and through the same gate, that's when everything started really kicking off. I was trying to keep as close to my family as possible, concerned more for my dad who was nearly 70 years old at the time. I remember him just saying to me to keep my head down and keep walking and if we got separated, to just head to the cemetery and out to the bus.

'We did get separated for a moment and I had to push my way through crowds of people fighting and throwing anything they could, with the police doing nothing from what I could see. At one point I was on my hands and knees crawling through people to get out. I can honestly say I've never been so frightened. I managed to find my dad and brothers at the cemetery and we just ran for the bus to get to safety. I've had a season ticket with Cardiff for about 15 years now, so I've watched them hundreds of times, but that's by far the worst experience I've ever had.'

At King's Road, there was one overwhelming feeling from supporters on both sides. Many felt there was an element of entrapment from the Metropolitan Police. It felt as though it was all supposed to happen, with a lack of intervention, and a lack of prevention as well. Cardiff City Supporters Club committee member Vince Alm says, 'I believe it was entrapment to take many known Chelsea/England hooligans prior to the 2010 World Cup in South Africa who had become active again. The known Chelsea hooligans were allowed to congregate outside the away end during the game, which enabled them to provoke Cardiff City supporters leaving the ground.

'Many of the Cardiff fans who got caught on the front line of the provocation reacted to it and ended up getting arrested. This included about 80-100 who were allowed to pursue a group of Chelsea fans who had provoked Cardiff fans from a side street on to the King's Road.'

It was clear from how narrow the roads are around Stamford Bridge that the two sets of fans, especially given their notorious reputations, could not be allowed to be let out on to the same street. So, why were known criminals and hooligans allowed to wait near the away end?

A visiting supporter, who wishes to remain anonymous, tells his version of events, and claims he saw banned fans who were allowed to wait near the away supporters' exit on the day of the game. 'Six coaches of us went to Enfield to get the Tube in and avoid police. While in Enfield, we had a call from two coaches of lads who were in Shepherd's Bush. There was 80 of them and they were all banned. They had phoned Spurs to tell them that they were there, and Spurs said they would be coming "tooled up".

'We caught the Tube to Shepherd's Bush and on leaving the station, we saw a large mob at the top of the street. We charged them thinking they were Spurs, and they charged at us, but it was actually the banned Cardiff lads. So we called Spurs again, hoping to ambush them, but they said they couldn't get the numbers, so we left for Chelsea, leaving the banned Cardiff supporters there.

'I got to Chelsea on my own at half-time and passed a pub full of Chelsea, some of the well-known lads. This pub was outside the away end, which is strange because when you are banned, you cannot go within two kilometres of the ground on a match day. I think police knew they were there and they were allowed to drink there until the Cardiff fans came out.

'Full-time came, out came the Cardiff fans, and there were hundreds of them waiting there for us, including the banned Chelsea fans. It was strange that the police allowed it, almost as if they were hoping for a row, so that they could film it.

'Anyway, Cardiff overwhelmed Chelsea outside the away end, the police just stood back and filmed it. The fighting kicked off when a Chelsea fan was walking up and down calling the Cardiff fans on. The police again did nothing. After a while, maybe 15 minutes, the Chelsea lads were gone and we had too many for them. We walked up towards the coaches and some Cardiff lads were telling everyone that Chelsea were at the bottom of a side street. I ran down there with about 50 others.

'I was towards the front of the group and I saw a woman with a baby in a pram, so I picked the pram up and carried it into a nearby shop, just before the mob came down the road. After I made sure they were okay, I didn't want to get picked off on my own, so I went back to the Cardiff lot who were relieving Tesco of all their booze.

'What happened down that side street is on YouTube. The fighting wasn't even the Soul Crew, there were all sorts of fans involved and I think police just allowed it to happen, so they could film it and get people jailed.'

It seems outrageous, doesn't it? Did the police really entrap supporters just to get the known hooligans (and subsequently others) locked up? The police will not comment on the matter, but when so many in attendance claim that's what happened, it's difficult to argue. When fans who have no previous link with trouble end up unprotected and somehow prosecuted, it seems like something has gone wrong, it feels like the police haven't done what their main purpose is to do – protect the public.

Vince Alm adds, 'They have never admitted any liability to this day, and there was some shocking policing, it all appeared to be set up to catch certain individuals with the number of cameras recording evidence, and the police being reactive rather than proactive.

'The evidence is pretty damning when they allowed 80–100 Cardiff fans down a side street on to the King's Road where Chelsea fans were congregated, and then a police line prevented any further Cardiff fans exiting down that street. This led to the fighting on the King's Road which the police filmed for a few minutes before taking any significant action.

'They let everyone down involved, including those who got caught up in it. All of it could have been prevented with better segregation or holding Cardiff fans back until the streets cleared. It was all unnecessary. The intelligence was there prior to the match, and the only thing the Met planned for was trouble, not to prevent trouble. It was dangerous for the police involved who had to eventually get in and break it up, poor all around.'

Amid years of violence and disorder, it seems to be forgotten that football supporters are members of the public. They have been given a category of their own, that of people who can be treated how police want them to be treated, with no set rules or rights. Vince provides more insight on why that is the case. He says, 'There has been a government-led crackdown on football violence since Hillsborough which has led to stiff sentencing. I believe there were two key reasons why such sentences were dished out in regards to jail. First one: the troubled happened on a Saturday afternoon in one of the busiest streets in London with many innocent people going about their own business shopping getting caught up in it, and secondly the London Olympics were due in 2012 and by the time sentencing took place it was 2011 and a message was sent out that the authorities would stand for no public disorder on the streets of London.'

Thankfully, the situation is improving with the Football Supporters' Federation and with football clubs now having supporter liaison officers, who are often fans themselves, and understand what it's like to attend a game of football, but trouble still occurs.

David, another Cardiff follower, holds a similar belief. He adds, 'I came out of the away end and a police officer told me to turn left towards the coaches. As soon as I got to King's Road, it was full of home fans, police on horses and police with dogs. I heard a window smash, which I think was a bin being put through a shop window, and then a group of Cardiff fans chased a few Chelsea lads up an alleyway.

'We missed the majority of the violence but heading back to the coaches, speaking to Chelsea fans, even they couldn't believe what had happened. The one thing that puzzled me was why both sets of fans were allowed out at the same time.'

One of the many people to be imprisoned after the violent incidents was Matthew Alm, son of Vince. Matthew received a ten-month sentence for two counts of affray but he was one of many supporters who would be imprisoned for actions that, on any other day, probably wouldn't have warranted any jail time. That feeling is represented in his father's comments to WalesOnline shortly after Matthew's sentencing in 2011. 'The sentence is obviously not very good news,' said Vince. 'The judge accepted Matthew showed no violence, he was not kicking or punching people, but that he was part of a large group that was surging. I'm quite proud of what my son has done, he had a mate of his getting hit by four Chelsea lads and he went across, pushed the Cardiff lad out of the way and ran back and for that in football is considered affray, not self-defence or helping your mate.

'I'm not ashamed of anything he did, I'm very proud of the restraint he showed while the violence was going on around him and I'm very proud that he's been so dignified all the way through it and accepted what's happened.'

Police weren't totally to blame, and it would be unfair to suggest that they were. Operation Ternhill, which saw a number of known criminals locked up, must have been seen as a success. Police officers were also hurt in the attack, with one losing four teeth after being hit by a rock. However, people can't just be seen as collateral damage, whether they are football fans or not. Whether this was set up to catch people or whether it was a genuine mistake that offenders were in the area at the time of the match, there should have been some leniency shown to others who were caught up as a result of this oversight.

There are so many stories like Matthew's, so many supporters whose lives changed, and it could have been prevented. Surely it's not a case of people's lives being changed forever for the sake of locking up these idiots who have given the sport a bad name for such a long time. Hopefully that wasn't the case, but even if it wasn't, even if this was a genuine mistake from the police force, they were wrong to allow it to happen. Supporters should not have paid the price for their mistakes. People should have been better protected and disorderly fans shouldn't have been given the opportunity to cause trouble.

The Sun, which covered the topic heavily, publishing appeals and regular updates throughout the long investigation, called this 'the end of a reign of terror'. In its final summary of the case, the newspaper failed to recognise the 'collateral damage'; the people who were affected for the sake of locking up these criminals. However the headline was a fitting one. This operation did seem to put an end to much of the violence. There's no doubt that football hooliganism was fizzling out anyway with banning orders and prison sentences becoming more common, and this made an impact with violence becoming less frequent afterwards.

It's something both clubs had been working hard towards for a number of years. Both developed strong reputations for football violence and it's not something either of them were proud of. Thankfully society progressed, and football would win its battle over violence.

These incidents have become far more isolated and it's now safe to travel to almost any football match. Supporters can now attend games without the fear of being hurt, and that's the overriding positive from this horrible sequence of events.

If at first you don't succeed

FOLLOWING DEFEAT in the play-off final in 2010, Cardiff had the arduous task of trying to pick themselves up off the canvas again and giving it another go, although, their preparations for the 2010/11 season were hardly ideal. After failing to secure the much-craved funds offered by the Premier League, the Bluebirds were left with bills piling up once again and this time they would be in serious trouble.

Thankfully, however, a Malaysian consortium arrived to take over the club and this is where we first meet a certain Tan Sri Vincent Tan, otherwise known as Vincent Tan. Tan was a background figure at this point, part of a consortium led by Chan Tien Ghee, which would buy the club from Peter Ridsdale for around £6m. Ridsdale actually got in contact with the Malaysian businessman after replying to Ghee's letter to a number of English clubs asking for them to offer his son, Nick, a trial. Ridsdale was the only to reply and it all snowballed from there.

And luckily so, with the Bluebirds in heaps of debt – £66m was believed to be the total sum – and the very existence of Cardiff City Football Club itself in serious doubt, until the takeover was completed. Within a month of completion, £1.9m was paid to HMRC, leading to the winding-up petition being withdrawn, and a further tax debt of £1.3m was paid a month later.

A summer of turbulence for the capital's club affected the footballing preparations, too, with a transfer embargo being put in place. That meant Dave Jones couldn't make any signings until 6

August, just days before the start of the new season, and even when the ban was lifted there was no money to spend.

But when has that stopped him before? He revels in being cash-strapped and it proved to be the case again. Four free signings arrived, including future England goalkeeper Tom Heaton, and then Jones set about signing five players on loan. Those included future Premier League winner Danny Drinkwater, Jason Koumas, Seyi Olofinjana, Andy Keogh and none other than Craig Bellamy.

The latter was the signing of the summer, and seldom will you have seen such anticipation for a Championship capture in your life. Bellamy, a Premier League star who is a Cardiff boy through and through, arriving back at his hometown club, shocked the nation. There were rumours to start and then there, on Sky Sports News, were images of Bellamy walking down to training in his club gear. Then a press conference, which you simply don't see for player signings in these parts, was held. 'I wanted to come home. I always wanted to come back, but I wanted it to be at the top of my game, not just at the end of my career,' said Bellamy, who would instantly become everyone's favourite Cardiff City player.

It was another Jones miracle in the transfer market and it wouldn't even cost the club too much money. The £90,000 per week he was receiving as a Manchester City player was being hugely subsidised by his parent club and Cardiff had won the lottery. Shirts were flying out of the club shop and tickets were being bought up like bottles of water in the apocalypse. Everyone wanted to be a part of what was happening.

It was important for the club to create that feeling after such a disappointing summer. The play-off final defeat left everyone feeling flat, and then came the departure of homegrown midfielder Joe Ledley, followed by fans'-favourite Ross McCormack, prior to the threat of the club being wiped out altogether – it was vitally important to give supporters a reason to go on, because at that time they were putting their money in but getting nothing in return but hurt and disappointment.

The signing of Bellamy and the strength of the squad as a whole offered hope despite having no money to spend: Dave managed to show supporters some ambition, which is what he managed to do back in that FA Cup Final season. It's almost a positive kind of deception. When there's nothing positive coming from the club, when there are financial troubles, almost every club sinks because there's no money to spend, the players signed are poor and the fans are quickly turned off by the lackl of quality in the signings and the subsequent standard of football.

However, Jones somehow always managed to avoid such a fate. He would network superbly with agents to get the right contacts and he would pull magnificent signings out of the bag with a shoestring budget. If there wasn't a large amount of money to spend, he would pile what he had into wages and sign loans or free agents, figuring that if you split the money between fees and wages, you'll get less bang for your buck. Of course, it wasn't ideal in terms of assets because Cardiff were effectively paying rent on players who were on loan, and wouldn't get any of that money back, but it was worth a chance if it gave the Bluebirds an opportunity to finish high in the league.

Cardiff started the 2010/11 season very brightly with four wins from their first five and Bellamy even managed to score a stunning free kick on his debut against Doncaster Rovers. More than 24,000 fans piled in for two of the first three home games and it felt as though Jones had built a promotion-worthy squad, especially when they lost just two of their first 14 matches, winning ten of them.

One of those victories would go down in Bluebirds folklore – 4-0 at Leeds United. Cardiff hadn't played Leeds very often over the previous ten years or so, but there was always a special rivalry between the two clubs, born out of that special FA Cup win of 2002, so this result – nobody had seen it coming, despite Cardiff's form – was special.

The Bluebirds, in their attractive new black and yellow away kit, ran riot with goals from Jay Bothroyd and Michael Chopra. Even Lee Naylor – much maligned by Bluebirds over the course of the season – got involved by scoring a screamer from the edge of the box. Those fans inside Elland Road and those watching on television knew at that point that the squad had the ability to take the Championship by storm.

But yet another poor November and December – typical of Jones's teams for some unknown reason – would stall the Bluebirds.

Marvin Emnes ensured Swansea came away from the capital with all three points, leaving Cardiff in danger of conceding the first league double in South Wales derby history, and even the new year kicked off with a 3-0 defeat to Severnside rivals Bristol City. Jones never really liked derbies.

In January the Bluebirds made a few squad improvements with the permanent signing of 'The Beast', Jon Parkin, who had something of a habit of scoring against Cardiff for Preston – if you can't beat them, sign them. Israeli defender Dekel Keinan also joined and there were a couple more loans too. High-profile Arsenal academy winger Jay Emmanuel-Thomas, AKA JET, arrived in South Wales and former Bluebirds midfielder Aaron Ramsey re-signed for a temporary move. Ramsey was one of the young stars of that FA Cup Final season and he returned in a bid to regain fitness following a horrific leg break the season before, which had kept him out for the best part of ten months.

Following an earlier loan spell with Nottingham Forest, Ramsey rejoined Cardiff for six games, and he made quite the impact, scoring on his debut against Leicester. Cardiff didn't lose at all during Ramsey's loan spell, but he wasn't the only January signing to make an impact. New striker Parkin – who only cost £100,000 – scored an absolute belter on his debut up in Norwich to grab a point, and he became a fans' favourite, though this was largely down to his stocky physique and outlandish character.

Parkin is very much his own man and he has this typical Yorkshire way about him. He comes across as rather frank and it means you either love him or hate him. During his podcast, *Under the Cosh*, he revealed a comical story about one of his first training sessions with Cardiff City. 'He [Bellamy] was all right with me but only after the first couple of training sessions,' said Parkin. 'I was injured when I went to Cardiff, so I wasn't training, but I was sitting next to him in the dressing room and he must have been looking at me, thinking what the fuck, we're trying to get promotion and we've just signed that!

'I get training and I'm on his team, we're doing some sort of shape. Someone played the ball to him and he's played it around the corner, then I laid to a midfielder – I thought I'd done all right – he starts shouting at me, "Fucking give me the ball back," so I said, "Woah, woah, woah, hold on a minute here. We just need to get one thing straight." I said, "You're not playing with fucking Carlos Tevez now mate, he cost £30m and I cost a hundred grand, you'll have to lower your standards a bit here, pal!" From then, he was good as gold with me. He started shaking his head or whatever. That was my second day training, I think.'

The Bluebirds enjoyed a good run in February, including a trip to the Liberty Stadium to take on Swansea. Cardiff hadn't won there in three attempts since the Swans' return to the second tier and defeat this time would mean Swansea would be the first of the two sides to do the double over their South Wales derby rivals. There was every chance, too, with the Swans going well under Brendan Rodgers, looking for a play-off spot.

Cardiff, however, delivered a fine performance at the Liberty. Paul Quinn, often an inconsistent left-back, had the game of his life to keep out the in-form Scott Sinclair and his team-mates did a superb defensive job all over the pitch. It looked as though it would be goalless as the game edged towards the 85th minute, and then came something special, a moment of genius. Bothroyd took the ball up the line, played a nice pass across the field to Bellamy, and now it's time to let the BBC commentator take over.

'Bellamy to Ramsey, Bellamy! Off the post and in! What a strike from Craig Bellamy, and he might just have won the derby for Cardiff,' he yelled as Bellamy curled in a stunning effort off the inside of the post from more than 25 yards out.

Wild celebrations ensued in the away end as the Bluebirds all but wrapped up their first win at the Liberty Stadium, and their first away South Wales derby victory since 1997. Bellamy, who had returned to his hometown club, just had to be the man to score the winner against their rivals. The victory that kept Cardiff in right on the tails of second place, just one point behind Nottingham Forest, and the Bluebirds would stay in touch almost right until the end.

Queens Park Rangers edged Cardiff all season, leading the Championship under Neil Warnock and with a strong squad as a result of heavy investment. The Hoops had beaten Cardiff 2-1 in a top-of-the-table clash at Loftus Road earlier in the season and the two teams didn't meet again until the fourth-from-last game season.

It was a huge occasion with more than 26,000 in attendance as Cardiff looked to close the gap on a beautiful day at the Cardiff City Stadium. Just six minutes in, Bothroyd scored an unbelievable goal with a curling effort. The ball clipped the woodwork and flicked into the net at a ridiculous speed for what truly was a goal to savour, perhaps second only to Peter Whittingham's stunning volley earlier in the season – which won the Football League Goal of the Year award.

QPR's star man Adel Taarabt then equalised four minutes later, before Bellamy restored the Bluebirds' lead before the break, although Taarabt would have the last laugh with an equaliser 19 minutes before time to pretty much wrap up the title for Rangers.

There was glory for Neil Warnock at the Cardiff City Stadium, and not for the last time in his career. It was, however, in controversial circumstances with a dispute over the signing of Alejandro Faurlin. QPR were threatened with a points deduction and the issue rumbled on into the last game of the season, but eventually they received a suspended deduction and a large fine, allowing them to lift the title.

Back to South Wales, and Cardiff continued their chase of second place, now occupied by Norwich, with a 1-0 away win over Preston – the Deepdale curse had been banished, perhaps it was Jon Parkin all along? So going into the last two games Norwich led by one point and Cardiff needed to beat Middlesbrough at home to continue the chase ahead of Norwich's game in the evening. Both matches were on television.

Cardiff slipped up in catastrophic fashion. Boro scored three goals in the first 21 minutes, ensuring a torturous afternoon for Bluebirds to sit and accept that it was all over. Fans listened to the Norwich game on the way home on the radio, and some watched in pubs and at home hoping for a favour. Portsmouth managed no such thing.

The Canaries did their job with a 1-0 win at Fratton Park and their promotion to the Premier League was confirmed. Cardiff had 'bottled it' again and disappointment turned to anger, especially with rumours beginning to circulate that the players had been out drinking the night before that huge Boro game.

That was later denied by players, including Michael Chopra, who said, 'It all got out of hand – it was crazy what people were saying and the record needs to be put straight. I was NOT out drinking on the Sunday night before the Middlesbrough game, no way, it would have been totally unprofessional.

'We were all at the presentation night [Friday] and myself and a couple of other players went out after the presentations were made. But this was three days before the Middlesbrough game on the Monday. I'm not a heavy drinker and that night I was drinking Red Bull.

'From that the whole story was blown out of proportion – it was ridiculous. We had a clause written into our contracts that there was no drinking alcohol 48 hours before the game, otherwise there were massive fines the club could impose on the players – and the fact remains none of the players have been fined. Supporters were saying that I was a disgrace and should be kicked out and that kind of stuff – I was very hurt and upset about the whole thing because the worst thing was it was not true. I would apologise to any Cardiff City supporter if they thought I was out getting drunk the night before a massive game like Middlesbrough, but I was not out that night.'

But there was no time for moping. Cardiff had a job to do and after allowing Swansea, of all teams, to leapfrog them on the final day, when Bellamy salvaged a late draw at Burnley, the Bluebirds finished fourth for the second successive season, meaning they would face fifth-placed Reading in the play-off semi-final, with the second leg at home.

With the two South Wales teams separated in the semi-final, all the talk was already about how great and equally chaotic it may be for them to meet in the final at Wembley.

First, though, both teams had to do their job, and Swansea were up first, drawing their away leg 0-0 against Nottingham Forest, before Cardiff managed the same result at Reading in a packed Madejski Stadium.

They left more concerned about Bellamy than anything else after he limped off just 17 minutes in. News would follow in the coming days that Bellamy was to miss the second leg. It was all to play for, though, with neither team having looked like scoring in the opening game. They could still be playing now, in 2018, and it would still be goalless.

Three days later, Swansea secured their place at Wembley in dramatic circumstances at the Liberty with a 3-1 win, including a superb long-range effort from Darren Pratley, and the pressure was on Cardiff the following day to do their bit to ensure a South Wales derby play-off final. They didn't. More than 25,000 – who were all given 'clappers' – watched on as Cardiff capitulated again, and to this day, if you were to hypnotise a Cardiff supporter into reliving this play-off semi-final, you would do so with the sound of a 'clapper'.

Shane Long opened the scoring when goalkeeper Stephen Bywater – whose name invites a chuckle from Cardiff fans these days – came running out of his goal, before kicking the ball against his own player and allowing Long to chip it into the net. Then on the stroke of half-time, Dekel Keinan wrestled down Matt Mills in the box to allow Long to make it two from the spot. It was all over from then, in effect, with many supporters already on their way home by the time former Bluebird Jobi McAnuff skipped through the heart of the Cardiff defence before driving the ball home and celebrating a play-off final spot amid a heap of Reading players in front of the away supporters.

It was yet another collapse and this time, there was no room for excuses. Yes, there was a transfer embargo, but with the loan signings made and with the quality of players already at the club, Dave Jones had a team good enough to compete for the title, and certainly good enough to finish second. In the end, they couldn't even match the achievements of the previous year, instead losing in the semi-final, and supporters really weren't happy.

Jones remained defiant, saying after the game, 'We were dominating the first half, but made a silly mistake and then conceded a penalty. You can't legislate for that. After that, we couldn't get the breakthrough and Reading earned their reward of a day out at Wembley. It's disappointing and at this moment, I feel lower than a snake's belly. However, I love my job and my

CV tells you that I can bounce back. I need time to get over the disappointment and the anger, but I certainly don't want to give up what I enjoy doing.'

It got a lot worse when Swansea beat Reading 4-2 in the final to secure their place in the Premier League. It was the ultimate insult, for Cardiff, who had been in the Championship for eight successive seasons, had made three real attempts for promotion and failed, then, within three seasons of being in the league, their neighbours had done it.

The Bluebirds were continuing to live up to their 'bottlers' nickname, and that mentality had clearly found its way through to the players. For having fallen down with a squad as good as this, someone had to pay, and that would be manager Jones. Just 13 days after the semi-final defeat, on 30 May, Jones was sacked after six years at the club and it signalled the end of an era for Cardiff City.

Dave Jones departs

'DAVE JONES leaves his post in the knowledge that he has left the club in a far better position than when he arrived,' said then chief executive Gethin Jenkins upon the sacking of the manager.

And he wasn't wrong. In 2005, Jones arrived at a club desperate to establish itself in the Championship, while harbouring dreams of a future in the Premier League. The Bluebirds had been in the second tier for two years when Jones first rocked up, but they looked far more likely to go down than to go up. The facilities matched those of a League 1 club and in truth, they were going nowhere. There were no real training facilities, Ninian Park continued to deteriorate and Jones was left with next to no money.

He revealed, 'Everybody thinks the club had money. After I signed I found they had no training ground, just a local pitch we nicknamed dogshit park, because we had to clear the dog crap up before we could train. They still owed vast amounts of money, no one would give the club credit. One reporter accused me of a "scorched earth policy". I had one every season because the players were only signed for one year or went back to their parent clubs. I started every season with exactly the same scenario. We were always firefighting. But we still got players, we still got close to promotion, got to the FA Cup Final. Each year we finished higher than we had ever done. Each year we got more points than they had ever done. People didn't know that we couldn't even afford Christmas decorations.'

Six years later, when Jones departed, the Bluebirds had proper training facilities and a new stadium, and had reached an FA Cup final, a play-off final and a semi-final. Jones didn't single-handedly achieve all that, but he has to be given a huge amount of credit for what he did on a shoestring budget.

He was a master of turning something into nothing and that's what he had to do in South Wales. With very little money, he created an excitement and a buzz seldom seen surrounding football at the time. The signings of Robbie Fowler and Jimmy Floyd Hasselbaink were absolutely huge, they put bums on seats and they gave the Bluebirds front pages aplenty. Realistically, Jones was never going to deliver league success in his first few years, but football fans can understand that. You do, however, need to give them excitement, a small bit of hope to keep coming back, and that's what those signings did. They also put Cardiff on the footballing map again and got people talking about the club who, just three years before, had still been knocking about in the third tier. Jones had a tough job at Cardiff, make no mistake about that, and in the modern day, you won't find many managers who will put up with what he did over the course of his six years.

His best players were sold year on year in a desperate attempt to keep the club afloat and even if someone left for £5m, Jones would barely see a penny. However he would rebuild, go again, and he is due plenty of credit for that. To still achieve relative success with his hands tied behind his back for most of it his time in charge is incredible. And back then he was seen as one of the most successful managers in the club's history. He took Cardiff to heights seldom seen for years and years, and it wasn't through financial means, just through a sheer ambition.

Supporters respond to that. They can get behind ambition, even if it's a little misplaced or over optimistic; they would rather see a club being ambitious than giving up and shutting up shop. Jones worked wonders with what he had and it's fair to say, as Jenkins alluded to, the club came on leaps and bounds over the course of his six years in charge.

They went from looking down in the Championship to being disappointed to be missing out on the Premier League. Without any money he gave them a platform to build on, and he left behind one of the best teams in the Championship, something supporters couldn't have imagined when he had been appointed.

In his statement, Jenkins added, 'Dave's tenure has seen Cardiff City Football Club develop from a standpoint of Championship stability through to becoming regular promotion contenders, while also having taken the team to an FA Cup Final. His efforts in the recruitment and development of players also meant that the sale of these players at times enabled the club to survive. He has also had a significant contribution in the development of training facilities and the stadium during his Cardiff City career.'

City's fortunes on the pitch were mixed. There are reasons Jones was sacked in 2011 – it wasn't all good. However, if in 2005 you'd have offered fans an opportunity to reach the FA Cup Final, the play-off final and a semi-final in the next six years, they'd have bitten your hand off, even if they knew their team would lose every single one of those fixtures. Having said that, Jones's final year in particular was something of a failure given the squad he had, and not just because Craig Bellamy was present. It can be difficult to gel loan players together, and it was a trickier task because of the lack of finance at the club to bring in permanent signings. However, even given all Jones had done for the club, there weren't too many disappointed when he was handed his P45.

It felt like the time was right for a change, and the 2010/11 season did feel like a failure. The Bluebirds were in the top two for most of it but they blew that and they blew the play-offs in spectacular fashion, at home, too, which is naturally a little more unforgivable.

Where did it all go wrong? Well, it's fair to say Jones's relaxed management style caught up with him in 2011. To his credit, he was brilliant at creating a good atmosphere in the dressing room and he would do that by giving the players freedom, allowing them to look after themselves and look after each other. He also knew which players to keep a close eye on, and who to use a more relaxed approach with – Michael Chopra, who enjoyed four different spells with Jones at Cardiff, is a prime example. Jones knew that Chopra didn't really respond to authority, so he would allow him to essentially get away with murder as long as he turned up and performed well on a Saturday, and he usually did, too.

Jon Parkin reveals, 'He was more lenient on them maybe, and obviously felt that was the best way to get the best out of them.

That was in everything, off the pitch, in training and in games. It was just little things like "Chops" used to go home all the time, back to Newcastle. He'd play a game on a Tuesday night, he'd drive to Newcastle, which was like five or six hours, and drive back on the Wednesday night for another six hours. You are not going to give yourself time to recover for the game on the Saturday if you are doing that.

'But Jay [Bothroyd] and "Chops" were scoring the goals, and that is the way football: if of you are going out on the Saturday, Sunday, Monday and Tuesday, but scoring on the Saturday, who is going to argue with you? Everyone knew what Jay and "Chops" were like, so we just dismissed it really. We let them get on with themselves.'

Jay Bothroyd's situation was much the same. And while it didn't appear so given their superb partnership on the pitch, Bothroyd and Chopra would often disagree in the dressing room – call it a clash of big egos. They would compete with their designer gear, with their expensive cars; it was just the sort personalities they were. Jones allowed them to marshal themselves, and you'd have to say it worked. The Bluebirds were close to promotion on two occasions and Bothroyd and Chopra were huge in pushing them in that direction. However, during the 2010/11 season it was a little different. Jones no longer had an excellent dressing room.

The players Jones had in previous years were used to how the dressing room was managed, they accepted that Chopra and Bothroyd would be allowed to set their own boundaries because it got the best out of them. Bothroyd later revealed, 'One thing about Dave Jones, there was a lot of personalities, Dave Jones is a manager, he was a man-manager. If he needed to shout at you he would, if you needed an arm around you he would, if you needed a few days off, he'd give you that. As long as you turned up on a Saturday and you performed you could basically do whatever you want.'

However, during the 2010/11 season Jones signed a few players who were of a different ilk, so to speak. Characters like Craig Bellamy and Jon Parkin were no-nonsense, they would say things how they were. They came from hard-working backgrounds where the team works hard together as one. They celebrated results in the same fashion, so it was never going to sit well with them that Chopra and Bothroyd, for example, could do what they liked, and this would cause disagreements, ultimately leading to a perhaps not totally unhealthy but certainly off-balance dressing room.

Jones's management style essentially would come back to haunt him in that sense, and this proved to be the case for some of his players as well. For example, Chopra would end up racking up a huge gambling debt and he actually left the Bluebirds to pay it off. It was a case of giving players too much leniency and while that can work, it has to be done in moderation, especially in the modern game when there are so many distractions, and so much money to pay for those distractions.

Another area in which Jones had his shortfalls was his lack of social skills. He was never really a fans' favourite in South Wales and that is probably down to his persona. With his achievements, he probably should have been highly thought of, but he often gave people reasons to dislike him. Supporters didn't like the way he would play down big derby games, which were embroiled in passion and history. To approach such an occasion like any other game is an insult to supporters – that attitude held him back.

He wasn't liked by sections of the media, either, especially not the main newspaper in the capital, the *South Wales Echo*, which was banned from many press conferences. Jones revoked access for its football correspondent Steve Tucker for a number of years, and was known to lose his temper with reporters if they had written a story that he didn't like.

Many share tales of him shouting and balling at reporters young and old for articles they had written, and given that the media ultimately portray his character to the general public and the supporters, that's never such a clever idea. Of course there will be disagreements between manager and media, especially if things aren't going well, but the way Jones acted on occasions meant he was disliked by many in the capital.

Speaking to WalesOnline in 2015, Jones reflected on his time at Cardiff. He said, 'As a manager the one thing you learn very quickly is you are never going to please everyone whether it be because of the team you pick, players not selected, the way you look and act on the touchline or answer questions. My style as a manager is to win, to trust my players and staff and to protect them and the club when and where I thought needed.

'The first time I walked into Cardiff I knew it was always going to be a struggle and an uphill battle just to keep the club afloat. The club was in a financial crisis with a run-down stadium, no training facilities, no players and, more importantly, no funds to buy players. It was imperative that our recruitment strategy was paramount if the club was to stay in the division and then slowly progress.

'The process was to get players in on free transfers and turn those players into valuable assets, work on the youth at the club and again use that as a source of income, the idea being to produce cheap and sell big. The problem we always faced, as we found and produced players, was that it got us to the point of having a chance to get promoted, but, as we also found to our cost, each year we had to sell our best players to survive, which always felt like one step forward and two or even three steps back.

'Although I had great times at Cardiff my biggest regret is not gaining promotion. I felt it was getting closer each year only to be disappointed and we could never buy at the time needed, only sell. Cardiff City would not be the club it is today without the daily dramas and as the old Cardiff Blues manager, Dai Young, said to me over coffee one day, both clubs where always one day away from disaster.

'I am proud of what we achieved at Cardiff though, an FA Cup final, near misses on promotion, reducing the debt, building a fantastic stadium, a state-of-the-art training facility, producing some great talent through the youth system, good recruitment of players who became crowd favourites and which put the club on the global stage. This, I believe, gave the fans a club to be proud of and one which their fantastic support deserves.'

There's a lot to consider in a six-year spell at a football club and such long terms are a rarity these days, but Jones's time was largely successful. Ultimately he failed to get promotion for one reason or another, partly his fault and partly through a lack of backing, but that inability to reach the promised land is what cost him a seventh year.

Having said that, it did feel like his time was up, and there were murmurings of discontent from supporters throughout what was a relatively successful season. And when people are unhappy despite things going right, it's probably an indication that your time is coming to an end.

Without Dave Jones, would Cardiff City be where they are in 2018? Absolutely not, and that, above all, is how his time at the club should be judged. It indicates that it was a successful six years. And given the way he transformed the club, with the help of others, of course, it was a success and the majority of fans will agree with that, regardless of whether they like Jones as a person. It was a pivotal six years in the modern history of the club and will show that Jones played a monumental part in the success that would follow.

Out with the old

FOLLOWING THE sacking of Dave Jones, the Bluebirds began their search for a new manager; someone to take them to the next level, to the Premier League. A number of high-profile applicants came forward but in the end, Cardiff decided to go and get their man rather than waiting for him to come to them.

They approached Watford to speak to their manager, Malky Mackay, and despite being turned away initially, they eventually got their permission and landed him on a three-year deal. The Watford job was Mackay's first in management, having represented the Hornets as a player. And it has to be said that he didn't do anything particularly eye-catching at Vicarage Road, achieving a 14th place finish having been 16th the season before. He won a third of his games during his time in charge.

That was enough to convince Cardiff, though, and there were reasons why. After six years with Jones they wanted something fresh, a new approach, and Malky, as he is referred to by Bluebirds fans, offered that. He talked the talk and he impressed the Cardiff hierarchy both before his interview and after. He was their man and they were going to get him.

It wasn't an easy time to be taking the Cardiff job given the play-off heartbreak that had gone before, but Mackay was fortunate in that he had a clean slate. Fans wanted something new, so he could come in and pitch whatever approach he wanted, in effect. There was no pressure on him as such, certainly not in his first year, but a play-off finish was expected, although that wasn't asking an awful lot given the infrastructure the club now had.

It may sound a strange contradiction to say there was no pressure but he was expected to reach the top six of one of the toughest leagues in the world, however that's how it was. He wasn't expected to reach the Premier League in his first season, but there was still an overall expectation that he should get Cardiff competing somewhere around that top six.

Unfortunately for Malky, he had a rebuilding job to do with Craig Bellamy moving to Liverpool from Manchester City, ruling out a stay, and more fans' favourites also departed. Michael Chopra left for reasons already alluded to, joining Ipswich Town for £1m, while Jay Bothroyd could not agree a new contract. He wanted big money after impressing the previous season and earning himself his sole England cap. Bothroyd joined Premier League new boys QPR, and Chris Burke, the Bluebirds' reliable winger, moved on to fulfil his ambition of returning to Scotland, but he would end up joining Birmingham – that didn't go down too well with supporters.

Mackay then went about rebuilding the squad with a whopping eight new signings, nine including loans, spending over £2m. Those signings included Mackay's favourite, Don Cowie, Craig Conway, Kenny Miller, Aron Gunnarsson, Joe Mason, Rudy Gestede, Ben Turner and a certain Robert Earnshaw, who made his fairytale return after a seven-year absence. To Mackay's credit, five of those signings were free, but the likes of Turner and Miller would require significant fees. Mackay also brought in many of his own staff, including David Kerslake, Joe McBride and head of recruitment Iain Moody. There's more to come about Moody later.

There was a quiet optimism about the club, but not quite like the season before. It was probably more directed at what sort of football the Bluebirds would play and what kind of team they would be under Mackay. Supporters were excited about a new direction rather than their promotion hopes, and that was quite healthy after what was essentially three years of heartbreak. The yellow returned to the new kit, which had a rather retro look to it with a thick V-neck collar and basic design, but the third kit – a superb black and yellow design – really grabbed the attention.

The fixtures saw Cardiff face newly (and surprisingly) relegated West Ham away from home on the first day of the season. An exciting occasion and the perfect way to put a new squad to the test. It was to be shown on television, but still, plenty would make the trip to Upton Park, many of whom were protesting about police restrictions for such away journeys. That didn't dampen their spirits, though, and the expectations were as high as ever on opening day.

When the season kicks off you can be favourites to go down but for a moment or two, when that ball is kicked for the first time, you have as good a chance as anyone to win the title – and that's one of the great things about the game we love.

Cardiff looked solid against the Championship favourites, so much so that they appeared to be going home with a very respectable point until the first memory of Mackay's reign was carved out before his very eyes. The clock struck 90 as successful triallist Rudy Gestede stole the ball on the far side, deep in the West Ham half. The lanky striker strode down the line and cuts it back, and although it looked as though it was going beyond Kenny Miller, the Scotsman showed his experience to get a touch before adjusting himself and striking it goalwards.

Robert Green stretched, not expecting the shot, and could only palm the ball into the net. He should have done better but no one in the away end cared. Unbelievable scenes unfolded, Miller ran towards the travelling fans doing the famous 'Ayatollah' and as he slipped to the ground before regaining his feet and standing arms open in front of the uncontrollable away following, he knew he had already installed himself as a fans' favourite. The Bluebirds stole all three points and Mackay's first competitive game in charge was a memorable one.

The form didn't last, however, despite a Severnside derby win against Bristol City the following week. Cardiff won just four of their first 12 games – Malky was really clinging on to that 33.3 per cent win percentage, wasn't he?

Matters would improve, however, and Cardiff established themselves as play-off contenders after a run of six wins from eight, with no defeats, and they wouldn't suffer another poor run until February, which wasn't without its reasons. The Bluebirds soared in the League Cup – something we'll touch on to later. That winter blip did cost Cardiff in the league, though, and the play-offs looked in doubt, especially after an extremely busy and equally dry March. Five draws from eight games and just one win saw them attempting to catch up, playing their games in hand caused by the League Cup run.

The one only win in March was a memorable one, mind you. The Bluebirds claimed a league double over Bristol City thanks to an 87th-minute own goal. But that aside, things weren't going at all well. And the poor run meant Cardiff would go into their last six games two points off the top six, still with a game in hand. First up it was a clash against top-six rivals Middlesbrough.

Cardiff often struggled when playing a long way from home but that was put to bed with a 2-0 win at the Riverside. A home draw with Mackay's former club Watford followed, before victories over Barnsley and Derby. Cardiff were handling the pressure, unlike in previous years, and it was a something the supporters were delighted with, unsurprisingly so after being let down so much in the past.

A draw against Leeds in the penultimate game left Cardiff needing just a point on the final day to secure their top-six spot, and they more than obliged with a stunning comeback victory at Crystal Palace. Middlesbrough lost, meaning Cardiff were there in any case, but it was made all the sweeter when Don Cowie rifled in a fine winner at Selhurst Park to send the Bluebirds into the play-offs for the third successive season.

Having said that, it felt a little different this time around. Cardiff's opponents in the semi-finals were West Ham, who had been tipped to win the league at the start of the campaign but were ultimately outdone by Reading and Southampton, who took the automatic promotion places.

The Hammers may have dropped down from the Premier League but they retained a cluster of talented players. Cardiff had won the regular-season clash at Upton Park and West Ham triumphed in Wales, so this looked like being a finely-poised encounter but in terms of the feeling from supporters, it was a little different compared to previous years. Nobody really expected Cardiff to win, partly because of how strong West Ham were, but also because there was a sensible realisation that this was the start of a new project.

There was more to come and in fact the Bluebirds probably weren't ready for the Premier League, as more needed to be done after pressing the reset button.

Things were finally settling down a little financially, off the field, and Mackay was beginning to build something. This wasn't like under Dave Jones when it was the end of a project, all that was missing in the previous years was promotion. Here, it felt more like a bonus to be competing in the play-offs, and looking back, that seems strange given that the Bluebirds had played in them for the previous two seasons.

Nevertheless, Cardiff were going to give it their best effort, of course, even if it was to no avail. They lost 2-0 at home thanks to two goals from Welsh international Jack Collison and it was all over. Cardiff went to Upton Park knowing that they had little chance of overturning a two-goal deficit when they had struggled so badly to contain West Ham in the first leg, but yet again, they gave it a go.

Plenty of supporter-filled buses arrived at Upton Park with fans holding on to the faint hope of a comeback. But there would be no miracle at the ground where the season had started for Mackay and his Bluebirds, no repeat of that memorable opening day. Kevin Nolan kicked off the action on the evening with a goal after just 15 minutes, and if it wasn't over then, it certainly was when Ricardo Vaz Te smashed in a stunner before the break. There was time for a third, too, when Nicky Maynard – that's not the last you'll hear of him – made it three on the night and 5-0 on aggregate.

As expected, the Bluebirds couldn't prevent the Hammers from reaching the play-off final and as it turned out, Blackpool couldn't prevent Sam Allardyce's men from returning to the Premier League, either. West Ham returned to the promised land at the first time of asking with a 2-1 final win against the Tangerines.

As for Cardiff, their search for promotion to the promised land would rumble on for yet another season, meaning it would be a tenth year in the second tier. But this time the heartbreak wasn't too much to take, for reasons discussed to earlier. This time, it was the start of something big and this time, there was a belief that next season, the outcome really would be better.

Another walk down Wembley Way

ONE OF the reasons why there wasn't as much disappointment surrounding that play-off final defeat was that the Bluebirds faithful would get another trip to Wembley during the 2011/12 season. It was a cup run that, just like in 2008, would take all the pressure off the league campaign and it's funny how that happens in football.

There's something awfully satisfying about a good run for football fans – admittedly that's heightened for a club like Cardiff City – and it can soak up a lot of expectation. Of course, Cardiff's expectations were solely in league competition, with what had become an obsession to reach the Premier League, something that had proved so elusive. The Bluebirds almost felt blessed to have seen their team reach an FA Cup Final at Wembley in 2008, and that was once in a lifetime, so any other good runs afterwards were appreciated, but elimination wasn't taken to heart.

Perhaps it's a little like your 21st birthday. You know it's your last big one for a while, you're getting older, so you appreciate anything you get each year after that no matter how small. The expectation of receiving exciting gifts as a child passes and in the same way, Cardiff's cup expectations were dramatically lowered. Perhaps that did them good, or perhaps it made no difference at all when they began their journey in the League Cup – then often referred to as the Carling Cup – in 2011.

It started at Oxford in the August, and the Bluebirds would spend far more time at the Kassam Stadium than they would have hoped. Simon Clist scored a first half equaliser to cancel out

Craig Conway's goal and there were no further replies so extra time beckoned. However, Cardiff were dominant despite their frustrations at having to play an additional 30 minutes of football so early in the season. Peter Whittingham scored with a fine effort eight minutes after the restart and youngster Nat Jarvis rounded things off right before the final whistle.

Huddersfield Town arrived at the Cardiff City Stadium in the next round and once again, lower-division opposition would prove tricky for the Bluebirds, although the Yorkshire side proved themselves to be a League 1 club with high standards by winning promotion to the Championship later that season.

Cardiff went 2-0 up with goals from Jon Parkin and Gabor Gyepes but they let it slip. Huddersfield equalised through Jordan Rhodes – who would go on to be a top Championship player – and Danny Ward, who would sign for the Bluebirds six years later. They even grabbed a third through Rhodes to completely swing the tie in their favour. But Cardiff couldn't let it lie, and Don Cowie scored with a fine header from the Bluebirds' last roll of the dice, three minutes into added time. Mackay's men had saved their cup hopes.

From that point, there was only going to be one winner, with Huddersfield looking dead on their feet for much of extra time. Conway, who provided the assist for the late equaliser, got a goal for himself to put his team ahead, and Cowie scored again at the death to ensure the Bluebirds progressed.

Next up, fellow Championship club Leicester City visited in South Wales and once again, it wouldn't be settled in 90 minutes. Cowie netted with another looping header, becoming quite the goalscorer in the competition, but the Bluebirds' joy didn't last. Steve Howard grabbed an equaliser before a huge mistake from Darcy Blake at the back allowed Leicester to break; Lloyd Dyer was the eventual scorer to put the Foxes ahead.

Once again, Cardiff went into the last ten minutes with a one-goal deficit but once again, they found a way to claw themselves back. Rudy Gestede got the equaliser with eight minutes remaining and it was some goal, too, a stunning effort from the edge of the box. Extra time once again ensued, but this time there was to be no running away with it and Cardiff required spot kicks. So, as in that play-off semi-final just 14 months earlier, Cardiff and Leicester went to penalties at the Cardiff City Stadium. Both teams scored their first six – there was no Yann Kermorgant to offer a chip down the middle this time – and it took until Leicester's seventh to see the turning point. Gelson Fernandes blasted over, and an unlikely penalty hero in Paul Quinn confidently dispatched his to win it for Cardiff and to send his team into round four.

After three rounds and three sets of extra time, Malky Mackay may have been hoping for a cup exit given that he was trying to orchestrate a play-off bid alongside this cup run. However, it must be stressed that expectations still weren't being raised at this point. Even in the fourth round, when another Championship club, Burnley, came to the Cardiff City Stadium, there were only 11,000 in attendance, an increase of just 3,000 from the Leicester tie.

Of course, the rather unflattering draw didn't help, but it did help Cardiff's chances, and playing on their own turf would prove favourable all the way through, as had happened in 2008. First, though, the Bluebirds had to book their place in the quarter-final and they did so with relative ease, beating Burnley 1-0. Joe Mason scored the all-important goal – it wouldn't be his last of the cup campaign – and they marched on, for the first time in the run, without the need for an extra 30 minutes.

In the quarter-final Cardiff were drawn against struggling Premier League club Blackburn Rovers and around 20,000 turned up to a game that whetted the appetite a lot more than the previous rounds. And the fact that it was a quarter-final was always going to make it all the more appealing. However, the occasion wasn't all about football, and that's because the game took place just two days after the death of Wales boss Gary Speed. The much-loved former player turned manager seemed to be turning things around for the Welsh national team, offering hope for the first time in more than a decade, before his tragic passing. It came out of nowhere, it shocked everyone, and it stood as a stinging reminder to everyone involved in the game that life goes beyond football.

Gary's death also served as a real wake-up call regarding mental health, especially given the circumstances. Gary took his own life just two days after appearing joyfully on television, and that appearance only made it more shocking to people who knew him as a person, and those who knew him as their favourite footballer, or their national team's manager. His death caused devastation not only to his family, but to the whole football community and especially those in Wales. The Bluebirds paid tribute to him prior to the match against Blackburn.

You could hear a pin drop during the minute's silence. It was as if everyone in the stadium went numb, before the singing of 'there's only one Gary Speed'. This wasn't an elderly former player who had passed away, this wasn't someone who many in the stadium didn't see, this was someone these supporters saw and backed on so many occasions, this was someone who was taken far too soon. Many of these supporters will watch every Wales fixture, home and away, and in that respect, Gary Speed was part of a family, a Welsh football family which has grown even stronger as part of his legacy. There should be no competition or comparison of how much a death affects a country, but seldom will you see one quite like this which left so many people lost for words, feeling as devastated as this. That deeply felt sorrow was reflected during the minute's silence and the other tributes ahead of kick-off.

Those pre-match events undoubtedly played a part in the atmosphere during the game. It would be a stretch to say the Cardiff players were performing to make Speed proud, as many of them wouldn't have known him. But there's no doubt that he was in the minds of supporters throughout and those tributes provoked an emotional reaction from them.

That emotion could be felt throughout the ground as the Bluebirds booked their place in the semi-finals of the League Cup for the first time since 1966. Kenny Miller grabbed a goal within the first 20 minutes and a fragile Blackburn side, who would go on to be relegated that season, were comprehensively beaten. Anthony Gerrard rounded things off five minutes after half-time and Cardiff came away with a 2-0 win to march on to the penultimate stage of the competition.

Fans eagerly awaited the draw, knowing their opponents would be either Liverpool, Manchester City or fellow Championship club Crystal Palace, who had knocked out Manchester United in extra time at Old Trafford. Unbelievably, the draw favoured Cardiff again and they faced Palace, meaning a second-tier club in the final was guaranteed. The Bluebirds were fancying their chances from the moment the draw was made and for the first time in the whole cup run, expectations were raised. Yes, Palace had beaten Manchester United away to reach this point, but they were enduring a rather awful league campaign, battling it out in the bottom half under Dougie Freedman.

More than 22,000 watched on at Selhurst Park in the first leg as Anthony Gardner edged it for Palace. The towering defender headed home a free kick after an initial flick-on, and that was all that separated the two sides amid a raucous atmosphere in south-east London.

Cardiff were still in it. It was only one goal after all, but Palace had done their bit, so the pressure was now on the Bluebirds. And with the knowledge that away goals were in force if the two sides couldn't be separated after extra time, Cardiff had to avoid conceding if they wanted any real chance of securing a spot at Wembley.

It was all set up for another big occasion at the Cardiff City Stadium, which was still in its infancy yet hosting historic moments at a rapid rate for a club the size of the Bluebirds. In the build-up to the second leg, Freedman decided to play a few mind games, claiming that Cardiff and their supporters were 'scared stiff of failure', Malky Mackay responded with class, saying, 'Needless to say, part of my team talk is done,' and beyond that, it gave the supporters a metaphorical bone to chew. It started off quietly, but by the end the whole stadium appeared to join in with a chorus of 'Dougie Freedman, we're not fucking scared.'

It was quite the atmosphere inside the ground for the evening kick-off with more than 25,000 in attendance, including plenty of Palace fans; with cup competitions requiring a larger allocation for away supporters, they were given half of the Family Stand as well as the usual corner.

Cardiff took just seven minutes to cancel out the lead Palace had worked so hard for in the first leg. Don Cowie whipped in a powerful cross and Anthony Gardner, who scored in the first leg, headed into his own net to cancel out that previous goal with an own goal.

Cardiff completely dominated from that point on, with more than 20 shots on goal. But they couldn't find their way past an excellent Julian Speroni who put in the performance of his life in the Palace goal, although he was also helped by the post and a couple of goal-line clearances. Palace's chances of reaching the final were diminishing and they weren't at all helped by defender Paddy McCarthy, who was sent off after two fouls on the lively Kenny Miller. But Cardiff still couldn't score, despite again hitting the crossbar. And even in the face of a dominant extra-time display from the hosts, Palace held on to give themselves as good a chance as they could have hoped for in a penalty shoot-out.

That Dougie Freedman song continued to echo around the Cardiff City Stadium and the Palace boss must have been regretting his comments after such a poor display from his team. Cardiff's dominance bred confidence heading into the shoot-out, but such is the nature of penalties, Palace had as good a chance as the Bluebirds despite having had 120 minutes to forget.

Now was a time for cool heads amid a bouncing Cardiff City Stadium. Miller stepped up first on the back of a fine performance, but he smashed the ball over the top and into the Palace fans. Then Wales international Jermaine Easter was denied by Tom Heaton, before Craig Conway confidently drove the ball down the middle. Sean Scannell then stepped up for Palace and missed with a dreadful effort, which was well read by Heaton. Rudy Gestede then briefly doubled Cardiff's lead with a shortl run-up and a cool finish, before Mile Jedinak got Palace on the scoreboard. Peter Whittingham wasn't going to miss, and after he dispatched his spot kick it was all on Jonathan Parr, who appeared to be the most nervous man in the stadium, as he stepped up to take the penalty in front of a sea of Palace fans to his left and another of Cardiff supporters to his right.

He leant back as he took the shot, sending the ball way wide and into the Palace fans. Delirium. Heaton sprinted up the line and to the bench where he was met by all the players, scenes of chaotic celebration ensuing both on the pitch and in the stands. The Bluebirds were heading back to Wembley for their first League Cup Final. Supporters may not have expected it, but perhaps that, and all the heartbreak of the previous league campaigns, made it all the sweeter. An unbelievable feat, and Wembley Way beckoned once more.

Just 24 hours later, it was confirmed that Liverpool would be their opponents. The Reds drew 2-2 in their second leg with Manchester City, sending them through following a 1-0 away win in the first leg. And that victory over City across two legs in itself highlighted the size of the task ahead of Cardiff as City went on to be Premier League champions that season. It was a Liverpool team with an array of talent, as the likes of Pepe Reina, Jamie Carragher, Steven Gerrard, Jordan Henderson, Luis Suarez, Andy Carrol and Dirk Kuyt were all involved, and don't forget Craig Bellamy, who was playing for the Bluebirds the previous season and would meet his former club in the final.

Kenny Dalglish was the man in charge of the Reds at the time, and he was in confident mood ahead of a cup final clash with a Championship club. In South Wales, that aforementioned expectation had dropped off again as all the talk was about the achievement of reaching a first final in the competition and little glory was expected. Of course, such is the beautiful game, many of the Bluebirds faithful had a small voice in the back of their head telling them that 'anything could happen', but the voice of reason said 'absolutely no chance'.

Supporter Callum Ellis recalls the mood ahead of the game: 'I don't think the optimism was too high heading into the game. I would say it was viewed as more of a day out in London – unlike both FA Cup games and the play-off final – I don't think the majority of fans thought we would have any chance of lifting the trophy.'

The day itself seemed to take an age to come around, with more than a month between the semi-final and final. Each club received just over 31,000 tickets and all were gobbled up rather quickly, as you might expect. Not only was this a final but you also have to bear in mind that many fans of Cardiff, as with any other club that seldom plays in the Premier League, will have second clubs that they support. For many in Wales, that is Liverpool due to their success achieved across so many decades. So this was a once-in-a-lifetime opportunity for many to see a cup final between Cardiff City and Liverpool. Usually it would feel like a once-in-a-lifetime chance to see Cardiff at Wembley, too, but this was the fourth time in as many years for the Bluebirds, so it was becoming a second home!

An impressive attendance of 89,041 filled Wembley for the final and the atmosphere was fantastic, two sets of passionate supporters with a sea of blue meeting a sea of red. Two great clubs, who come from very different backgrounds: Liverpool, looking to end a silverware drought spanning six years, and Cardiff, just looking to do themselves proud after surpassing everyone's expectations to reach the final, as they had done four years earlier.

The game kicked off and it really was a cauldron of noise inside Wembley as Liverpool started brightly. Just a minute and a half in, Glenn Johnson hit the underside of the crossbar with a long-range effort. It was going to be a long evening for Cardiff – or was it? The Bluebirds settled down nicely, withstanding Liverpool's pressure. Then, after 19 minutes, Kevin McNaughton's cross was cleared back out and he got another chance to deliver, but instead chose to pick out fellow Scotsman Kenny Miller on the edge of the box.

Miller threaded a fine ball through to find young striker Joe Mason and 'it's Cardiff City who score first against all the odds', according to the commentary, as Mason rolled the ball under Reina and into the bottom corner. There was unbridled joy at the other end of the stadium as Cardiff fans celebrated wildly, catching glimpses of each other looking stunned, not believing what was going on. It was a truly wonderful moment for the Bluebirds and for 20-year-old Mason, who was the coolest man in the stadium as he slotted the ball past an experienced World Cup-winning goalkeeper in Reina.

Cardiff held out until half-time, but Liverpool piled on the pressure in the second half, almost suffocating the Bluebirds, who tried desperately to give themselves an outlet. On the hour mark the inevitable goal arrived. Stewart Downing delivered a fine corner and Luis Suarez managed to connect to the initial tame header, flicking the ball on but hitting the post. It came back out and Martin Skrtel reacted quickest, pouncing before cleverly rolling it under Tom Heaton from close range. Scenes of joy in the Liverpool end followed but it said something about the difference in these two clubs when the Liverpool players barely celebrated as they were more interested in retrieving the ball and restarting the game to get a winner.

But they wouldn't get one in normal time, with Cardiff putting in a superb defensive display, not least from Mark Hudson and Ben Turner. It seemed Liverpool would romp on after getting an equaliser, but Cardiff just wouldn't allow it, they wouldn't lie down. In fact, they should have won it late on when Miller had a golden chance in front of goal, but somehow he managed to lift the ball over the bar, so for the fifth time in eight League Cup ties during 2011/12, Cardiff would require extra time.

Liverpool again dominated with Cardiff beginning to tire, but still they stood tall and made it difficult despite the introduction of Craig Bellamy. Liverpool did get their goal, however, just three minutes into the second half of extra time. Substitute Dirk Kuyt misplaced his original effort but it was inadvertently sent straight back to him and the Dutch striker adjusted excellently to fire a powerful effort past Heaton from the edge of the box.

Once again it felt like the final was Liverpool's to win and Cardiff would be powerless to stop them, but this club rewrites the script. In the 26th minute of extra time, Aron Gunnarsson launched a ball into the box despite hobbling with an injury, and Liverpool cleared for a corner. Peter Whittingham delivered it superbly, Reina spilled the ball and Filip Kiss saw an effort cleared off the line. That was Cardiff's chance.

They say you always get that one opportunity, and that was it. They had another corner, but supporters looked at each other, they thought they knew – but they were wrong. Whittingham delivered another world-class set piece and it came to the back post. Time seemed to stop. Turner almost looked as if he was trying to work out where the ball was as Kuyt tried to clear while on the floor. The ball stopped in front of Turner and he stabbed it home from a yard out, sparking some of the most brilliant scenes many Bluebirds have ever witnessed. The players ran off in different directions, in disbelief, and Turner, who looked more like a rugby player in build, went behind the goal, swinging his shirt over his head. Cardiff fans jumped with joy, some fell to their knees and some fell down rows of seats as they tried to turn their feelings into actions.

ANOTHER WALK DOWN WEMBLEY WAY

Joshua Slack recalls his experience: 'It was indescribable. Everyone was grabbing on to anyone they could find, I think I fell down about four rows. It meant so much to every Cardiff fan to come all that way, to score a goal in those circumstances, and that made it all the more special and it is one of, if not, the proudest I have been since I started supporting the club.'

Callum Ellis adds, 'If I was to choose three of the wildest goal celebrations from my 12 years following the club, I would say that would be right up there – delirium. The goal coming so late on made it extra special for the fans – I didn't think we would draw level after going behind.'

Cardiff City, against all odds, were taking Liverpool to penalties in the League Cup Final.

The shoot-out came around all too quickly, with both sets of fans too nervous to speak, biting their nails as they watched on. Liverpool won the toss, meaning the penalties would be taken in front of their supporters and they would go first. Cardiff had won twice from the spot twice on their road to the final and if they could do it just once more they would lift the League Cup.

Steven Gerrard stepped up first and everyone inside the stadium expected him to score – he didn't. Heaton produced a wonderful save, tipping the ball on to the bar with an outstretched arm, and Cardiff fans remained in wonderland. They'd be brought back down to earth, though, when Miller sent the keeper the wrong way only to hit the post. Charlie Adam was up next, a man who had scored against Cardiff at Wembley for Blackpool in 2010, but he put the ball a long way over the bar. Cardiff had another chance. Cowie, who had been a hero throughout the campaign, stepped up and took advantage, slotting the ball high into the top corner. Then Kuyt slotted his penalty home with ease, piling the pressure on Rudy Gestede. Looking tired, but still employing his slow run-up, Gestede strolled up to the ball before hitting the post with his penalty. Downing then put the pressure back on Cardiff, but Whittingham didn't miss. He never did. Then Johnson emphatically put Liverpool back ahead to ensure Anthony Gerrard of Cardiff, cousin of Liverpool's Steven Gerrard, had to score. He didn't. Gerrard put the ball wide and Liverpool had their eighth League Cup.

He later reflected on that crushing moment. 'I was fifth designated penalty taker in the match against Crystal Palace [semi-final], but Jonathan Parr missed their fourth, so 'Bungle' [Tom Heaton] was the hero because he saved one. Afterwards I said to him, "You took my limelight." I was number five because I was one of the best penalty takers there.

'At Wembley, I just got told "you all right for number five" and I said "no problem". Obviously, he [Mackay] knew what I was capable of in taking penalties. Out of 100 penalties, if you told me I've got to either hit the top left-hand corner as you look at it, or the bottom left-hand corner, I'd hit 90 per cent and that's no exaggeration. That was my corner.

'But on the day, I absolutely pulled it and it clipped the post. I was fully confident of putting it exactly where I wanted to, but it just didn't happen, and that's a cross I have to bear and people will also remember me for it, those Cardiff fans and stuff like that. After that game we had a party, we would have had a party if we had lost it in 90 minutes. We were underdogs, like the lads in the FA Cup Final [against Portsmouth]. They went there as underdogs, gave it a good go and just lost 1-0. If that had happened in the Liverpool game, everybody would have thought Liverpool were expected to win.

'It was just unfortunate it went to penalties and I was the one to miss the penalty. But people tend to forget that two strikers [Kenny Miller and Rudy Gestede] missed their penalties as well, and one of the greatest players to grace the Premier League [Steven Gerrard] missed the first one. At the party, my family were there for me, and Lee Naylor and his partner at the time were unbelievable for me. They didn't leave me alone, making sure I was okay. I must have drunk about 30 bottles of Heineken, at the party and we went out after it, and I'm not joking, to this day I was stone cold sober going home. I could have drunk petrol, I could have drunk white spirit, nothing could have got me drunk and let me forget that penalty, nothing at all.'

City fans at the other end fell to their knees, to their chairs and into each other's arms in devastation. They were crushed and most of all, they were exhausted. Joshua Slack adds, 'It was gut-wrenching,

I think that goes for all the other City fans as well. But then again, I was proud of what we had achieved as a club – Malky and the lads put everything into that final and not one of them players on the pitch could be ashamed of losing to Liverpool, because every one of them put their hearts on the line for the club. It is some of the best football I have seen in terms of pure grit and determination, and we were very unfortunate to lose on penalties in my opinion. It was hard to take, of course, but the lads could definitely take a lot of positives heading into the rest of the Championship campaign that season.'

It was a game of so many emotions, a game that started with Cardiff having little more than an outside chance and it ended with them having so many chances, it seemed, to win it. Only Cardiff could give you hope and then send you crashing back down like this and that's how it felt so often for these fans, not least on this memorable night, but there was no time to hold such a belief.

This time, the Bluebirds had done themselves proud; this time, they had made the world stop and look, to take notice when everyone expected to see a whitewash. A club on the verge of extinction just a couple of years before was still creating history, whether they won or not, and against opponents imbued with a history of success, they came within inches of winning the League Cup.

Malky Mackay said after the game, 'We wanted to come here and win today but the players have done the club proud. I think today we were playing against a top team and I think we have got a lot to be proud of. You have seen two teams who have put everything into that game. We can take a lot of self-belief from getting to the final of a 92-club competition and taking a team at the top of the Premier League to penalties. We will patch up our squad and give it the best shot. We have got from now until the end of the season. For most of them it's the first time they've been anywhere near something like this. There is a lot of emotion out there because it is a young side and emotions are running high. We had a chance in the last minute of the game but Kenny [Miller] just blazed over. The way we came back, I'm so proud of them. We lost with dignity.'

It just wasn't to be and, just like in 2008, Cardiff fans left a cup final at Wembley feeling distraught but again, and this time more than before, there was an immense feeling of pride, that their team had proved something and defied the odds.

Joshua Slack continues, 'There was of course disappointment when me and my dad left the Wembley concourses, because we had come so far, but we could all hold our heads high because we saw the Bluebirds put in an unbelievable shift against one of the best teams in Europe.'

It was league success that the Bluebirds craved so badly, but how occasions like this whet the appetite for that success. It also set the foundations for future improvements and now supporters really believed in Mackay. If he could implement and execute a game plan worthy of stopping a team like Liverpool for 120 minutes, he could get this club out of the Championship if, given the time. And so the Bluebirds faithful walked back down Wembley Way again disappointed but this time heads were held a little higher, this time, they left knowing that it was just a matter of time until success came knocking on Cardiff City's door.

The rebrand

ON TUESDAY, 8 May 2012, just one day after Cardiff's defeat in the play-off second leg at West Ham, the club called a meeting with supporters. The people who attended would leave distraught, heartbroken and stunned. Members from Cardiff City Supporters Club, Cardiff City Supporters' Trust and even supporters who run popular message boards were called in as a representation of the Bluebirds faithful to hear a damning message. Chaired by Alan Whiteley and attended by other club officials, the meeting was held to tell this select group of supporters that things had to change.

Despite the arrival of new owners in the last couple of years, the club was failing. Money was pouring into a bottomless well by the bucket load and any income was getting swallowed up. The Bluebirds were meandering towards possible administration unless there was significant investment. Not only that, but the Langston debt owed to former chairman Sam Hammam continued to hang over the capital's club.

These supporters were then given an ultimatum, in effect, with Whiteley delivering the message that Vincent Tan was willing to plough £100m into the club. That included reducing debt, spending big on next season's squad, a new training base and a stadium extension. However, he would only do this if there was an overhaul of the club's image. He wanted a red kit, so that Cardiff City resonated with the Asian market, and to go with it, a red badge with a large Welsh dragon. The fans in attendance were shown the new badge proposal, which was different to the eventual design, and the bluebird was nowhere to be seen.

The fans had been put in an unfair position. They had to gauge whether their fellow supporters would prefer to become a lower-division club again, possibly flirting with administration, or instead change everything – the kit colour, the badge – and lose such a huge part of their identity in exchange for success. It's not a choice any football fan should have to make, but while it wasn't all down to what was conveyed by the supporters in this meeting, there certainly was a huge responsibility on their shoulders to give a reaction that would represent their peers.

And that in itself is unfair to ask. One can only give his or her own opinion – you can never predict what everyone else is thinking, especially not more than 20,000 fans. In the meeting, most supporters gave a straight up 'no', saying they'd prefer to take their chances in blue. Two weren't sure and one more was completely in favour.

It was a choice between survival and progress or potentially losing more than 100 years of history, of heritage and culture. Those who were against it knew that by taking the risk, they may not end up with a club to support, or in any case that it could end up a shadow of the club they supported. But to lose everything they loved while growing up about Cardiff City Football Club was it really worth making progress and was it worth surviving?

The message was clear from the supporters at that meeting; the majority didn't want change and that was received by Whiteley and his colleagues. It was then communicated to the Malaysians, and a statement was released two days later which said that there would be no changes to the colours of the club or to the badge, but now the club had to live within its means and there would be no investment.

Coming from then CEO Dato Chan, it read, 'It is clear to all concerned that the club cannot continue to function in its current state, effectively losing large amounts of money each month, while acquiring more and more debt. We have continued along this path until the end of the current season, but the club inevitably now faces bold and real-world decisions should we want to see the club survive.

'As romantic and simplistic a notion as it may seem, maintaining our current course without growth or chance, is not, and cannot be an option. In light of the vociferous opposition by a number of the fans to the proposals being considered, as expressed directly to our local management and through various media and other outlets, we will not proceed with the proposed change of colour and logo and the team will continue to play in blue for the next season with the current badge. We will now reassess in conjunction with the board of the club the future strategy and the further ongoing investment necessary to allow the club to continue to trade. This may include looking for new and additional partners and investors.'

That was not good news either. A club striving for promotion year on year was now in danger of becoming one that had to battle for survival. That's the reality of it in the Championship. Cardiff were losing about £1m per month with a debt of £70m and with player and staff wages at a whopping 90 per cent of the turnover. A business cannot survive like that so turning such damning finances around wasn't going to be easy.

In reality, it wasn't going to be fixed without investment, which had now been passed up, and supporters started to question whether the right decision was made, whether indeed it was worth changing things to make progress or even to stay alive. It wasn't their fault. Others will say Cardiff fans, or at least those who were in favour, sold their soul, but there are crucial considerations. These supporters shouldn't have been given such a choice, and they hadn't exactly had it easy in the past. There had been so many heartbreaks going for promotion and now the very idea of promotion could be completely removed, and this is a club that had spent far too long in the shadows.

Ben Price was one of the many supporters left torn. He recalls, 'The rebrand for me was a difficult one. I understood why fans were so opposed to it but I was also tempted by the end reward that was promotion. I had seen Cardiff fail so many times that I was desperate to see my club playing in the top flight.'

It took until 2003 to get out of League 1, or the Second Division as it was then known, and even after that, years of mediocrity followed. It's not all about success in football and Cardiff fans, at least the regular 12,000 to 15,000, aren't about success. They would be long gone if that was the case, but they had waited their turn, backed the club through such dark days, and many of them weren't about to quit. Many of them didn't follow the club because of its badge or because it was blue, they followed the team which is such a big part of many people's lives. If it was indeed 'red or dead' as it was made out to be, then for many, it simply had to be red.

Was it 'red or dead'? Probably not in the strictest sense. The club would have ended up dropping a division or two if they had not found an investor. But while some will disagree, a huge number chose red over that fate and there's no shame in that. It was choosing between a rock and a hard place. That's what Vincent Tan and his peers did very cleverly. They appeared to tease the idea of the rebrand, then take it away, leaving fans to realise that they may in fact be in deeper trouble not taking the deal, forcing supporters to question their ideals, and it really did change a lot of minds when the statement came out saying there would be no more investment. It was a relief to many, but to others it was a terminal diagnosis.

Then, out of the blue, on 6 June, just under a month after the original meeting with supporters, a statement was made by Alan Whitely, confirming that the rebrand would go ahead. It read, 'This club will always be Cardiff City Football Club and its name and heart will never change nor are any of the changes meant to destroy any part of its history or culture. The adoption of the new badge incorporating the proud symbol of the Welsh dragon, which was the symbol on the club's badge on the only occasion the FA Cup left England, with the iconic Bluebird and the new red home strip very proudly places Cardiff as the capital city of Wales, while also recognising its history and creates a symbolic fusion with Asia which will allow us to fly the Welsh flag on behalf of Cardiff wherever we go.'

The day had arrived, the rebrand was going to happen. And one cannot put into words the confusion that took place inside the heads of so many supporters. Many were outraged, a minority were pleased and then there were others who didn't know what to feel.

Ben Price continues, 'I was conflicted, I was watching a team who had Cardiff City on the badge, but it wasn't the club I supported. The red, the badge, the infighting with the fans, I can safely look back on that time and say it wasn't worth a second of it.'

A state of numbness ensued for so many. On one hand, the club was saved, and this was its golden chance to progress, a one-way ticket to success and perhaps the only chance to clear a long-standing debt that had threatened the capital's club for so long. On the other hand, so much that fans fell in love with as a child had been wiped out in one fell swoop. The history behind Cardiff City would remain – nobody could ever take it away – but now so much was going to change overnight. Everything about this club is blue and now it would be red. The club was famous for the nickname the 'Bluebirds' and now what? 'The Dragons'? There were so many questions and the Bluebirds faithful were never going to like the answers. The positives? The debt would be more or less cleared. The club would strive for success via financial means in the same way that Leicester City had done through Asian investment, and the club's very future was guaranteed.

The new badge was released and this time it did feature a bluebird, albeit a very small one, and it also included a large Welsh dragon and the words 'Fire and Passion' also included. The common consensus was that it looked like a beer mat and very few – even those who weren't as bothered by the rebrand – liked that logo. It was very poorly designed, and it had no resemblance to Cardiff City.

The inferior bluebird under the dragon was seen as an insult more than anything else – it was met with fierce opposition. The new kit wasn't so bad, it was nicely designed by Puma with the same design for the home and away kit in different colours. There was, at least, a blue and yellow away kit that many bought instead to wear to home games and the red and black home kit predictably wasn't so popular. Even so, it still sold well, and it was quite an attractive design with all the connotations aside. When it was released, however, there was still an element of disbelief around what was happening. And that probably didn't settle in until the actual team walked out at the Cardiff City Stadium in that red and black strip.

This wasn't the first time a club had been rebranded – although it was new ground in the English Football League – with plenty of clubs overseas going through such changes, although most of them were through sponsorship like Red Bull Salzburg, for example. That sort of switch also came with a new name, shared with the energy drink, the makers of which are, of course, the club's owners. You also see it with clubs in the USA, but they are more franchised and it's more common practice there, where in the past people would support different franchises each year. That wasn't the case with Salzburg and many of their fans were left, like Cardiff supporters, devastated when they saw their club rebranded.

Unfortunately, however, there's not an awful lot fans can do about it but protest and Cardiff fans struggled to get anything off the ground with the success that would follow on the pitch. There are no rules in the Football League to prevent such a change; they only require that supporters are consulted beforehand, so Cardiff were left on their own, in the dark and at the mercy of their owner, Vincent Tan, who became a villain overnight in South Wales.

Unsurprisingly, it took a little while for him to say anything. But he did eventually put pen to paper to address the outraged faithful. His statement read, 'For all concerned I would like to emphasise that I hold no desire to trample on club history or heritage and would be saddened if supporters thought that this was my intention. I have the greatest respect for the Welsh national symbol of the red dragon. I believe it to be a symbol of great strength and I was surprised it had such little coverage on the club's badge.

'Whether people agree with this decision or not, I firmly believe that this change in colour and stature will give this club a new focus and a dynamism, linking as it does the symbolism of the colour red and the new focus on the Welsh dragon, along with the retention of the long-standing Bluebird element. With the powerful images these portray in both Wales and the Asian marketplaces I am prepared to back this vision with the investment that we have outlined above, which I would hope demonstrates both my commitment and confidence in that strategy.

'Given our commitment to date, I sincerely would like to see our supporters join us on this journey with the sole desire of making Cardiff City Football Club the best it can be. There is no reason why any existing supporter needs to feel disenfranchised. This is and will always remain your club.'

Tan arrived at the club as part of a consortium but over time he became the outright owner, taking up more shares to become the controlling force behind the club. And he had exercised that control to the extreme with the rebrand. He gave Cardiff the money they wanted, the money they needed, but at such a price that it was almost cruel in that sense. He felt that he could make Cardiff more popular in Asia, a huge market, but he failed to gauge that it could and would cost the club so much money in its current base. And while the Asian market is based on success, the fans who go week-in, week-out aren't, so if you lose them, when times are tough, you've lost everyone.

It turned out that Tan didn't lose everyone, however, and some were on board with the changes. Perhaps that's generous; it's probably a better fit to say many put up with the changes to see their club thrive and to see the threat of extinction disappear. Survival was ensured by Tan, who ploughed in £35m, which included a war chest for Malky Mackay, £10m to settle the Langston debt and a further £12m for a stadium expansion. Tan had already made other investments into the club and with money clearing further debts around the club, his total investment would, as promised, be taken to £100m.

That was enough to win some supporters over, or at least it was a comfort for fans to deal with what was happening. But for others, like Thomas Griffiths, it was simply too much to take. He recalls, 'On the way back from West Ham in the play-offs, rumours were flying around the bus of a change of colour and identity in line with Mr Tan's dreams of becoming more successful. These were rightly laughed off at the time.

'As the summer passed and the changes occurred, confusion surrounded the club and the fans. As I had already renewed my season ticket, as I had the ten years previously, I decided that I would still give it a shot. You can't slate something that you haven't tried, right? I lasted 45 minutes at the first game. It was soulless. Something was massively missing for me. Something I couldn't quite put my finger on.

'As most football fans would agree, when you start following a football team home and away, you feel part of something. As the years went go by, the fans stood next you at Ninian Park, the Cardiff City Stadium and other grounds around the country, become more like family. I felt part of something. I felt like I mattered. My voice and my need to follow 11 complete strangers around the country week in, week out, it mattered. I attempted a few more games that season.

'I can honestly say I felt five per cent of the joy that I used to feel when the Blues scored. I started to question why I still bothered. As the season went on, it finally made sense. Football is a business. It no longer felt like I mattered. Vincent Tan didn't care about whether it was a loyal bum sitting on that seat, he only cared that a bum was sat on that seat. I felt anger towards my fellow fans, who seemed blinded by success. I no longer purchased anything from the club shop or in the ground as I didn't want to line the tyrant's pockets.

'I was bitter. Very bitter. Towards my fellow fans and people who touted that Tan was saving the club. I hated all the in-fighting. People were singled out and threatened for not being pro red. Months turned to years and I completely lost of track of goings-on. I could set my watch by whether City were at home or away, but now I found myself checking the internet to see if it was safe to go to Leckwith at 3pm to do some shopping.

'I can honestly say now looking back that Vincent Tan has done me a favour. I'm happier. I now spend my money on things that make me happier rather than pissing it up the wall. I'm on the verge of buying my own home and getting married. I holiday regularly and go to watch music gigs weekly. Maybe football is a business, but it certainly isn't the business for me anymore.'

Thomas wasn't alone. Around 70 supporters requested refunds on season tickets and many others simply stayed away. Even those who remained could understand the reasoning from others. Ben Price adds, 'I completely understood why people walked away. My uncle got me into supporting Cardiff, he loved the club from a young lad but even he couldn't go anymore. It wasn't the same club and I was close to not renewing after relegation, but I guess I was just a sucker for punishment.'

There's absolutely no doubt that the majority stuck around. There was an attendance of more than 21,000 for the first game of the season, against Huddersfield, and that was only down by around 1,000 from the first home game of the campaign before, which was against local rivals Bristol City, so in reality it probably wasn't less than expected at all. Having said that, many did stay away and that was their right, their choice. They weren't wrong to do that and the supporters who stayed weren't right.

In some cases, you can say that supporters should be loyal no matter what, but this wasn't one of them. This was an extenuating circumstance and it was about everyone making the choice for themselves. Unfortunately, it wasn't all that easy. People who bought the red shirts were taunted at games and taunted online by those who walked away or those who stayed and only wore blue, and that was the saddest thing about the whole saga.

Inadvertently, Vincent Tan had managed to turn Cardiff City fans against each other and there were regularly heated arguments whether it was at a game or via social media. The supporters were hurt, and they were forced to take it out on each other.

Ben Price says, 'I soon regretted my decision [to continue despite the rebrand], the divide between the fans was not worth those few months in the top flight. I kept on watching Cardiff but from November onwards it became a chore. For the first time I can remember I wasn't excited to head to the stadium, I didn't get the buzz I used to get when I saw the pitch as I walked to my seat. It was sad, I love football and I love Cardiff City but that season in the Premier League with the rebrand pushed me as close as I have ever come to walking away from the sport altogether.'

The club, with the knowledge it was going to be ruthlessly criticised, closed its doors to supporters, it cut them off and that just left them at each other's throats. That was the start of it, in many ways. Success on the pitch is temporary but a club's culture is not.

At this point, it was only showing in the form of arguments between fans and a couple of small-scale protests, but the rot had started and even if it would take a couple of years, it was eventually going to swallow the club up. Meanwhile, fans still had to get used to the idea of their team playing in red. And it was quickly going to become a reality with the new season fast approaching. It was even strange for players like Robert Earnshaw, who had come through of the club as a youngster before returning in 2011. Speaking to BBC Sport, he said, 'To be honest it's still not quite sinking in. It's like someone playing a little bit of a joke. It's going to be weird, though. For me at 16 coming through I was playing in blue and I've always played in blue. Coming back last year it was blue. All the fans who have supported the team going back years, maybe even before my time, they've always known blue. It's going to be really strange, but we'll see how it goes.'

Ultimately, the players had a job to do and that's how they had to approach the season, despite being taken aback by what had happened and the subsequent fall-out. Speaking to Scott Johnson in his book, *Cardiff City: Rebranded*, then captain Mark Hudson talks about the reaction. He says, 'I think we were at the training ground. It wasn't as if we were sat down and told this was going to happen, it was filtered down from the top. It's very difficult to understand. For a club that's always been blue, to change their history is always going to be a shock to everyone involved.

'I found it very strange. I had never heard of it happening in football before and you understand the feelings of the fans completely, what their problems were with it. It's difficult for a player employed by the club to have any issue with it, we had to get our heads down and concentrate on what the task was, which was getting promotion.

'We were never told not to talk about it. We talked about it all the time, it's a big thing to happen to a club. It was something that we all went through as a group; staff, players and fans. If you're a Cardiff City player and walk through the city, fans do come up to you, which is great. It's something that I loved. It was always in fans' minds, what is Tan's reason behind it, but we could only answer for ourselves. That was what he thought was best for the club, what he wanted to do.'

It was a strange situation for the players, who couldn't do an awful lot to help. Perhaps not at all clubs, but the majority of players care about the supporters as the supporters are the ones who sing their names each week, they make them feel loved and welcomed. Fans are the ones who stop them in the street, as Hudson alluded to, and you're nothing special unless you're made to feel special by the people. Celebrity status is given to footballers, but that's only because of the media attention and the love supporters have for them.

If supporters all decided to not look twice when they saw a footballer in the street, they would soon lose any sense of importance and the majority of them don't forget that, regardless of what wages they receive. Most players who make it to the top are from a working-class background and most are down to earth. That is forgotten given the level of celebrity in the industry these days but it's still true, especially for clubs at Championship level and lower. The fans are important to the players and when they are so clearly hurting, it can be difficult going out and doing your job. You'll see it all the time, when a football club is run badly, and the supporters make their protests heard on match day, it can soon change the fortunes on the pitch, and Cardiff found that out later on.

However, at this point, Cardiff were aiming for promotion and they simply had to make the most of the money that was made available. And that's how much-loved club legend Kev McNaughton remembers it. Also speaking in *Cardiff City: Rebranded*, he says, 'I think as players it was just a case of knuckling down and getting on with your job. The squad at the time, in terms of professionalism, was probably the best we had at my time at the club. Looking back, I can't remember anyone kicking up a fuss about it. We were pretty focused on the job in hand. I think when you spend a good deal of time at a club, you do feel part of it. It becomes your club.

'So, when the fans are suffering, it does have an effect on you. No player enjoys seeing supporters divided or unhappy. At the time, I don't think the players felt there was much they could do in terms of speaking to guys at the top. Looking back now, maybe we could have spoken to them about it. Whether it would have made a difference, I don't know.'

One thing the players could affect was their fortunes on the pitch and promotion was very much the target from the off. This level of investment does not come around too often for Championship clubs and the Bluebirds – yes, that remained their nickname – were desperate to take advantage, especially on the back of an encouraging previous season. Failure wasn't an option. This opportunity to reward the fans for sticking around in the hardest time that any supporter could possibly imagine, just had to be taken advantage of.

The ~~Blues~~ Reds
are going up

AMID THE chaos of the rebrand, Malky Mackay set about building a promotion-worthy squad with a healthy war chest to spend on players, provided, as promised, by Vincent Tan. Mackay would spend around £10m in total during the summer and that saw some top-quality Championship names arriving through the doors at the Cardiff City Stadium.

Craig Bellamy returned on a free transfer, taking a pay cut to become a permanent Bluebird with the view of ending his career in South Wales. Another experienced forward in Heidar Helguson also arrived on a free transfer. Mackay's biggest outlay was for former Bristol City and West Ham striker Nicky Maynard, who cost £2.5m, while a further £2m was spent on South Korean talent Kim-Bo-Kyung. Filip Kiss joined permanently for £500,000 and he was joined by Matthew Connolly and Tommy Smith on relatively small fees. Craig Noone and Jordon Mutch cost another £3m between them and Cardiff also took a punt on Slovenian striker Etien Velikonja for over £1.5m. Answers on a postcard.

There were plenty of outgoings as well, as Mackay set about reshaping his squad despite the relative success of the season before. The likes of Anthony Gerrard, Kenny Miller, Jon Parkin, Tom Heaton and Darcy Blake all departed among a list of 14 outgoing players.

The Bluebirds were confident after a strong pre-season which saw them demolish Premier League club Newcastle United at home, although you never can read too much into friendlies – that's rule number one of the new season. There wasn't any over-confidence but with fans feeling as if they were trading their soul for success, it was almost expected.

Mark Hudson made the Bluebirds' intentions clear early on. He said, 'Top two is the main aim for us. I don't think anyone wants to see us go through the play-offs again. I definitely don't. But with the squad we've got this year and the way we've gelled over the last 12 to 13 months, as a group we're a lot more solid now.'

The rebrand aside, Cardiff had been close for years despite working on a limited budget, so a simple probability test tells you that spending £10m on top of that will likely bring you that elusive promotion. However, it doesn't always work like that in football and fans had learned not to get their hopes up by now. That was a foolish move which would only result in disappointment.

In terms of 'buying success', plenty of teams have tried in the Championship and beyond but it doesn't always work, especially in England's second tier, where you have to get the balance of the squad right to go up. Even promotion expert Neil Warnock recognises that. He claims, 'It's all right having money, but you've still got to spend it right. You've still got to get a dressing room behind you. Sometimes it's more difficult when you've got money.'

If you buy too many egos, too many players who are used to success, then you'll end up with egg on your face. It's made out to be easy if you have money, but it's just as difficult, only the challenges are different.

That was for Mackay and his coaching staff to worry about, and on the outside, they continued to instil a belief and a confidence around the Cardiff City Stadium that wasn't there before. Mackay wasn't cocky as such in public, but whereas with Dave Jones it was a little 'we will see what we can do' or 'we will give it our best shot', Malky was very much 'we know how good we are, and we have to prove it.'

He didn't hide from the players that they were expected to perform. This was a group that included some of the best names in the Championship and pressure comes with that. Malky spread confidence around the squad and that level of expectation, which wasn't there during his first season, became a mainstay. That wasn't just his doing, though. The rebrand placed a real pressure upon

Malky and his team because the only thing that would make it all worse is if it was all for nothing.

Fan Jordan Jones says, 'With the promised investment after the rebrand, the promotion had to happen. Any slip-up while we were playing in foreign colours, would be used against the rebrand. The season before, it was just a feeling of pride to be competing in the play-offs after a gruelling League Cup Final. We knew it was a project and we're excited for what the future held for us.'

Cardiff kicked off the season with a home clash with newly-promoted Huddersfield Town, a team they had needed extra time to beat in the League Cup the season before. More than 21,000 turned up to see the new stars in action but the game didn't take off in the way it was expected to. Huddersfield were resolute at the back, making it difficult for the home side, but the manner in which the winner came – captain Mark Hudson turning home a stoppage-time goal – provided a significant boost to Cardiff's confidence.

That gave the Bluebirds an early sense of 'we can always find a way' and it wasn't the last time a late opening-day goal would set the tone for their season. Cardiff went on to draw their next game, against Brighton, which saw Etien Velikonja miss from about two yards out, before losing away to Severnside rivals Bristol City.

A record of a win, a draw and a defeat was hardly flattering from the first three games but Cardiff were just finding their stride. They won their next three games, first of all thanks to a Peter Whittingham hat-trick at home to Wolves – it was a good job they had turned down a bid for him in the summer. Then came a victory over Leeds – which saw Bellamy get his first goal back in Cardiff's adopted colours, – and an away win over Millwall to round off a purple patch, although that that last result left a bitter taste in the mouth, with big summer signing Maynard suffering an almost season-ending knee injury.

Cardiff then lost three of their next five but after that, they seldom looked back and soared to the top of the Championship with an incredible run of 13 wins from 16 games, with just one defeat, ensuring they were the ones to catch.

The winter signing of Fraizer Campbell really pushed the Bluebirds, giving them the boost they needed. Campbell, who, in some ways was a little reminiscent of the outgoing legend Robert Earnshaw, scored the winner at Leeds on his debut. And he would go on to get five goals in his first five games, helping Cardiff to three crucial victories. It was a very astute signing, and he wasn't the only one. Defender Leon Barnett joined on loan in March for a month or so and he filled the void left by injured captain Mark Hudson superbly. He is another player who many look back on as being a pivotal signing during the course of the season.

The performances weren't all that pretty, in truth, and Mackay didn't employ a particularly pretty style of play. It was resolute at the back with the knowledge that they had the talent up top to hurt teams when they did venture forward. The reserved game plan was also shown in the scores, as in 11 of those 13 victories, the Bluebirds came out on top by just one goal. That's how things were under Mackay, who by this point had developed a reputation of being a man of the people.

The Scotsman had become loved with his fist pumps after games and he seemed to take time to connect with supporters. True entertainment was limited to the odd occasions when Cardiff blew teams away, like in a memorable 4-1 win at Ewood Park. It went down as one of the best away performances in a long, long time. The level of talent on display that night was enough to win over even the most cynical Cardiff fan, so this team were capable of scoring goals as well as playing it a little safer. Mind you, with a squad with that level of talent, it was hardly surprising.

It was, however, the steely, hard-working side of Cardiff that carried them towards success. They were difficult to beat and that was shown in pivotal results like an away victory over Ipswich when Heidar Helguson scored twice to ensure a successful comeback, and when Tommy Smith's deflected long-range effort won it at Blackpool. With characters like Aron Gunnarsson, Ben Turner, Mark Hudson – who would suffer a season-ending injury in March – and Craig Bellamy, the Bluebirds just weren't going to lie down. And they demanded 100 per cent from each other, 100 per cent of the time. That was made clear when youngster Ben Nugent scored an own goal against Bristol City to give the away team a lifeline – he got an absolute bollocking!

It was also expected by the manager. Mackay was quite intense in his methods, he always expected 100 per cent and those who didn't give that didn't make the grade. We'll later discover that it was part of Malky's downfall but for now, it was working, and to terrific effect.

Cardiff won just one in five games and there seemed to be a wobble taking place as the end of the season drew closer, but that run in the middle months had given them a buffer. Even after that stutter the Bluebirds held a four-point gap over second-placed Hull and were six clear of third place, and with a game in hand over both. After a big home win over Blackburn and a crucial away draw against promotion rivals Watford – much to the thanks of David Marshall's heroics in goal – Cardiff were on their way, although for many fans that nagging doubt remained.

If anyone could mess up such an opportunity it was the Bluebirds, and that feeling was given some merit when Barnsley took a point at the Cardiff City Stadium to ensure the home team's game in hand went to waste. In typical Cardiff fashion, Barnsley grabbed a stoppage-time equaliser thanks to a huge deflection which sent Marshall one way and the ball, travelling at the slowest possible speed, went in the other direction. 'Here we go again' murmured fans leaving the stadium.

There was a real sense that Cardiff needed to put things right the following Saturday at home to Nottingham Forest, and they did so in some style with a 3-0 win in about as one-sided a game as you could wish to see – it would prove to be Cardiff's last victory of the season, too. The doubts were vanquished, especially when the table indicated that the Bluebirds only needed to avoid defeat in their next game to get promoted.

More than 26,000 supporters turned out to see the moment the club had been waiting for, a home clash with Charlton Athletic, and all they needed to do was avoid defeat to secure their place in the Premier League.

Chances came and went but news was filtering through that Watford had gone 1-0 down in the 83rd minute and that meant Cardiff would be up regardless of the result in the Welsh capital, if things stayed as they were.

Charlton, who had beaten Cardiff 5-4 in a spectacular game earlier in the season, had done well under Chris Powell but they had little to play for that evening. It probably helped Cardiff come through the test, and it meant there were few nerves late on. Charlton players were more worried about getting mobbed by on-rushing supporters than grabbing a late goal, and you can bet those home fans were already plotting their route on to the pitch as Powell turned to Mackay to shake his hand before the final whistle.

Then it was confirmed. Referee Scott Mathieson blew the final whistle and relief poured out of the stands as supporters ran on. Cardiff were promoted. exactly 53 years since their last elevation to the top flight and after three consecutive seasons of play-off heartbreak. Craig Bellamy collapsed on to his backside in tears as supporters around him expressed their gratitude and delight. Cardiff had finally made it to the Premier League after years of heartbreak and beyond that, years of disappointment in the lower leagues.

Many felt this wasn't their club being promoted, it was not the way they wanted to see Cardiff City reach the Premier League following the rebrand. And it did take the edge off celebrations, as supporter Jordan Jones remembers: 'I would say the rebrand did affect the celebrations, as there was a contingent of supporters who stopped supporting the club due to the rebrand and, of course, that left a small hole. I enjoyed it myself, as it was my club being promoted to the top flight, where we would be pitted against some top sides.'

However, for most, it was forgotten for a moment, even if it was just for that moment. You can take away the badge, you can change the shirt, but it will always be Cardiff City to the majority of fans and this was what everyone lay in bed dreaming about. They had been beaten to the post by Swansea City two years previously, but this was their turn and my goodness they were going to celebrate it.

The players celebrated too. There's a famous image of Kev McNaughton being carried by supporters with a smile across his face, celebrating as one of the supporters, which is what fans really loved about him. He gave 100 per cent in every single game, he'd leave the pitch on his last legs and that aside, he displayed the passion of a supporter. In recent times, you'll seldom see a player loved quite like Kev was by Cardiff City fans in his ten years at the club, and he will always be remembered in South Wales. Perhaps more so after he stuck around, despite suffering so much disappointment, and then became one of the players to get Cardiff over the line. That was a terrific night of never-to-be-forgotten celebration for fans.

Regardless of the red shirts and the comical badge, the Bluebirds were finally there, at the pinnacle. Malky Mackay also expressed his delight by saying, 'I'm very proud of the football club. There has been a lot of disappointment in the last few years, but a great deal of money has gone into this football club over the last four years and I'm delighted for everyone involved. As a manager it's about looking after a group of people and asking them to come back time and again. That is why I am so proud and pleased with what has happened.

'The owner has been into the dressing room and he is someone who has been really hands-on. A lot of credit has to go to him. For him to come over here and put trust in myself and the players is wonderful. He has made sure that we have got a blend of good players and good people in the backroom. You have to have good people to achieve something like this. It is a very tough division to get out of and we have achieved that.

'We have been there at the top since November and that brings with it its own pressures. But we have continued to respect our opposition, and that has been key to our success. I won't prevent the boys from celebrating. I don't think I will have any choice in the matter.'

Skipper Mark Hudson added, 'We had 12 professionals when he arrived, and he needed to sign a lot of players that first summer. We made the play-offs last season, but it wasn't to be. But he has done a fantastic job and the chairman, too. He has backed the manager throughout. The fans have been patient, too. They have been fantastic. It's been good for them. Since November we have shown a consistency that you need in this league.

'You ask the boys in there and it is the best squad they have been involved in. We have put everything into every game and into training too and we have finally done it. All the manager has said is for us to show consistency, seven days a week. That is what we have given him. I would have loved to have been in the shirt today, but it was not to be. But that's football, you get injured. But I have been in there throughout, right up until kick-off, and it's a great dressing room. The best I have been in.'

The celebrations continued into the following weeks, but there was still a job to be done, particularly a few days later when Cardiff could win the title with a point, while Burnley needed one of their own to secure Championship safety. Cardiff took the lead through Craig Conway but they were pegged back in injury time, meaning another draw and another set of celebrations. This time the Bluebirds were crowned title winners and around 1,000 fans made the long trip up to Lancashire to enjoy another special occasion with the players. Those fans had flags and banners to commemorate the fact they were crowned the best team in the Championship.

However, the real celebrations took place back at home just one week later. The draw with Bolton was followed by a post-match presentation of the Championship trophy. Another big crowd of more than 26,000 squeezed inside the Cardiff City Stadium to see a moment that fans had been awaiting for such a long time. That extended to the man who presented the trophy, too. Stuart Beasley, a representative from then Championship sponsors nPower, decided to get in on the celebrations, presenting the trophy to Mark Hudson before turning and celebrating it with the players. Craig Bellamy then gave him a shove off the stage in what was a rather strange turn of events, but who can blame him for taking his opportunity?

It was another day to remember and one without stress unlike so many other promotion battles. Supporters could sit back, relax and enjoy the celebrations as their team lifted the trophy that crowned them the best in the Championship. After years of disappointment they wouldn't have cared if they finished 15th and by some miracle got promoted because of a good disciplinary record, so to come out on top was just the icing on the cake and another reason to celebrate a memorable season.

But the season wasn't quite over yet. Still One game remained and that meant there was still time for another draw, their fourth in a row to finish the campaign – talk about limping over the line. They still had a big part to play, however, in an enjoyable day out in Hull which saw fans go in fancy dress, as is traditional, for a fun away trip on the final day, and there haven't been many of those down the years for Cardiff fans.

Hull were second on 78 points, which is desperately low for a Championship team looking to finish as runners-up. But they were still in a position where, if they could match or better Watford's result, they would be promoted. Cardiff didn't exactly help. Fraizer Campbell opened the scoring against his former club to put the cat among the pigeons and after Watford equalised against Leeds before half-time, Hull fans went into the break feeling rather sick about the situation. A Nick Proschwitz equaliser helped their cause in the second half and Paul McShane grabbed what the Tigers hoped would be the winner, especially after Andrew Taylor was sent off for Cardiff.

The Premier League was in sight for Steve Bruce and his men, especially when Ben Nugent conceded a penalty in stoppage time and many home fans spilled on to the pitch to celebrate, despite the game not being over. They were finally ushered back into the stands as Proschwitz stepped up and Bruce turned away, unable to watch, with good reason as David Marshall saved the spot kick.

Cardiff cleared and in one of the next phases of play, from a throw-in, the ball hit on to a Hull hand and a Cardiff penalty was awarded. A state of shock descended upon the KC Stadium, while the Cardiff fans behind the goal celebrated, mostly with laughter at Hull's expense. It was an unbelievable turn of events which took another twist when Nicky Maynard, who was making his first appearance off the bench since that near season-ending knee injury, stepped up and dispatched the penalty into the bottom corner. Bedlam followed behind the goal in the Cardiff end while the Hull fans watched on, devastated, thinking their Premier League dream was over – but it wasn't.

The all-important Watford v Leeds game was around 15 minutes behind, meaning an anxious wait for Hull at the final whistle, and when former Cardiff striker Ross McCormack scored a 90th-minute penalty for Leeds it meant the celebrations could begin. Hull fans surged on to the pitch and it crowned off a memorable season for both teams.

Hull had grabbed second with a strangely low total of 79 points, but they didn't care. Both clubs had been promoted and in a rare football moment, both sets of fans celebrated together in the sunshine on Humberside. Some fans swapped shirts and the rest sung Premier League songs together. A wonderful moment, the sort you don't see enough of in football.

The Premier League awaited and the supporters enjoyed the thought of that. A historic season had come to an end for Cardiff City. And so did a 53-year absence from the top flight.

'Next season, Bluebirds, we're dining in style.'

'We've finally made it'

REACHING THE Premier League became an obsession for Cardiff over the course of five years. It started with that desperate heartbreak of missing out on the play-offs by one goal and it grew ever stronger. It was setback after setback, but each teary-eyed occasion only enhanced the Bluebirds' desperate lust to reach the promised land.

It's strange when you think about it, how a club only promoted from League 1 in 2003 could develop such a craving for the Premier League, but few outfits develop quite so quickly as Cardiff had in these years, even with a few hiccups along the way.

The Bluebirds were a big club in days of the past, so it was a case of revamping that belief after being one of the many 'sleeping giants' in English football. Cardiff aren't on the level – in terms of size and stature – of the likes of Leeds and Aston Villa, others who will claim to be 'sleeping giants', but they certainly weren't a League 1 club. The Championship? Perhaps. That seems to be Cardiff's true level if ever one did exist. But that didn't stop the dreamers in South Wales and fortunately, or perhaps by good selection, Cardiff ended up with a couple of dreamers in Dave Jones and Malky Mackay, both of whom played their part in finally bringing Premier League football to the Welsh capital. They were managers who thought with their hearts and not their heads, men who had ambition beyond what was realistic, an ambition that went beyond scepticism.

Cardiff were in the Championship for a decade, which should not be discounted as a short space of time – that's how long it took for the Bluebirds to reach the top after promotion from League 1. Teams have done it in far shorter timescales, not least Swansea City.

The success achieved down the M4 by Swansea, who many at the time they were promoted believed to be a smaller club following their years in the doldrums of the Football League, only heightened Cardiff's sense of urgency.

Football rivalry is a funny thing and it has many strings to its bow. Ultimately, it's about competition, who's doing better, and that applies both at board level with financial competition and signing the best young players in the country, and at the fans' level, with supporters gloating with their mates in the pubs. For Swansea to go up and stay up in the way that they did when everyone expected them to fail was impressive – even Cardiff fans had to admit it. There was jealousy, of course there was, with Swansea playing the best teams in the country while Cardiff were going up and down the country on a Tuesday evening, and all that contributed to this desperate need to be promoted.

For many, that desire to see Cardiff go up took a back seat when supporters realised that it may not be in blue anymore, but an average attendance of more than 22,000 during the promotion year – up by 1,000 or so from the previous season – tells you that the desire for success even outweighed any grudge with the rebrand. There are a cohort of loyal supporters at Cardiff, perhaps 10,000 or so, who would be there even in the darkest days of the lowest division, and perhaps it's a little unfair to say they turn up to see success – their presence during such unsuccessful times has proved any thought of that wrong. However, it's true to say that many of these supporters became as obsessed with promotion as the players and the staff at the football club. Probably because it was so close on so many occasions, probably because in that play-off final in 2010, for parts of that game, supporters and players could taste the Premier League, only to have it snatched away, almost like opening up your favourite chocolate bar before dropping it in a puddle.

With the financial issues, it appeared that the hope of promotion would become a distant memory. It was just so elusive and that left everyone desperate to end the nightmare., which was often compounded by the reputation of being 'bottlers'. Many in the Championship, as well as Swansea fans, which would take the opportunity to remind Cardiff fans of that reputation that their club had attracted during all those nearly occasions. The Bluebirds were the nearly men and that had to be put to bed, a mentality had to be overcome and it took a leader to make that happen.

Step forward Malky Mackay, who had his drawbacks, something we will discover later, but who was a leader, both as a player and a manager. He was exactly what Cardiff needed in such difficult circumstances, someone to show passion, unlike his predecessor, someone who embodied the traits of a Cardiff supporter. Possessing those traits allowed him to unite the fans, who had split over the departure of Jones and particularly the rebrand. There was a crack enforced upon the Cardiff fanbase that would take many years to heal, but Mackay did a good job of patching it up. So many supporters clung on to him and his ideals – or at least the public ones – and he got the supporters believing again, which was important, given so many lost belief from so many last gasp failures.

Many couldn't believe in the club anymore, it was a club that had failed them by altering their identity. But even many of those supporters still backed and believed in the team through the culture Mackay created. His fist pumps after games were almost a reassurance, offering comfort that the club was still one of passion and solidarity. You could wax lyrical about Mackay but there's no doubt that Cardiff got the right man at the right time when they appointed him in 2011, and ultimately, the proof was in the pudding.

In the end, it took a lot of money for Cardiff to secure promotion and it was no underdog story like it would have been five years previously. This was a team built on cash, it had a seasoned top-class pro in Craig Bellamy and others on large wages. Mackay was given a big pot to build on an already relatively successful team that had finished in the top six and taken Liverpool to penalties the season before. Cardiff were also considered one of the top Championship sides anyway by this point, after finishing in the top seven for four consecutive seasons, reaching the play-offs three times in a row. Predicted Championship tables usually end up way off, such is the nature of the division, but Cardiff would always be tipped for the top six by supporters and pundits alike. They were already a successful Championship team, one that many of the strugglers would aspire to replicate – on the pitch – and so when you add a £12m budget to that, you've always got a chance.

The website Transfermarkt estimates that the total value of arrivals in the 2012/13 season was in excess of £23m and for a Championship club at that time, it means bucket-loads of quality. Money doesn't make it easy, the Championship simply doesn't work like that, but with a steward like Mackay to guide the Bluebirds they seemed destined for the top as soon as Mark Hudson bundled in a late winner in that first game of the season.

There were setbacks, of course there were, but from the quality of goals being scored, it was clear this team simply had too much quality and the Premier League, albeit with a points total that would quite often only get you third place, was secured with comfort. That in itself was fitting given all the heartbreak Cardiff City fans had suffered while chasing promotion. To do it without any stress or worries was something the Bluebirds faithful really needed at this point – mind you, they certainly would have taken a stressful promotion if it meant the same result.

In terms of what it meant to supporters, that much was clear from the celebrations after making the top flight. There were fans in tears, and many others expressed their emotions with the help of an abundance of alcohol and even pyrotechnics, but it clearly meant the world to them. Not just because it was so elusive, either. As a football fan, you go along to all the meaningless occasions down the years with a hope and a dream of just one day seeing your team achieve success. Many don't even get to see that in their lifetime. And for a long list of loyal supporters – there are too many to name – they don't get to experience the emotion of seeing their team achieve that success before time runs out. However, it makes the celebrations more poignant for those in attendance who know how lucky they are to see such an occasion, in red or any other colour.

For supporters big or small, this was all that they had waited for, it's what they stared at the ceiling at night dreaming of. Non-football fans won't quite understand why, but Cardiff City Football Club is many people's lives. Other than family – and even that sometimes – nothing takes priority over the football. They put all their money and time into it and get so little back, so you can only imagine the outpouring of emotion when they finally do get to taste success. They deserve it, too.

Players and managers, they come and go, but supporters don't, they are there throughout. They stand in the rain, the sun, the snow and the wind. They put gallons of petrol in their cars and they buy extortionately priced train tickets all in the name of Cardiff City, and while the success is ultimately achieved by the exertions of the players themselves, promotion should be celebrated by supporters more than anyone, and indeed it was in this case.

As fans'-favourite Kev McNaughton was lifted aloft amid the sea of fans on the playing surface, that was evident and neither nobody nor nothing could spoil that moment, in which everything, the red kit, the change of badge, the hatred towards the owner and everything else was forgotten. For a section of fans, it was just a moment, for others it was a day, a month or a year, but 99 per cent of supporters had at least a moment to enjoy and savour.

Now the Premier League awaited. Gone were the days of Ipswich Town, Barnsley and Nottingham Forest. All those tiresome same away trips year on year. Now it was time for the bright lights of the top flight, new experiences and a chance to put Cardiff City on the map, to give the world an opportunity to get to know this football club.

The excitement was unbearable for supporters and while plenty of scepticism remained – that's born out of years ofBluebirds-like failure – this felt like a new dawn for the club and a real treat; an opportunity for fans to see talented players play in their city every other week, some of whom actually belonged to the club. They weren't playing for the opposing team, they weren't on loan, these were going to be Cardiff's players and that all factored in to the excitement, along with playing teams like Arsenal and Manchester United, visiting stadiums like the Emirates and Old Trafford.

It was a fantastic time to be a Cardiff fan and the summer simply couldn't go quickly enough as the countdown to the Premier League began.

It wasn't supposed to be this way

IT STARTED rather well, with so much excitement and optimism, and it would end with a whimper, with disappointment and anger. Cardiff City's Premier League season, their first campaign in the top flight since 1961/62, was highly anticipated. Season tickets flew off the shelves and there were sell-outs aplenty for fixtures at home and away. The Bluebirds faithful were unsurprisingly keen to seize their chance to see top flight football in the Welsh capital for the first time in 51 years.

Malky Mackay set about building his Premier League squad and he wasn't short of backing from Vincent Tan and the club's board. The Scotsman spent around £30m on transfer fees in total and five players left, four on frees while Heidar Helguson hung up his boots. Of the signings, Gary Medel was the most eye-catching, joining from Sevilla for a club record fee of £9.5m, and the defensive midfielder known as 'The Pitbull' didn't disappoint. Also in were Andreas Cornelius, a young Danish striker who was signed for £8m, and defender Steven Caulker, for a similar fee. Players like Kevin Theophile-Catherine and Peter Odemwingie also signed up for the Bluebirds' Premier League adventure. But the transfer fees for those players didn't come close to matching the big three, one of whom would go on to cause a fair bit of controversy.

Cardiff seemed to have a decent squad to go into the Premier League – there weren't too many big signings, but the players who did come in for big fees were going to supplement an already very talented group that had been built up before the previous season.

Those players already in place were worth well in excess of £30m which, for the Championship, was some squad, as the league table proved.

Malky and the supporters had real belief in players like Mark Hudson and Ben Turner despite their fitness issues, and it was clear that many others had the ability to play in the Premier League. Fraizer Campbell, Kim Bo-Kyung, Jordon Mutch and Craig Noone all seemed to possess a quality beyond the standard of the second tier, so they were entrusted to represent the Bluebirds in the top flight. The supporters were happy with that, too. They fully trusted Mackay's judgement at this point and they weren't going to question his signings, especially not after seeing Cornelius's best bits on YouTube, but there's a lesson to be learned there.

The excitement began to reach boiling point as the season arrived. And that was helped by the national media, who finally seemed to be taking notice of City now that they had secured a spot in the big time. Jim White from Sky Sports News was flying around all the Premier League grounds in a helicopter and his arrival at Cardiff was highly anticipated by supporters watching on. It's all a bit trivial, but it was also all very new for supporters, who weren't used to seeing their club being taken so seriously. This is the Premier League and while it was all a little strange in some ways, it proved to be a stark difference to the Championship lifestyle fans had grown used to in the previous ten years.

The very thought of finally getting to see the Bluebirds at the top table was sending the blood pressure through the roof. It was a long summer as fans began to count down the hours, especially when the fixtures were released. And the first home game was to be Manchester City, though Cardiff would kick off against West Ham away from home, a trip they hadn't long made twice in one season when the Hammers were in the Championship. Still, it was all a little different from a Championship game and the Premier League's introduction of a pre-match anthem, similar to the soundtrack of the Champions League, and the branded trimmings on the pitch pre-match, made every game feel like an occasion.

Now you probably wouldn't feel that if you were a fan of a Premier League club, but when you've come from the Championship

– which is a great league by the way – and you get used to the format. To get promotion and see how much more of a show every game is, it lights up your eyes. Cardiff fans were no different and it took a while for that novelty to wear off.

Before all that, before the drama of the season itself, arrived match day one. For Cardiff, it proved to be an early reality check when Joe Cole put West Ham in front within 13 minutes and Kevin Nolan finished the game off late on.

The Bluebirds simply didn't turn up and they got punished – welcome to the Premier League. That didn't destroy any belief, though. It takes more than that to kill early season optimism and Cardiff were yet to enjoy their first home fixture, against the 2011/12 champions Manchester City.

Manuel Pellegrini had spent big over the summer and he had an incredible level of talent at his disposal, so much so that they would win the league later that season. But way before they could even consider that possibility, they arrived in South Wales to a packed-out Cardiff City Stadium with more than 27,000 in attendance. Cardiff have a good history against the Citizens and there's one great memory in particular with Nathan Blake scoring a winner against them in an FA Cup home tie in 1994. No such upset was expected here, however, and on a beautiful August afternoon, home fans fans turned out in their numbers expecting to see some beautiful football, admittedly by the away side.

Cardiff did really well in the first half and it was a masterclass from Mackay, who knew how to set up an organised defence. However, top-flight quality shone through when Edin Dzeko still managed to break the deadlock in the 52nd minute with a thunderbolt from long range. That's one of the many difficult elements of the Premier League, however organised you are. You just cannot stop moments of magic from world-class players. And that can be so frustrating for a club like Cardiff.

But they responded excellently and the Sky Blues were the ones left stunned nine minutes later when Aron Gunnarsson dispatched a rebound from close range to pull Cardiff level. The celebrations were wild, but they were nothing compared to the 78th minute when Fraizer Campbell headed them into the lead. What on earth is happening, asked the fans in the stands as they jumped with joy and disbelief.

It would get better, too. City just didn't learn their lesson and with moments remaining, Campbell again climbed up to head home a corner and the scenes were simply unbelievable, an early souvenir from the Premier League. Alvaro Negredo managed to find the net in stoppage time, forcing a nervy final four minutes, but Cardiff held on to make a real statement of intent. They weren't just going to be the whipping boys, they were there to make an impact, or so it felt.

Celebrations continued long into the night after that very special win, and it was followed by two decent results, draws against Everton and Hull respectively. The Bluebirds were then seconds away from holding Tottenham in Wales before Paulinho scored a stunning back-heel to win it in stoppage time – there's that aforementioned sucker punch again.

Then came another chance to celebrate and another souvenir to take home from the Premier League, a 2-1 win at Fulham, where this time Cardiff were on the right side of a late goal. Jordon Mutch scored an absolute screamer, a curled effort from long range two minutes into stoppage time to send thousands of travelling fans into delirium. Again, however, Mackay's men were sent crashing back down to earth with a home defeat against Newcastle and a controversial 4-1 loss at Chelsea.

That's what supporters found so difficult in the Premier League. The good moments are fantastic, they're usually unexpected so they are celebrated wildly, but they are few and far between. Cardiff won just two of their first eight Premier League games and while that's not such a bad record alongside two draws – it's not quite relegation form – the Bluebirds had been used to winning for large parts of the previous five years. In the Premier League you can't get too down about bad runs but, that is easier said than done when you've been in the Championship for so long, doing well, and then all of a sudden, the good moments become few and far between. For clubs with a history of being mid-table in the Premier League, they are used to it and they appear content, but it takes a while for supporters to fall into that mindset.

It's a strange transition, especially for those who have spent so long in the division below.

The Bluebirds did have a few good moments to celebrate in November, and the month kicked off with the hotly-anticipated first Premier League South Wales derby, at the Cardiff City Stadium. There was a sell-out crowd, of course, and plenty of Swans fans made the trip down the M4, though their numbers were limited due to policing restrictions.

There was a strange confidence about the visiting supporters, which is seldom seen in a derby fixture. Usually, regardless of the difference in standard between the two teams, fans are cautious and nervous because they know anything can happen, but on this occasion, for some reason, the Swans appeared to be very confident. They brought with them a new song to tease the Cardiff faithful about their new red colour – you expect no less from rival supporters – and they expected to win. They had reason to, mind you; their squad was impressive, with the likes of Michu lighting up the Premier League in recent years, and manager Michael Laudrup had done well. He had lead the Swans to League Cup glory the season before, and then into Europe this season via the qualifiers.

Swansea were clear favourites, but it's always a mistake being confident in a derby. You'll often end up with egg on your face and Swansea supporters did when their former loan player Steven Caulker headed Cardiff in front in the second half to cue wild celebrations. The underdogs were doing it again, this time against their biggest rivals.

Swansea actually did quite well early on, but the game completely changed after a thumping Ben Turner challenge jolted Cardiff into gear. Swansea looked second best throughout after that and they never really looked like scoring. In fact, Cardiff looked to be getting a second when Campbell beat out-rushing goalkeeper Michel Vorm to the ball. The Dutchman's sending-off in injury time was celebrated like a goal. There was no way back for Swansea, who now had to put defender Angel Rangel in goal, and while they kept the score to one, they couldn't keep Cardiff from taking all three points. It's safe to say Swansea fans didn't look as relaxed leaving the stadium as they did entering it.

Once again, it felt like Cardiff had lift off after the derby, but once again they were sent crashing back down to earth with a defeat, this time to Aston Villa. There was another occasion to remember after that when Kim Bo-Kyung scored a last-minute equaliser to take a point from Manchester United at home, but the situation would take a turn for the worse soon after. In mid-December, Cardiff got their first win since that Swansea game thanks to a 1-0 success at home to West Brom, but then the cracks which had started to appear earlier meant the ceiling started to give way and water was flowing through at an alarming rate.

There had been murmurs of Mackay being under pressure as far back as November, but supporters continued to back their manager, with banners and all. In the October, Cardiff had parted company with head of recruitment Iain Moody out of the blue, replacing him with Kazakhstani Alisher Apsalyamov, a friend of Vincent Tan's son who was primarily a painter, or so reports claimed. Mackay brought Moody to the club when he joined in 2011; he was a trusted member of the staff, and as expected, his exit didn't sit well with the Scotsman.

At the time, BBC Sport Wales correspondent Rob Phillips said, not knowing the news that would follow, 'Moody has been an unobtrusive, yet hugely significant, influence at Cardiff City. The worry for Cardiff fans will be the unsettling of Mackay – a highly rated young manager – after a decent start to the season. With Mackay pinning much faith in the team ethic throughout the club, these will be worrying developments.'

Mackay's position was becoming a little pressured with a poor run of results sending Cardiff closer and closer to the relegation zone. An abject performance in a 2-0 defeat at Crystal Palace left Cardiff a place above the bottom three and Mackay on the edge. After that display, many Cardiff fans inside Selhurst Park struggled to back their boss. For one reason or another, performances were getting worse and a relatively good start felt a lifetime away, not least for Mackay himself. That Palace game came before the West Brom win, so there was momentary respite for Mackay, until a trip to Liverpool changed everything.

Between that, Tan and Malky exchanged an indirect public war of words where Tan revealed, via Peter Lim, that Mackay had overspent. And in giving that statement, Iain Moody's sacking was quickly cleared up. Mackay was given a summer budget of £35m and with add-ons, which was how Moody and Mackay used to pull off such good signings, but the spending rose to around £50m. That meant Tan would be providing no money for the winter window, telling Malky, again via Lim's statement, that he would have to go with what he had got. 'The owner believes that the manager has been given the best possible chance of retaining our Premier League status,' the statement read.

He was right in some ways. Cardiff were the biggest spenders of the promoted clubs and the problem with Mackay and Moody – and Cardiff would find out the true consequences of this later on – is that they would always sign players with smaller fees and bigger add-ons, bigger bonuses and bigger sell-on clauses in order to get the deal done, but financially, that doesn't benefit the club. It's also likely that it contributed to a huge overspending of £15m which the Bluebirds didn't have to waste.

Cardiff travelled to Liverpool for their last game before Christmas and more than 3,000 supporters made the long trip to Anfield to see their team outclassed 3-1 in the Bluebirds' first trip to the famous old venue since a 2007 League Cup defeat. However, after the game, the majority of fans stayed behind to make a clear message. The fans chanted 'Don't sack Mackay' during the game and they continued to sing it on repeat for 45 minutes after the full-time whistle. That action goes beyond any words to epitomise what Mackay meant to the fans, how much they trusted him and how he had united them.

The caveat was that fans didn't have full knowledge of the way Mackay worked. And Vincent Tan then pressed send on a pivotal e-mail. He told Mackay – who refused to resign – that it was time to walk away or he would be sacked. The e-mail also included lots of evidence against the Scotsman, from poor performances to dodgy dealings, and it even included behavioural complaints, which we will come on to in greater detail later on. Mackay took charge for the following game, a shoddy 3-0 defeat to Southampton, but he didn't survive for 24 hours after that. The inevitable statement arrived.

In it came the first hint that there was more to this than fans were aware of. Tan said, 'There has been a good deal of publicity generated by, and about, Mr Malky Mackay for the last few months. I have deliberately not responded to this, hoping that the club can be judged on its football rather than personalised arguments about who said what to whom. I have, however, regretfully concluded that it is no longer fair to the club, its players, its fans and the public more generally for this uncomfortable state of affairs to continue. Cardiff City Football Club means far too much to us all for it to be distracted by this.'

However, fans weren't interested in any reasoning at the time, and what reason did they have to believe Tan, a man who had upset them time and again in the past? They felt he had changed their club's identity and now he had taken away a leader they wholly trusted. There's no doubt Mackay contributed to the hate towards Tan at the time, too, kicking up a stink on his way through the door, but without any real reason given for the sacking it was always going to reflect badly on Tan, who fans already felt they couldn't trust or indeed like.

Now began the search for a new manager amid all that chaos. It was almost as if the next boss was set up to fail, with a daunting set of fixtures ahead, and with Cardiff sitting just one point above the drop zone. However, that's the stressful life of a manager and it didn't by any means translate to Cardiff going down. There were plenty of points available, they just needed a manager who was going to deliver them.

Cardiff didn't have anyone in particular lined up, but it only took six days for to find the man who would succeed Mackay. Step forward Ole Gunnar Solskjaer, remember him? Once a star of world football, renowned for his Champions League Final heroics with Manchester United, the original super sub. Since his retirement from football, he had returned to his homeland, Norway, to manage Molde. He did well there, winning the league twice in his two full seasons in charge. That was enough to impress the City hierarchy and he was given the job.

His appointment was a strange one, but at that time, hiring a young manager with bright ideas was in fashion so it wasn't completely unprecedented, even if it did feel a little unambitious given the position Cardiff were in. Just a few days after his appointment, Solskjaer won his first game in charge, too, coming from behind to beat Newcastle United away from home in the FA Cup, and that certainly helped raise spirits and indeed belief that he could do a good job. Not that it lasted long, with three defeats from three following, though two of them were against Manchester United and Manchester City away and the latter did see Cardiff score twice against the eventual Premier League champions.

Solskjaer set about improving his squad from the moment he arrived in South Wales, and despite Mackay having no budget for January, the new boss was given funds to spend. Andreas Cornelius was sold back to Copenhagen just months after arriving for £8m and cost Cardiff a sizeable chunk in the process. Cornelius struggled with a nasty injury during his time in South Wales but when he was fit, he didn't play, or certainly not enough. Mackay reiterated that he was a project, one for the future, and that left Vincent Tan furious. 'What did we get? We paid £10.5m [including losses] for Cornelius, who didn't even play 45 minutes and then the manager said he was a project. I'm in the Premier League, I need to survive. What an idiot he [Mackay] is,' said Tan, and on this rare occasion, it was difficult to disagree.

The man who is said to know nothing about football was right, you don't spend that much on a player you're not going to play when you first go into the Premier League. You need players who will keep you up, players who will at least give 100 per cent, even if they're not guaranteed to succeed. So, Cornelius left, leaving a raging anger inside Tan aimed towards Mackay, but at least for Solskjaer, it meant he had some money to spend – and he would put lots of trust in some of his countrymen.

Three Norwegians arrived in the form of Joe Inge Berget, Magnus Wolff Eikrem and Mats Moller Daehli. Those players would cost more than £6m and only one would ever be classed as good enough to make an impact. Experienced striker Kenwyne Jones also signed up, joining on a swap deal which saw Peter Odemwingie go the other way to Stoke City just months after joining the club. Former Manchester United defender Fabio also joined permanently, along with Juan Cala, and Old Trafford starlet Wilfried Zaha signed on loan. Solskjaer was putting his United contacts into full use and that did excite fans in South Wales.

What wasn't so exciting was Cardiff's form. It didn't improve under Solskjaer, not remotely, and he only managed three wins in 11, two of which were in the cup and the other was a comeback at home to Norwich. The Bluebirds were even eliminated from the FA Cup with an embarrassing home defeat to Wigan Athletic of the division below.

There were two real turning points in this torrid run which really seemed to end hope for supporters, even as early as February. The Bluebirds travelled to Swansea for the second South Wales derby of the season with the hope of becoming the first of the two teams to complete a league double over the other. Swansea were struggling themselves after sacking Michael Laudrup and replacing him with player Garry Monk, who would be in charge for the first time. Cardiff should have had a real chance, despite their poor form, but once the game kicked off they had no chance. An abject display in a match that requires passion, determination and pride in one's performance left them on the wrong end of a 3-0 hammering from their biggest rivals, and heads really began to drop.

During the following week they had had to hold on for dear life to take a point at home to Aston Villa and David Marshall – who was really turning heads with his displays – put in the performance of his life, making a save that you had to see to believe to ensure his team took a point. However, 11 days later arrived another key defeat when Cardiff put in probably their worst display across the whole of the Premier League season, against fellow promoted club Hull City. The Tigers romped to a 4-0 victory in South Wales and the level of performance wouldn't even have been good enough to get a draw in the Championship. All belief in Solskjaer drifted away from that point. There was still hope of survival – there always is until the curtain has fully closed – but the reality of it was that Cardiff simply weren't good enough and it was showing on the pitch.

The Bluebirds did pick up another win when Fulham came to town, completing a rare double, but title-chasing Liverpool dampened spirits two weeks later by winning 6-3 in the Welsh capital. It was actually one of Cardiff's better displays under Solskjaer, they really gave it a go, but defensive errors and a world-class Luis Suarez meant it was to be another defeat.

The following week there was another flicker of hope, and that's what's so difficult for supporters when a team is in this sort of situation. It's all ups and downs. One week there's hope, the next it's taken away, and sometimes it's more humane to go quickly, isn't it? Nevertheless, the latest flicker of hope arrived on a short trip to The Hawthorns to face West Brom. It was the same old story early on when the home side raced into a two-goal lead within ten minutes and at that point, those in the away end felt it was done and dusted, back to Championship life, back to reality. However, much to their delight, Solskjaer's men pulled it back to 2-2 with goals either side of half-time. That wasn't all. Four minutes into added time, Thievy scored for West Brom and the home supporters leant over the barriers to gloat; they had effectively sent Cardiff down after the Bluebirds had come back strongly only to lose.

But they hadn't lost yet. It seemed all over, though, and Cardiff fans looked at each other, stunned, some even left, and then Zaha marched down the right-hand side and smashed a low ball across the floor and into the box. It came to Ben Turner, who struggled to get it under his spell with a defender close by, but he managed to stab it on while falling to the ground.

Time stood still as Norwegian youngster Daehli – who had become something of a fans' favourite with his trickery and neat technical play – controlled the ball, set his body and took aim. The ball lifted up and hit the net after clipping the top of the post to spark some of the most incredible scenes ever witnessed in a Cardiff City away end.

Police needlessly rushed in towards the Cardiff fans, who had completely lost the plot – in a positive way. The celebrations were wild as the Cardiff players carried out their own in front of the away end. And by this time police were wrestling some fans to the floor, some rather harshly despite West Brom fans being allowed to celebrate how they wished moments before. This is life as an away fan these days. But it couldn't dampen the spirits of these supporters who couldn't believe what they had seen. They had conceded in the

94th minute, it was all over, wasn't it? Somehow, Cardiff had stolen time that didn't seem to exist and grabbed a goal out of nothing. An unbelievable goal and another souvenir from the Premier League, another memory to treasure.

The pattern of ups and downs continued after the celebrations had subsided in the West Midlands. Another terrible performance at home saw Crystal Palace become the latest team to make easy work of it in the Welsh capital. There was still time for some more hope when Cardiff won against all odds at Southampton and drew at home to Stoke, and all roads lead to the Stadium of Light. Sunderland v Cardiff City with just three games remaining. Sunderland, the great escapologists of the Premier League, were sat bottom, one point behind Cardiff in 19th and three points from safety, but both teams knew that Norwich, who occupied the final safety spot, had an awful run-in, and that meant there was a spot still up for grabs.

This was win or bust for both teams and it really was billed as the season's survival clash, with Sky Sports broadcasting the fixture live. It couldn't have gone worse for Cardiff. Connor Wickham scored after 26 minutes and Fabio Borini made it two from the spot just before half-time following a much talked about Juan Cala sending-off. Cala, the hero from two weeks previous when he scored the winner at Southampton, quickly descended to zero after pulling back his man just inside the area.

There was no way back for Cardiff, who had, in truth, been poor for weeks. And Sunderland made a statement by scoring two more to send the Welsh side to the brink of relegation. This Sunderland team, who had taken a point from the Bluebirds after coming from two behind with a stoppage-time equaliser earlier in the season – that was another key moment – were giving themselves hope and ending what little hope Solskjaer's men had left. Supporters continued to do the maths, they continued to work out what results Cardiff needed from different teams, and as supporters do in such circumstances, they carved out any slice of hope they could find and they took it to Newcastle for the penultimate game of the season.

Cardiff were now five points behind Sunderland – who now occupied the last safety spot – and the Black Cats possessed a game in hand. The Bluebirds had to win at Newcastle to have even the slightest hope of survival going into the final week, when Sunderland could still send them down before Chelsea arrived in Wales. In truth, very few believed that any sort of miracle could occur at this point and even fewer believed the Bluebirds deserved one. Even the players knew the reality of the situation and it was reflected in their abject performance in losing 3-0 at Newcastle.

Craig Bellamy was sat on the pitch in tears as he had been almost a year previously, but this time they weren't tears of joy, far from it. His career was going to end with his hometown club suffering relegation from the Premier League at the first time of asking. 'The realisation that we're down is hard to take,' said Solskjaer following confirmation of the Bluebirds' relegation.

'It's the lowest moment of my career and it's the same for many of my players. The threat of relegation has been lurking there for quite a while, but now comes the realisation. You've just got to face the facts, and I'll face the situation head-on. From a personal viewpoint, I didn't make the impact I'd hoped for and believed I would, and that's something for me to chew on now for a little while. Now is not the time to reflect on what's gone on this season; when a team's at the bottom, there's many things that have gone against them, and there are things we've not managed to put in our favour both on and off the pitch. That needs a bigger evaluation than is possible just sitting here now. It's very disappointing, we're very low and the dressing room is a quiet place right now. It's not a nice feeling, but we've got to show we can bounce back.'

A season of so many hopes and dreams had all gone wrong. Why? Where do we start? It was chaos from top to bottom and it probably stemmed from Malky Mackay's poor behaviour and his defiance of Vincent Tan, who was far from blameless himself. His public outbursts were ill-timed and caused only further harm to the Bluebirds' season, which in itself was disastrous. From management on the sidelines, to management at the top, and even in terms of players' performances, Cardiff deserved to be relegated and supporters often hold a biased view, which tells them their club never deserves the worst. But it says something when supporters even admitted they deserved to go back down. The feeling that far outweighed the devastation of relegation was that it felt like it was the beginning of the end, and that was frightening for supporters.

This didn't feel like a club that could bounce back, partly because of the chaotic nature in which it was being run, but it also felt weak. It felt broken and who on earth had the tools to repair it? All the hope and belief that fans started the season with had been sapped, and they didn't want to know about football for the summer. They had seen enough, they were exhausted after two years which saw a rebrand, a promotion and a relegation. It wasn't supposed to be this way and that was the overriding feeling in the final game of the season, a home fixture against Chelsea won 2-1 by Jose Mourinho's team despite Cardiff taking the lead. Supporters watched on wondering what could have been. It shouldn't have been this sour, it shouldn't have turned this poisonous. But Cardiff had gone down a very bumpy road and they couldn't turn back. This club, across the course of the rebrand and relegation – despite the band aid of a promotion – had been wounded, and they were losing too much blood.

This time it wasn't about money or success. Cardiff were used to fighting for their lives in that sense, and supporters would fight with them. This was a battle about identity and a club that was becoming less like Cardiff City by the day. It wasn't just about the colour or the badge, either. The way in which the club was being run that forced a void between the club and the supporters which grew bigger with every passing moment.

Supporters didn't feel close to their club and that wasn't helped by the fact that the club no longer embodied the values that it had instilled into its fans. It was all going to go wrong from here, and as Cardiff returned to the Championship, just 12 months after leaving it, there was a serious concern about what would follow.

How would this proud club stop itself from rotting from the inside? How would it repair a seemingly unrepairable crack?

The end of
Malky Mackay

THE SACKING of Malky Mackay was all a little nasty and while the decision to dismiss the manager did not result in Cardiff City's relegation, the manner in which it unfolded significantly contributed towards their downfall in the context of the season. Could Mackay have kept Cardiff in the Premier League? Of course, but there were no guarantees. Many will point out the fact that the Bluebirds were outside the relegation zone when he was handed his P45, but you've got to consider the wretched run of fixtures that was heading Cardiff's way, plus the fact that he wouldn't have been able to build on the squad in the January window.

The performances under Mackay, whether affected by surrounding circumstances or not, were becoming poorer by the week and the results he achieved towards the end of his reign were a contributing factor. Near the end of his time his team put in the most awful performance at Crystal Palace and they weren't much better in a goalless draw at Stoke against a side who were there for the taking.

Some fans on the busses on the way back from Stoke actually changed that 'Don't sack Mackay' chant to 'Please sack Mackay', so there wasn't the fierce opposition from everyone that some like to think. What supporters were upset about more than anything was the character leaving, it wasn't the football because that wasn't anything special; tactical masterclasses there were some, but they were few and far between and in terms of pure tactical management,

Malky didn't have anything special, and that was proven in his career beyond South Wales.

As mentioned earlier, Mackay was a fantastic leader of men, both as a player and as a manager, and he appeared brave and bold in his approach. He also offered a level-headedness in a time of crisis off the field. It's probably overestimating it a little but to give an idea, Mackay was a little like a father figure for Cardiff fans, offering them assurances during a troubled period. He earned the trust of the Bluebirds' faithful but he also went on to abuse it. And there's the media, who he played to a tee, attempting to manipulate them on to his side – and it really did become a game of sides, as school-playgroundish as that sounds. When Mackay was being threatened with losing his job he played everything out in the public eye, defending himself, reminding people of what he had done and refusing to resign. 'I won't be walking away,' he told BT Sport. 'That's the first thing. I'm proud to be the manager of Cardiff City. I'm a proud and passionate man to lead this football club and lead this team. I have done for two and a half years. I couldn't look at myself resigning.'

He made Vincent Tan look the bad guy and he knew what he was doing, although he knew it was going to be easy given that Tan was already a villain to many in South Wales. So when the owner turned up in black leather gloves at Anfield on the day that supporters backed Mackay to the hilt he truly was cast as the Bond villain, but there was far more to the sacking than met the eye, and there is some credit due to Tan for not going public with issues that he was aware of. Tan could have flipped the tables in an instant if he had released at the time of the sacking what would come out later on. However, curiously, he kept it to himself – whether that was for investigative purposes or not – and he took the brunt of it from fans on the chin.

Fans remained unsure about the Mackay situation and many remained angry for a long while, until beyond the Premier League season. Much mystery lingered and with Tan claiming there was more to it with his statement, so there was a real curiosity and a clamour to find out what was going on. Mackay played the innocent game, making statements to the League Managers' Association

Wembley winners: Joe Ledley fires Cardiff City into the FA Cup Final.

Pride in defeat: Bluebirds defeated in the FA Cup Final.

Glorious: Ninian Park in all its beauty during its final year.

The end of an era: Ninian Park is demolished.

Devastation: Homegrown talent Joe Ledley sobs as Cardiff City lose the 2010 play-off final to unlikely Blackpool.

Ecstasy: Ben Turner scores an extra-time leveller to take Liverpool to penalties in the 2012 League Cup Final.

The love of my life: Kev McNaughton celebrates promotion to the Premier League with the Bluebirds faithful.

Champions: Cardiff City lift the Championship trophy.

Dreamland: Cardiff City defeat Manchester City in their first Premier League home fixture.

Lift-off: Former Swansea City player Steven Caulker ensures Cardiff City win the first ever Premier League derby.

Don't sack Mackay: Vincent Tan appears villain-esque at Anfield as he plots to fire the Bluebirds boss.

Back in blue: Cardiff City walk out in blue at home for the first time in more than two years.

A master at work: Peter Whittingham will go down as a Cardiff City legend.

'We're back': Cardiff City lift the Championship runner-up trophy in front of delighted supporters.

How things change: Vincent Tan celebrates promotion with his manager Neil Warnock.

Mobbed: Bluebirds captain Sean Morrison celebrates promotion with supporters.

Into the blue: Cardiff City fans celebrate promotion in the city. (Callum Ellis)

Into the blue: Cardiff City fans celebrate promotion in the city. (Callum Ellis)

Captain fantastic: Sean Morrison entertains Cardiff City fans on stage following the open-top bus parade. (Callum Ellis)

Warnock wonder: The Bluebirds boss drinks in the promotion celebrations, the eighth of his record-breaking career. (Callum Ellis)

(LMA) and then reportedly filing a law suit against the club for damages and then suspiciously, everything changed. Mackay made a grovelling apology to Tan out of the blue.

His statement read, 'Today I have reached a settlement agreement dropping all claims I have made against Cardiff City Football Club. I have enjoyed my time at Cardiff City and I am most grateful to the board of Cardiff City and Vincent Tan for giving me the opportunity. The club's owner Mr Vincent Tan invested heavily in the club and supported our decisions in our push for promotion to the Premier League. Without him this would not have been possible. My thanks to all those at the club and the fans who have supported me during my time in Wales. If I have caused any offence to anyone during this time, especially to Vincent Tan, then I apologise without reservation. I wish everyone associated with Cardiff City FC all the best for the future and thank them for their support.'

Immediately it was clear that there was more to this, someone had something against Mackay and as it always does, the truth would come out. Mackay had fought his case furiously and he was so intent on his innocence that for this statement to just appear as such a big surprise, to say sorry like he did to Tan, something was about to blow. Cardiff quickly confirmed that legal proceedings had been dropped and Tan, in an interview with WalesOnline, piled further misery on Mackay while also hinting at the mystery. He said, 'The main person responsible is Malky Mackay, the hero of the fans. They should ask why he apologises. They should find out from him. Legally, I'm not supposed to say. I wish I could, but I can't.'

Then in August they came out. The damaging allegations that everyone was waiting for. The *Daily Mail* released the juicy details after Mackay and his old mate Iain Moody applied for the Crystal Palace job and let's just say the references part of the application didn't go so well for Mackay.

The newspaper revealed that Mackay had sent racist, homophobic and sexist texts during his time at Cardiff. The club had obtained thousands of e-mails and messages during a raid of Moody's home carried out as part of an investigation into the pair's wrongdoing relating to the overspending done the previous summer. Moody was also thought to have held back transfer documents. And while all this was going on, there was a concern that Crystal Palace, before their 3-0 win over Cardiff towards the end of the season, had somehow received the Bluebirds' team sheet well in advance of the game.

Moody had joined Palace after being sacked by Cardiff and was still said to be receiving tactical information from a small group of players. The allegations towards Mackay and Moody, aside from 'spygate', were absolutely astonishing. Mackay had sent Moody texts like 'Fkn chinkys' in relation to new South Korean signing Kim Bo-Kyung's representatives. Messages between the pair also included 'Nothing like a Jew that sees money slipping through his fingers,' 'Who struck me as an independently minded young homo,' and one in relation to a female football agent which read 'I bet you'd love a bounce on her falsies.' They were horrifying, they were obscene, and with them fell Mackay's spell over Cardiff fans.

Cardiff had possession of this evidence months before, seizing it as part of that investigation, and all of a sudden everything all made sense; Mackay's fight for innocence, trying to stay on the front foot from minute, one and then his tiresome and desperate apology to Tan. It was a set of circumstances that supporters felt could only happen at Cardiff, a club becoming a circus. It was a case of new day, new story, and the local and national media just couldn't get enough. Mackay apologised shortly afterwards via the LMA, which itself had to apologise after claiming Mackay's texts were 'banter', a rather outrageous thing to say.

Then Mackay did an interview on Sky Sports where he appeared sheepishly saying sorry, in what looked more like a man trying to save his career than sincerely apologising, but that's just speculation. He said, 'Obviously the texts are things that I absolutely have to explain by talking to you today. Out of 10,000 text messages in and out of someone's phone I sent three that, looking at them, are completely unacceptable and inappropriate. For that, and for any offence they caused, I sincerely apologise. It's something I did and there's no excuse for that. I did it in a period where I was under immense pressure and stress in terms of the relationships that were not going too well at my football club.

'Once again, that doesn't actually excuse anything. It was unacceptable for a manager. I'm a human being and I made a mistake. I suppose I would humbly ask people to ask themselves that if their own phone was taken and every text was scrutinised, if there'd be a certain amount of embarrassing texts for everyone. It was something that was unacceptable, but I've been in a multicultural environment for 20 years. I love British football and I'm no racist, no sexist, no homophobe and no anti-Semite. The people that know me, know that. I know it's the people that don't know me that I've got to convince of that. I'm sincerely apologetic for those three texts and for any offence that was taken. It was wrong and it's something that isn't in my character.

'Anyone that knows me knows it's a mistake that I've made. I know it's not what people see of me when they meet me and talk to me. It was someone else's phone that had a vast array of 10,000 texts lifted from it. I received some but the three I've sent that are in question, I'm accountable for. I've been speaking to my union about the equality and diversity training and it's something that I'll be going forward with. Organisations like Kick It Out and Stonewall too. I know I have to prove to people who don't know me that I'm someone who's passionate about football and this is not who I am.

'There's an FA investigation going on at the moment and I'm 100 per cent confident that the investigation will show I am guilty of absolutely no wrongdoing in terms of transfers at the club. Secondly, I signed a non-disclosure agreement with Mehmet Dalman at Cardiff City and I have to hold my end of the bargain up. I have to comply with the FA in this investigation to the letter of the law. Anything they need from me, I'll be available here. What I've done is made a mistake. I sincerely apologise for that. These are testing times, but I've got values and resilience. I will come back from this. I hope I'm given the opportunity. The last 20 years, I've worked with huge diversity, different ethnicities, colours and creeds. Many people have had dealings with me in football.'

There's no doubt that Mackay, even amid an FA investigation instigated by Cardiff when they found the documents, was trying to save what was left of his quickly deteriorating career. In terms of the transfers, to cut a complicated story short, Mackay and Moody were accused of overpaying agents and covering it up by withholding documents. All that nasty business was mixed with all these terrible texts, which received plenty of front pages across Britain. The FA also investigated the texts; however, no action would be taken because they were sent with a legitimate expectation of privacy. Mackay and Moody were given a stern talking to by the FA but aside from that, they had done far greater damage to their careers, and their names would be forever tarnished.

Deservedly so, as there's no place for such behaviour in football, in a sport that is trying desperately to rid itself of old-fashioned views, a sport that is trying to make progress, to promote equality. These are the type of people who are holding the game back and their vile culture of racism and sexism (among other isms), whether they were meant to be offensive or not, and whether they were intended as private or not, cannot be accepted in any form. Legally, they got away with it but people within such a progressive sport will not forgive people for this type of behaviour and Mackay would find that as he tried to rebuild his now broken career.

The racism went beyond private texts, too, and that became clear when former Cardiff youngster Ibrahim Farah came out with a social media post which read, 'Malky Mackay is a racist, wish the people at Cardiff City seen it sooner. To treat certain players how he did at Cardiff was disgusting.' Welsh-born Farah continued his Twitter rant, 'Malky Mackay always used to call me a wee Egyptian and laugh his head off. No one knows what happens behind the scenes in football clubs. At the time when you're a young pro no one will listen. People would listen to the manager and not me, so I chose to keep my mouth shut. Every manager has his views on his players I wasn't his type of player but to treat certain player on how he did at Cardiff was disgusting. Oxford away a young Somali boy was at the gates and Malky shouted look at that black Somali kid at the gates, look it's Ibby [Farah]'s brother. He then started laughing at him and coaching staff. Cardiff were treated poor by Malky and his coaching staff were scared to speak around him let alone ask him for help on the training pitch.'

Farah's story gives an insight to the culture some people create at football clubs. And it's not easy for players in a world where speaking out of line can cost you your place in a team or cost you a place at a club where you could win promotion. However, we need to create a culture in football where the players on that bus to Oxford stand up and tell Mackay he's out of line. Nobody should be allowed to make racist statements and if managers are in positions where they feel they can't be questioned, as though they're untouchable, then the game is broken, we have a problem.

We must have a culture in football where players, or members of staff from the cooks to the cleaners, are encouraged to speak out against comments like Mackay's. Clubs' employees shouldn't be afraid to report people, whether it's the chairman or the manager making the comments. That's something we should be striving for in football and that's something Cardiff City made progress towards when sacking Mackay. And you would hope that even if results were going well in the Premier League, these comments, messages and texts wouldn't have been overlooked and the result would have been the same.

Mackay's treatment of players in general also left a lot to the be desired. While speaking on his podcast *Under the Cosh*, former Bluebird Jon Parkin revealed, 'He just came in and he absolutely hated me. From minute one, he came in during the summer and he was like an army sergeant. He wanted this, this and this, and I wasn't that. The problem is, I could never keep my mouth shut. If I think something isn't right, I'll say. Come pre-season, it was West Ham away, I was on the bench and he fetched a kid on, obviously I was thinking that if he did that then I'm not playing. We won that game 1-0.

'It gets to the Tuesday night and we have a game and I'm not even in the squad. I got home after the game and I tweeted "Does anyone need a gardener because I'm looking for work." By Thursday or Friday, I'm in the paper. He got me in and I was just like, "it is what it is" and from then, he just hated me. I was training with the kids, then I just went out on loan. It got to the point, the way he was treating me, he was making me train at daft times, making me train with the kids. The first two rounds of the League Cup, I played, we ended up getting to the final and I never even got invited. I had to make my own way up from Scunny [Scunthorpe] with my pals, the club never invited me to it, I never got a medal and we ended up finishing runners-up.'

Mackay would go on to fail with Wigan Athletic, who, with Dave Whelan – another man accused of racist comments – in charge were willing to take a chance on the disgraced Scotsman. He ended up contributing to the Latics' relegation from the Championship to League 1 and he returned to Scotland. Mackay became the Scottish Football Association's director of performance in December 2016 and he was backed by anti-racism group Kick It Out, which acknowledged that he had received equality and diversity training from the English FA. Mackay then went on to take caretaker charge of the Scotland national team following Gordon Strachan's departure, but he wasn't given the full-time job.

The press continue to label Mackay as a shamed ex-Cardiff boss in the present day, and while some have forgiven him, accepting that he made a mistake, many others will not, maintaining their view that he's a man with ancient principles, and a man who abused his position, while expressing shameful views on ethnic and sexual minorities.

As for Cardiff, they drew a big line under it all ahead of the new season; though legal proceedings would rumble on in the background, the club had to move on. Mind you, Tan would go on to make his feeling clear about Mackay plenty of times for a number of years to follow, including in 2014, when he questioned appointing Mackay in the first place.

He said, 'He didn't do very well at Watford, but somehow our CEO and our chairman hired him and replaced Dave Jones. Dave Jones actually did much better. So, I think Malky got lucky when he came to Cardiff. I invested a lot of money and then we went up. Do you think that Malky would have got us promoted without my investment?'

And Tan still to this day maligns the signing of Andreas Cornelius, which cost him a dollar or two, to put it mildly. The fans, however, had moved on and it all served as closure for so many who believed they had been hard done by through the sacking of a manager they liked. Now they knew why, and they could move on, accepting that it was completely and utterly the correct decision regardless of form and performances on the pitch.

The fall from grace

AMID THE devastation of relegation and the chaotic rumbling-on of Malky Mackay's departure it was easy to forget that Cardiff had to adjust to life back in the Championship. It would be a stretch to say supporters were looking forward to life back in the second tier, but there's something in that. The Premier League had been an absolute car crash, a catastrophe, and had seen the club turn into a circus. That aside, wins were few and far between – Cardiff managed just seven from 38 games – and that's not what supporters were used to.

It comes with the territory when you step up a division; you become a small fish in a big pond, but in truth, Cardiff fans probably enjoyed being the big fish, competing year on year. The club and its supporters became desperate to get promotion, but the grass isn't always greener.

Of course, the Premier League was still where Cardiff wanted to be, even after relegation, but not like this, not while everything was going so badly off the field. You have to be ready and you have to go about it right, and at this club, at this time, there were very few aspects that were 'right'. So, with that in mind, there wasn't such a resentment towards dropping back down to the Championship given all the wonderful memories – as well as the odd bad ones – it had provided for supporters.

Cardiff now had a shiny new stand, with an extension completed above the Ninian Stand ahead of the UEFA Super Cup, which the stadium hosted in August 2014, although there was a backlash to the new seats being predominantly red, something the club and its board members furiously defended. And in their defence, while it wasn't good timing with so many supporters upset about the colour change and with many holding fears that bit by bit, the club would be changed further.

When completed, the stand looked rather attractive with the rest of the lower bowl in blue. The Bluebirds also had a far less attractive new kit which was made by Cosway Sports, a brand many claimed to be from Malaysia with connections to Vincent Tan. That wasn't at all true. Cosway Sports was based in Cardiff. The number of shirts and amount of training wear a football club requires is always going to put huge demands on a locally based company. The quality of the kit was also well below what is usually produced by the likes of Puma and Adidas, and that was noticed by supporters and players alike. The design of the shirt itself wasn't too bad, but it wasn't great either. The home and away kits were essentially the same design, but the blue away kit had a collar and there was also a white and red third kit which would go on to cause a stir.

On to the football, and the worry was that Ole Gunnar Solskjaer remained in charge and few thought he had the ability to get Cardiff back up. However, that would change a little when his budget for the new season was unveiled. The Bluebirds made a good chunk of money over the summer when the likes of Gary Medel, Steven Caulker, Jordon Mutch and Fraizer Campbell departed, raising around £25m. Supporters were saddened to see Mark Hudson depart on deadline day, meaning his last contribution was a late own goal at Wolves, leading to a defeat.

It was a sad sight, and indeed a shock, to see the captain leave. But he admitted to WalesOnline that he wasn't surprised, 'I'm sad to leave Cardiff of course, me and my family love the area and the people are wonderful. I have some great memories. It was a little difficult. All summer I had been told my future was at Cardiff, I was captain and that was the way it would remain and then the day before the Fulham match, I was informed I wasn't needed and had to find another club. It's hard in a way because clubs who had expressed an interest in me through the summer had been sent away and told I wasn't for sale.

'But I half expected it, I wasn't so surprised. You don't spend £10m on two centre-halves for nothing so I suspected it. It's football anyway, these things happen, you've got to roll with it. Anyway, as you see those new players coming in you realise maybe your chance has gone and you are not going to get the opportunities you might want. That's fine. I want to play. I waited patiently for my chances last season and was playing under Ole and then I got injured which was frustrating.'

The departures, 17 first-team players in all across the whole season and including the retirement of Craig Bellamy, allowed Solskjaer to spend big as he plotted the Bluebirds' route back to the Premier League – they did, however, manage to keep hold of the previous season's star performer, David Marshall, against all odds. Spending money had worked for Tan in the past at Cardiff and he was looking to do the same again, except this time, he could still make a profit because of the departing players, even if he had taken a big hit on Andreas Cornelius during the previous season.

Solskjaer would only spend around £4m but on paper, he would be getting good value for money with the likes of Kagisho Dikgacoi, Federico Macheda, Danny Gabbidon and Javi Guerra arriving on free transfers – all were big names, in one way or another. The Bluebirds spent big on Reading striker Adam Le Fondre and defender Sean Morrison, both costing more than £2m, but Gabon international defender Bruno Ecuele Manga commanded the biggest fee. The deadline-day signing would cost more than £4m, but he truly would be value for money in years to come. Other smaller signings included Guido Burgstaller, Anthony Pilkington and Tom Adeyemi. There were 12 incomings, signalling a real overhaul of the squad given that there were 19 departures including loans in the summer window.

The mass business brought excitement back for supporters, who were given belief and confidence that the club were going to give it another go – and they were, undeterred by the disastrous campaign of last season. With the likes of Morrison and Le Fondre arriving, Cardiff were dominating the Championship market, securing some of the best players in the division. That inevitably translates to optimism in the stands, and the Bluebirds took that into their first three games with Solskjaer keen to put relegation behind him.

He said, 'I spent a long time getting over it, I've thought long and hard about what happened, what should have happened, and what could have happened. If you've got about three days, I could sit and talk to you about what could have been done differently. But I don't have time. When I used to win the league at Manchester United or at Molde, you just have a party, wake up the next day and move on, this wasn't easy.

'You want to reach your targets. When you don't, you dwell on it longer. We've looked forward to this [first game of the season] ever since we got relegated. We want to show we're a good team, we want to bounce back. And for Cardiff, bouncing back is the only acceptable outcome this season.'

A draw away to Blackburn on the opening day was followed by two wins – a better start than the promotion season two years previous. But Cardiff lost three of their next four and Solskjaer was gone, just like that. His final match in charge was a poor home display against Middlesbrough in which the Bluebirds went behind after less than two minutes and never recovered, and that was it. Two days later Solskjaer was handed his notice and off he went. The Norwegian amassed a record of two wins, two draws and three defeats in his first seven games of the season, and less than two months in he had been sacked with Cardiff sitting 17th. However, it's worth pointing out that Solskjaer had also overseen a hopeless survival bid the previous season and he left with a win percentage of just 30 per cent despite only taking charge of 30 games.

It wasn't a sour departure. He hadn't made too many friends during his eight-month stay in South Wales and much of that was down to his approach. He liked to constantly tinker with the team from game to game, constantly changing players, and you could see the effect that was having on the squad. There was no real shape to what Cardiff were doing, despite having a talented squad given the signings and the players still at the club, such as Kenwyne Jones, Mats Moller Daehli and Kim Bo-Kyung. This was an impressive group for the Championship and they looked gutless, clueless and fed up from minute one. As a fan, a neutral or even a pundit, you can tell when a player believes in what they're doing, if they believe in their manager, and this didn't resemble that. There were no tears shed upon the news of Solskjaer's departure, especially given the lowly position Cardiff now found themselves in.

Attention quickly turned to finding a new man to take charge and until a new manager was found, Danny Gabbidon – still registered as a player – took joint temporary charge alongside Scott Young, another former fans' favourite. The two oversaw an okay run of form, drawing two – although one of those saw the Bluebirds lose a two-goal lead at Derby – and winning one, before their last game together, at the start of October: a trip to Blackpool, who hadn't won all season. The Tangerines had just three points to their name from a possible 30 following a complete breakdown at the club which saw fans protesting against the owner, and then Cardiff arrived for a live televised game. Strangely, so did their new manager, former Leyton Orient boss Russell Slade, who climbed off the bus with the players despite this being Young and Gabbidon's final game in charge. The night would prove to be one of the low points for the club in the last ten years.

It epitomised everything that was wrong at the time and it also highlighted why the Bluebirds were going nowhere. The players stepped off the bus, ignoring their supporters who had travelled more than 200 miles on a cold Tuesday night. It sounds like nothing, a casualty of modern football, but that was never Cardiff City. Occasionally, perhaps, under Malky Mackay at away games, but not when fans travelled so far on weekdays, not when the supporters were backing a team in such bleak circumstances.

It was all summed up by the most abject performance you're likely to see. Blackpool got their first win of the season at the 11th attempt and it just had to be Cardiff who allowed it to happen, a team worth millions with wages far beyond so many others in the division – and therein, perhaps, lay the problem. Aron Gunnarsson didn't stop during that game, he barked out instructions to team-mates, but they did not respond to his rallying calls. They didn't care enough about the club, the team or the badge they represented. Perhaps they were upset by the way Solskjaer had run the team, maybe they were disappointed that he was gone and felt that suddenly, this wasn't what they had signed up for. But if there's something fans will not put up with, it's a lack of effort, a lack of respect for the club you're representing, and the supporters inside Bloomfield Road let that be known after the game.

Three days later, Slade was formally appointed. And while it wasn't exactly the most ambitious of choices from the outside, after seeing such a lack of effort from the players in recent weeks, supporters just wanted someone to grab the bull by the horns. Slade was the man tasked with that and he arrived on the back of a decent career. He had taken Leyton Orient to the League 1 play-off final the season before only to lose out on penalties, and he had done a great job overall with the Londoners. The concern was that he wasn't exactly a young manager with fresh ideas, nor was he an experienced Championship boss, so his appointment didn't exactly get supporters off their seats – and attendances had already dropped to around 20,000 on return to the Championship.

Fans certainly weren't as excited as Vincent Tan, who was piling praise on his new man, while slipping in another dig at Mackay. He said, 'Look at Russell's track record. He certainly deserves to be given a chance. After all, Cardiff gave a chance to a mediocre manager from Watford [Mackay] and he took the club to the Premier League. I did, however, give him a lot of money to spend for that – in fact, too much money.'

Having said that, after such a shocking start to the campaign, the form could only get better, you felt, and it did, just not in an attractive manner. Slade, who had watched that gutless display at Blackpool, made it clear that he wanted these players to work harder. He said, 'I'm grateful to Vincent for giving me this opportunity as Cardiff City is a fantastic football club. We have a large squad and it's more than putting out the best eleven players on paper. We need the best group of players out there with the right balance and chemistry. It's now about building a relationship with the players and installing a strong ethos and work ethic. That's what I want us to take on to the pitch every week.'

The Bluebirds lost just two of their next nine games, Slade won his first two in charge, and Cardiff climbed up to ninth in the Championship. Still, however, supporters weren't altogether pleased. The football was pretty horrible at times, in truth, with lots of direct balls up to Kenwyne Jones, and not in the way Dave Jones used to play direct football, for example. This really was pure route one and nothing else.

Slade did have to instill a style of football that was going to get Cardiff up the table and it did seem to be working, for a time at least. The new Cardiff boss was also quite lucky in the sense that by the time he oversaw a torrid run of form through Christmas and New Year, the attention of the Bluebirds' faithful had firmly switched from football to getting the club back to blue. We'll come on to this in far greater detail later on, but during this season, serious efforts were being made by a number of parties to return Cardiff to their native blue and as the season went on, the demonstrations picked up more and more traction.

Why at that point? When the club first turned to red, supporters could put up with it, partly because of the success but more so because the club itself hadn't changed completely, and there was also a leader they could relate to with Malky Mackay in charge. They didn't have that connection with Solskjaer and they certainly didn't have it with Slade, who had no personality with the media; the former PE teacher almost looked like a teacher character in the way he celebrated in his tracksuits after games. That's not to make fun of Slade, but when compared with the slick and suited-up Mackay, who epitomised professionalism – in the public domain – that's how supporters saw him.

Including the appointment of Slade, all the club's decisions were contributing to them becoming more and more distant from supporters. The fans had reached their limit. Ben Price says, 'I was conflicted, I was watching a team who had Cardiff City on the badge, but it wasn't the club I supported. The red, the badge, the infighting with the fans, I can safely look back on that time and say it wasn't worth a second of it. The highs of the wins against Man City and Swansea were not worth the fights and misery that the fans went through during the rebrand. I think every fan feels the same. Even the night we got promotion against Charlton it didn't feel as good as I thought it would.'

The rot had finally taken over and the club was falling apart. Supporters turned up each week to sing 'we'll always be blue' with their scarves held aloft, and for many fans, it was the only reason they came along. Demonstrations continued, and, on 9 January 2015, it was announced at a press conference that Vincent Tan had agreed to return the club to its native blue; another turning point in this Cardiff City story.

The day after that press conference, Cardiff welcomed fellow relegated club Fulham to the Cardiff City Stadium and for the first time since 3 May 2012 they walked out at home wearing their traditional blue kit. And they won, too!

Fortunately, the away kit for the season was essentially a mirror image of the home, just blue instead of red and with a collar, so it was a simple case of swapping the two. When the team walked out in blue once again, it truly was a special moment for everyone who fought for the return of the traditional colours. And it was also announced that there would be a new badge, which would give the fans their bluebird back, while compromising on the dragon to please Tan – all supporters ever asked for – at the end of the season ready for the new kit and the new season. That meant that for supporters, the end of the season couldn't come quickly enough. Especially when Slade made a number of unexciting transfers, including Alex Revell, Eoin Doyle and Scott Malone, all from the division below or bottom-half Championship clubs.

All three Norwegians were allowed to leave for free, including the talented Mats Moller Daehli who, in truth, just didn't have the physicality for the Championship. Kim Bo-Kyung also went for nothing and so did Guido Burgstaller, who had cost £800,000 just months earlier. Star signing Adam Le Fondre also unbelievably left on loan for the rest of the season after joining for more than £2m in the summer. He endured a torrid time of it in South Wales, or in other words, he couldn't hit a barn door. He ended up joining Bolton on loan for personal reasons. It was all a little farcical, really, and the season, which started with plenty of optimism, became a real write-off.

There was a silver lining bigger than many could have wished for in the return to blue but the end of the season just couldn't come quickly enough. Especially with the dire football that was being played out in front of fans each week.

In Slade's defence, he had to manage a chaotic dressing room full to the brim with players. A total of 28 featured throughout the season and there were plenty more who didn't. There were far too many pros at the club and far too many egos, too. Danny Gabbidon later revealed to WalesOnline, 'Credit where credit is due. Russell had a tough job when he came in, I know because I was there, there was a lot of stuff going on. There were players who needed to be shifted, bad eggs. The squad was very large, there were two groups. Pre-season had just been too easy for them. They had not done enough fitness work. After 45 minutes of a game they were out of gas. We spent four weeks getting them up to speed really and then Russell came in.

'The last couple of years, the direction the club has been going in, that's where fans have become disgruntled. You've got to get the right people in place. Vincent Tan has spent so much money, but it's about having the right people in the right places doing the right jobs to manage that money in the right way, to get the best out of the team or get the club going where you want it to go. The last couple of years, when it comes to matters on the field and off it, there's been no real direction. There's been no philosophy of play. There's so many things that need putting in place there. It's going to be a slow process. But with the money that's been invested the club should not really be in this kind of situation.'

Even Ravel Morrison, a loan signing from West Ham, had come and gone. He arrived touted as a bright young talent but was suddenly sent back early by Slade and told he had no future in South Wales. It was a crazy situation at the club and Slade was charged with doing a lot of the dirty work. He may have thought he was going to join a club going for promotion, but little did he know, he had to completely reshape the dressing room first. For him, it was like buying a house and then finding out it needed gutting from top to bottom. All of that was going to take time – it couldn't be fixed in one January window. It would take at least another summer and that probably left Slade looking forward to the summer as much as the supporters. Cardiff meandered into a top-half finish which, given the circumstances, wasn't such a bad result. This was a club in turmoil on and off the pitch and it needed a reboot.

The Bluebirds may have spent heaps of money in the summer, but this season could have been a lot worse. Having said that, for supporters, it felt like the longest in a very long time. Even in a relegation battle you have something to fight for, but in the position Cardiff were in there was nothing to cheer about. They were so stuck in mid-table that they loaned defender Matthew Connolly and striker Kenwyne Jones out in March to help fellow Championship clubs Watford and Bournemouth secure promotion. Slade had his hands tied behind his back and no one would release them for a long time afterwards.

There were some good moments, but the one that stands out above all was the 2-1 win at play-off chasing Brentford. Cardiff went behind when goalkeeper Simon Moore dropped the ball into the path of Andre Gray and it looked to be another unsuccessful away day for the Bluebirds until Federico Macheda equalised in the second half after a howling mistake from Brentford's own goalie, David Button. Then, against all odds, Alex Revell, who hadn't exactly won over the fans, broke through and scored with a stunning chip from an angle to catch out Button, who really was all over the place, coming well out of his area with little reason. That moment probably sparked the biggest celebrations of the season.

Beyond the goals, Cardiff had Macheda and Kadeem Harris sent off late in the second half, and they fought tooth and nail to hold on to the unlikely win. They showed the fight and determination that had completely deserted them during the early part of the season, something that they didn't have, for example, on that grim night at Bloomfield Road. The win, and the manner of it, served as a real positive, and one of the few indications that Slade, if given time and the necessary tools, could do a decent job in South Wales.

The end of the season finally arrived after back-to-back wins to round off a forgettable campaign which did little to drum up support having returned to the Championship, and with a new stand – soon to be temporarily mothballed – paid for, that didn't exactly bode well for the club.

Having said that, there was much to look forward to with a return to the blue home kit and a new badge, which was hotly anticipated. As for Slade, he had done the dirty work and now it was time for him to prove himself going into the next season. Many supporters didn't like him from the off because of his style of play and he did get defensive at times in press conferences, walking out of one in particular. However, he was quite down to earth, just not exciting as such, and he couldn't muster up a unity in the way Malky Mackay had, though even the Scot might have found that difficult in such a horrid set of circumstances.

All attention now turned to embracing the return to blue and putting this disastrous season in the rear-view mirror, going forward as a united club, and for the football club itself, serious steps were finally going to be taken to rebuild relationships with fans in an attempt to get back to the core values that make Cardiff City so unique.

Back to blue

ON 9 January 2015, a press conference was called at the Cardiff City Stadium. Seated at the top table were CEO Ken Choo, chairman Mehmet Dalman, Cardiff City Supporters Club representative Vince Alm and Bluebirds Unite founder Sian Branson.

Dalman began, 'We have had a board meeting, and we would like to share the outcome of that meeting with you all, but before we do so, I would like to ask our chief executive, Ken Choo, to read a short statement from Vincent Tan.'

Then Choo begun to say some of the most important words in Cardiff City's recent history: 'I am very proud to read this statement on behalf of Tan Sri Vincent Tan. The statement is dated today, 9 January 2015. It reads, "The Christmas and New Year period has given me time to reflect on the events of the last year. Spending time with my family has a profound effect on me. My mother Madam Low Siew Beng, a devoted Buddhist, who attended Cardiff City Football Club to watch them play, spoke to me on the importance of togetherness, unity and happiness. Cardiff City Football Club is important to me and I wish to see it united and happy.

'"With the guidance, blessing and influence of my mother, I asked my chairman, Mehmet Dalman, and my chief executive officer, Ken Choo, for their advice and to consult with a cross section of the fanbase. This meeting took place last night when some seven representatives from our supporters were present. My thanks and gratitude to those who gave up their evening to be there. I'm informed that this was a very productive and frank exchange of views, but all with the same objective – to strengthen our club. The views were also added to by a large group of e-mails that were sent to the club in the last 24 hours by a larger group of supporters.

"'As said so well by John F. Kennedy, 'Let us never negotiate out of fear, but let us never fear to negotiate.' My wish is to unite and make the club successful and in order to do this, I fully support the board's decision to implement the following changes: point one, starting from Saturday 10 January 2015 and until the end of the season, our home kit shall be blue, our away kit shall be red. I would like to thank the Football League for facilitating my request. Point two, for the 2015/16 season, Cardiff City's home kit colour shall be blue, our away kit colour shall be red. Point three, the club badge will be redesigned to reflect the dominance of the bluebird, while celebrating the proud history and heritage of the club. I also wish to incorporate elements representative of my culture and beliefs, which I hope are respected. Point four, as the chairman has explained, the debt-to-equity resolution is not straightforward. We will deal with this in due course, with all decisions made in the best interest of the club. Point five, for the 2015/16 season, non-price-freeze season tickets will be reduced, and price-freeze season tickets shall be adjusted accordingly to match these prices. I very much hope these steps will bring unity, success and happiness to our club. The challenge ahead for us is enormous and I truly believe we will overcome these obstacles as a united club. I believe with divine blessings, Cardiff City Football Club will achieve great success.'"

Cardiff City were back in blue. After almost three years of discontent and squabbling, the Bluebirds were returning to their traditional colour. However, this press conference was just the end, so, for the start of this long, hard battle for identity, we have to go back almost a year.

The protests against the red diminish during the season of promotion to the Premier League. Fans had waited so long for their shot at the promised land that they weren't going to waste what could be their only opportunity, but there was a shift. As the following season went on, after Malky Mackay's departure and the circus it created, fans began to realise that this was becoming less and less their club. It would be naïve to say it was down to a lack of success. It wasn't all about that. If Cardiff had won the Premier League or finished in the top half then maybe it could have been different, yes, but the lack of success lead to poor decisions by the manager, the board and just about everyone. It was becoming embarrassing and while Cardiff have been through plenty of ups and downs in the past, with the red kit and the red badge to boot, they were becoming completely disenfranchised.

The club continued to move further out of reach of the fanbase, closing its doors to supporters to protect themselves and it all went a little wrong, both on the pitch and off it. There were smaller protests before, but the first large protest took place before Cardiff's 6-3 defeat to Liverpool at home in March. Sian Branson had set up the Bluebirds Unite group during the promotion season and she gained a fair bit of traction surrounding the protest, in an attempt to get people together. Sian was also helped by message board owners as well as other supporters. It's fair to say the protest before the Liverpool game was the first that possessed any clout. It was the first that fans really got involved in, with many staying away for previous attempts. Around 10,000 marched to the ground in a bid to remind Tan that the club remained blue at its core, regardless of the current kit colour.

The Liverpool game also saw the birth of something that would become a staple at fixtures for the best part of a year after. Supporters would sing 'We'll always be blue, we'll always be blue, we're Cardiff City, we'll always be blue' when the clock struck 19.27, the year the Bluebirds famously lifted the FA Cup. It continued during the rest of the Premier League games and into the Championship, and it was a peaceful way of reminding everyone that supporters were still fighting for their identity and that they were still at heart a blue club trapped underneath the red veil. Following relegation, WalesOnline put together a powerful piece in which it spoke to four former captains, all of whom wished for the club to be turned back to blue.

The front page of the *South Wales Echo* read 'Now turn our club blue again Mr Tan'. Inside, former players like Phil Dwyer gave their opinion. He said, 'But then I saw the way fans reacted and have talked things over with many people who are Cardiff City through and through. I honestly didn't realise at first how much passion there is among supporters about the blue kit. I know ardent supporters who simply won't go to the Cardiff City Stadium anymore because their team are playing in red. Vincent Tan came into the club and maybe didn't realise the consequences of his rebranding decision. He is a highly successful businessman, but when it comes to football and club tradition he still has an awful lot to learn.

'Personally, I would love to see Cardiff City back playing in blue, but I really can't see Vincent Tan changing his mind on this. I played in all sorts of colours during my time at the club, but it was always mainly blue. It's about tradition with supporters. Players, in the main, don't mind about the colour of their shirts, but it means a lot to fans and they are hugely important at any club. The Bluebirds' faithful really surprised me with their passion to see this rebranding decision overturned.

'We waited so long for our club to get into Premier League football. I never thought I would see that in my lifetime. But Cardiff made the step up and we all celebrated. But this issue has taken the edge off what should have been a season to remember. The final nail in the coffin, of course, was relegation, and I fear it will take a long time for Cardiff City to regain top-flight status.'

Dwyer's words hit home for many in a cleverly timed piece, just when Cardiff were relegated and when the supporters were hurting most. WalesOnline continued to drum up support for the blue agenda in the following weeks and fans did the same, many turning out in blue for the final game of the season when there were blue balloons aplenty. Mind you, it wasn't exactly fully backed and you're never going to achieve that in the Premier League where you have a few thousand fans who are inevitably there to watch the opponents more than the home team.

After that defeat to Chelsea, the football season ended and momentum was lost. Everything shuts down during the summer and with no games, you have no stage as a supporter, no platform to make your voice heard. That meant any progress was at best reduced and the protesting supporters would have to go again the following season.

They did, too, but Tan replied with a stern response, telling Sky Sports on Christmas Day, of all days, 'I would like to tell them this: protesting will not make me change my mind. Cardiff will stay red and we hope the fans will think carefully and support the club so that we can get promoted to the Premier League. They should know that when I first invested in the club I said I would put in £100m if they would let me change the colour to red, use the red dragon as the symbol and replace the Bluebird emblem. After all, the red dragon is the symbol and national flag of Wales. At the time everyone agreed, and I kept my end of the bargain. I have invested now more than £100m, so if they are protesting, are they keeping their end of the bargain?'

Those comments came after two protests were planned. The first was at a home clash against Brighton and Hove Albion on a Tuesday night, in which supporters were asked to deck themselves out in blue. The second was a full march during a game with Derby County. The Brighton protest was to be very fitting, too, because after the change to red, Cardiff played Brighton on a cold night and the club gave each supporter a red scarf printed with the new logo – a PR exercise. Many refused the offer, throwing away their scarves, while others kept them.

For those who were against the rebrand, the evening went down as a real low point, and it forced some to never return. Now fans were going to hit back on another Tuesday night against Brighton, but this time they were going to paint the stadium blue, not red. Tan's statement was something of a setback for campaigners, especially as before the start of the season he had hinted at revisiting the rebrand decision at the end of the 2014/15 season, but now there seemed no chance of that happening.

By this point, it was all turning sour between supporters, with some still on board, not caring what colour the team played in, and others completely against it. You would see constant bickering and a 5-3 defeat at Bournemouth stands out. Cardiff played in a third kit that day, a white and red number, when arguably, they could have played in blue. Many were left furious and seldom will you see a more poisonous atmosphere in an away end. There were fans squabbling left, right and centre.

It was becoming a chore to watch Cardiff, partly because of the poor standard of football and also because of the bad atmosphere, and the disagreements between fans who had supported the club shoulder-to-shoulder for so many years and shared so many great memories. Perhaps the most damaging aspect of the rebrand was that it turned fans against each other, which is awful to experience. It had a profound impact on attendances, too, and in January just 4,194 turned up for the FA Cup third round tie with Colchester United – a new record low for the stadium. It was because of the poor standard of football during the season, there's no doubt about that, and the Friday evening kick-off played its part, too. However, supporters were just becoming so distant. They were finding other things to do, as we found out with Thomas Griffiths in an earlier chapter, rather than having to put themselves through the stress of it all, and that was starting to really show in terms of attendance numbers.

The drop seemed to hit home for Tan and just six days later, a crisis meeting of sorts was called. Officials promised to listen to supporters on their views of the future of the club. The meeting would see around 70 people attending, a cross section including representatives from travel groups, message boards, local government, campaign groups, supporter organisations and stakeholders. Everyone else was invited to send their views to an e-mail address and more than 1,000 took up this opportunity to let the club know how they felt. Some emails were shared with the people at the meeting. Finally, they were willing to listen, and finally, there was a breakthrough. The supporters in attendance made their views clear to the club's representatives, who included CEO Ken Choo, chairman Mehmet Dalman and director Steve Borley among others.

In Scott Johnson's book *Cardiff City: Rebranded* he reveals that Choo admitted on the evening that he was 'surprised by the level of respect shown for Vincent Tan' and that it could 'sway the decision significantly'. Dalman then offered significant hope by saying, 'If Vincent was here, I think he would have made the decision right now.' The respect for Tan may surprise some, especially non-Cardiff fans. But ultimately this was a man that saved the club. He could have been loved and adored if he hadn't made some catastrophic decisions along the way and he would go some way in rebuilding those bridges at a later stage.

He became disliked because of the rebrand decision and for little else. Even the sacking of Malky Mackay proved to be the correct decision, and supporters who quickly slated the Malaysian would soon change their stance when the truth emerged. Tan put in over £100m and you can't doubt that someone who offers up that level of finance wants what's best for the club. But the rebrand decision was the one choice, albeit a huge one, that fell out of line with that. It was catastrophic and it overwhelmed anything else for such a large section of supporters. Now, almost three years on, they were happy to forgive him, but only if he took up the opportunity to change back, to admit he was wrong and to start building those bridges before it was too late.

Dalman echoed that in his interview with WalesOnline after the meeting. He said, 'The feeling I took away was that fans want to unite with Vincent Tan. That desire was clear. If that means we have to reconsider the kit colour and badge, then we must. Only a strong character, a strong man like Vincent Tan, could ask for a forum like this to meet. I think he will be touched by what happened at this meeting. It was about building bridges. We gave fans a platform to air their views and it was a very constructive meeting. I also hope the fans appreciate some of the views the club have. The meeting was about listening and finding ways we can be together. It was clear from the audience they want to find a solution. That is very good for Cardiff City.'

Less than 24 hours later all was done and dusted. Cardiff had returned to blue and Vince Alm, who was at the top table during the now-historic press conference, shared his delight. He added, 'I'm not one to get emotional but I have filled up twice today and I think that's what will happen tomorrow. I can't wait for tomorrow – to get back to where we were. We have got a great set of fans when we are together, and I am really buzzing about that.'

Sian Branson said, 'I would like to say a big thanks to the club and Vincent Tan for making the meeting happen last night. We are very, very grateful for the investment put into the club, but more so very grateful we can be moving forward represented and recognising our proud traditions and heritage. On behalf of myself and many other fans, the subject of our kit colour and the predominant bluebird being on our badge is of utmost importance to us. We don't want to be at odds with the club so it's nice to see us all come together. I hope this is an opportunity for Cardiff City to go from strength to strength and be the strongest it has ever been under the leadership of Vincent Tan and his board.'

The next day, Cardiff would host Fulham and wear their native blue, thanks to permission from the Football League, which was needed due to a regulation which states clubs cannot change the colours of their kits during the season. More than 22,000 turned up and so many of them were dressed in blue for a celebration of the club's colour and identity officially returning. The Bluebirds, now actually blue, won that game and it really was an occasion to remember. The day Cardiff City returned to blue.

Choo and Dalman walked around the pitch pre-match and got their deserved applause. They, as well as the fans who fought so hard for the change back to blue, made a huge impact and the two would continue to do so. Particularly Ken because he – unlike his chairman – works full-time for Cardiff City, and spends a lot of time greeting supporters. He's a CEO with a difference, someone who will stop at the services on the way to away games to mix with fans; he often goes around to the away end before a game to speak to supporters, which makes a big impact on them.

This was a club that shut its doors previously, and Choo was one of the hierarchy who hid away amid the storm, but you can only make up for your actions, you can't change them, not that Choo did anything overly bad. Nonetheless, he made every attempt to connect with supporters and it was steps like that which helped the club become close with its supporters again. And that's crucial, especially if you're hoping for success on the field. That would take some time, even back in blue, and in truth, there were no instant rewards for returning to blue, not from a business point of view.

Attendances continued to drop at a steady pace, which was inevitable with no return to the Premier League in sight. However, at least now there was a platform upon which Cardiff could build relationships. They could rebuild the club as one of the community and supporters could back them without any guilt, squabbling or pain. Some would never return, some would, but at least now

Vincent Tan had done everything he could to put the situation right.

Cost-cutting would follow, but it was all necessary following the financial mistakes of the past and there was a silver lining in that the historic Langston debt was finally settled. The debt was essentially created by former owner Sam Hammam who, in short, took loans out in the club's name from his credit company, Langston, and everything stemmed from there. When Hammam left, Cardiff City then owed him £24m. The case would be tried in court but eventually it was settled, ending with a £5m payment from Tan and the club in 2016 after several more payments across the course of many years. The debt became a real concern at a number of points, but it was another obstacle cleared.

Back to the return to blue, and on 9 March 2015 the new logo, as promised by Tan, was released. To mixed views, it has to be said, as with anything new, but supporters seemed to like it. The bluebird was once again dominant and the dragon, now an Asian dragon which was probably the only aspect that divided opinion, sat below. A shield was the outline and the sort that Cardiff have used in the past, so that went down well, as did the prominent blue which made up the exterior of the shield.

The club statement upon release of the new crest read, 'Decisions were made with a view to producing a crest that everyone associated with Cardiff City could identify with and embrace. Our primary focus throughout the design and testing process was for the crest to demonstrate strong, historic links, while the modern and focused design is also seen as a strong visual step forward for Cardiff City. We very much hope you enjoy the final results, which includes the return to prominence of the Bluebird, as linked to the welcome return to traditional colours in January 2015.

'The 2015 dragon was created using three distinct influences, with a view to showcasing a design that was very much unique to Cardiff City. Projecting our Welsh heritage, the stance was taken from the national flag, as has been seen on our crest or shirt for a number of years. Celebrating Asian linked culture, design and tradition influences, we also looked to create a dragon that could be primarily owned and appreciated locally. To achieve this the main influence was drawn from the dragon placed on top of Cardiff City Hall, as has been the case since 1904. The dragon has been integral to the Welsh capital for over 100 years.'

The dragon was, in fact, the main source of conversation from this design but it's probably quite fitting that it's of an Asian design. The dragon was what Tan insisted upon, it was the part that dominated the old rebranded badge, albeit a Welsh one, and now it served as a compromise, and in that sense, the Asian design makes a lot of sense, though that will also divide opinion.

The badge would go on to settle nicely in the coming years and fans in the present day think of it as their own badge; it's not seen as a redesign or anything of the sort. It's the club logo and they are happy with it. After all, the badge had been redesigned a number of times in the past anyway; so long as it offers identity and a large bluebird, the supporters are happy.

Former WalesOnline writer Terry Phillips said at the time, 'The bluebird is back, big and proud. That, for me, is the big plus. I like the shape and don't even mind the red trim just inside the blue. City's new badge will feature on home and away shirts from the start of 2015/16 and, yes, it's the thumbs-up from me. The only negative thought I have is the small oriental dragon. It looks a bit of an afterthought to me, put down the bottom. But I certainly would not want the dragon any bigger than it is so even that is acceptable. Club owner Vincent Tan deserves great credit for making this possible. There is a little red on the badge and that is acceptable for me, too. Blue and the Bluebird have been a part of Cardiff City history. They are back.'

If fans were happy with that, then they were elated when the first kit since the return to blue was released. It was to be made by Adidas after the signing of a new four-year deal to bring a a super-brand, if you will, to the club for the first time. The design was sensational and almost everyone was thrilled. It was a mix between dark blue and a slightly lighter royal blue, with the traditional white three stripes, and it was accompanied by blue shorts and socks. It was a kit that looked special and looked more than a plain Adidas design. That too was fitting, given it was Cardiff City's first blue home kit to start the season since 2011.

A red away kit followed and there were no arguments; it was part of the compromise and Cardiff had used red away kits plenty of times in the past – it is a Welsh club after all. And with a strange yellow and black-striped third kit which would only be given to kit sponsors was also released, however it was never once worn.

So that was it, the return to blue was complete. The stadium front was given a nice new, blue, design, the kit was blue, the badge was blue, and the club were no longer in hiding.

Cardiff City returned to being the club we all know them to be.

'We're not shopping in Harrods anymore'

THE 2015/16 season began with fresh optimism created by a stunning home kit design and a new badge that fans actually liked. Cardiff City were back in blue but a lot more still needed to be sorted. Reversing the rebrand ensured that some supporters returned, and others got their love for the club back. That certainly helped ahead of the new season while Russell Slade continued to do his weeding, offloading all the dead wood at the club in an attempt to create a much healthier environment for playing staff.

The summer saw a few departures of note, including Nicky Maynard, one of the big signings of the promotion season. He would have to look back on his time at Cardiff as a failure, but how different might it have been if he hadn't suffered a serious knee injury during his first campaign in South Wales? Kev McNaughton was also released, and his departure would be felt throughout the fanbase. McNaughton became a Cardiff legend during his ten years at the club, experiencing the ups and downs, and as previously mentioned, the passion he displayed on the pitch made him a real fans' favourite.

McNaughton joined Wigan and he left with the knowledge that he had given Cardiff everything. You don't see many players who spend ten years at one club and that makes Kev rather unique, especially when you consider the club he signed for compared to the one he left. He was part of a roller-coaster journey and his contribution had earned him a place in the heart of the Bluebirds faithful forever.

The other departure of note was Javi Guerra, the Spanish forward, who returned to his home country to join Rayo Vallecano. Guerra simply wasn't given a chance for one reason or another in South Wales, and he's one in a long list of players during this period who will look back on their decision to join the Bluebirds as a bad one. Another who comes under that category, albeit he was given much more of a chance, was Adam Le Fondre, and he went out on loan again ahead of the 2015/16 season, joining Wolves.

Tom Adeyemi also left for a temporary move, along with Eoin Doyle, Filip Kiss and Etien Velikonja. There were just five signings and only three would be for the first team. Sammy Ameobi joined on loan from Newcastle, striker Idriss Saadi came from Clermont Foot and Gabriel Tamas, a Romanian defender who was unattached at the time, joined too. The number of incomings and the level of those players disappointed Cardiff fans, who knew their team needed more after scraping a mid-table finish in the season previous. On the back of that, many of the most talented players departed, and they weren't being adequately replaced.

However, Slade had put things rather bluntly during his first transfer window in charge, the previous January. He said, 'We are not shopping at Harrods now, we are shopping in a different area. We are going through a time of transition. Our wage bill is not sustainable. The only way forward is to reduce it to a sustainable level. We have come down a level and when you come down wage bills are astronomical, and you have to get down to a sensible level. It's not uncommon.'

Slade had a very tough job to do and his hands were tied behind his back, like many before him. Ahead of the 2015/16 season he had to continue chopping the squad, getting rid of the big earners and bad attitudes, while not having the money to replace them. Amid all the departures, Slade signed only one player who would feature regularly for the first team in the shape of Ameobi, an inexperienced youngster. That only highlights the size of the task that lay ahead of Slade, who was still expected to put together a play-off push.

Having said that, the former Leyton Orient boss still had a good team at his disposal with the likes of David Marshall, Fabio, Sean Morrison, Bruno Ecuele Manga, Ben Turner, Craig Noone, Peter

Whittingham, Anthony Pilkington and Kenwyne Jones. This was seen as a very decent team, but things had gone so wrong during the previous season that optimism was capped. However, a good pre-season which featured a trip to the Netherlands helped supporters raise their expectations a little. The Bluebirds beat Premier League clubs Watford and Bournemouth, and Joe Mason, who had returned to fitness, impressed throughout, indicating that he may finally have been ready to fulfil his potential.

The season itself started with a couple of dramatic draws, beginning with a 1-1 stalemate against Fulham thanks to a late Craig Noone stunner. Cardiff did it again the following week when they travelled to QPR and went two down within an hour. Sean Morrison got one back and Scott Malone scored a wonder-goal in injury time to grab another late equaliser.

After three draws to kick off the season three wins followed, including a televised success at home to Wolves that indicated a decent season could be on the cards after all. A steady run of form ensued, and Cardiff looked rather solid over the opening months, claiming a respectable draw against a Brighton side who were quick out of the blocks and stealing a late home win against Middlesbrough.

Attendances were down to the 14,000-mark but that was little surprise given the club had suffered two disappointing seasons and many had suffered a little too much during the rebrand fiasco. There was a section of fans who didn't take to Slade's football but those supporters tend to back the club anyway, they just make their disappointment heard. Slade was unfortunate in that respect, but he will have known that he wasn't going to be adored when he first viewed the criteria of his job.

The Bluebirds went into the Christmas period looking good with two entertaining 2-2 draws in the space of three games. But sandwiched between those was a two-goal collapse which saw Sheffield Wednesday complete a comeback to secure a draw in South Wales.

Still, though, Cardiff went into the Christmas games just one point from the play-offs and they looked genuine contenders. There were too many draws but wins like a 3-2 away victory over Bolton indicated that Slade's men were capable of turning the single-pointers into victories.

Mind you, their form was helped by the short-term loan signing of Tony Watt from Charlton, who impressed from the off, bringing energy and pace. There was a real feeling that he needed to be signed up until at least the end of the season, especially with Kenwyne Jones's stay looking tenuous. Rumours surrounded the Trinidadian striker, suggesting that he was being told he had to lower his wages or leave, and that looked to be true when he scored a 93rd-minute winner against Brentford and didn't celebrate; the hallmark of an unhappy striker.

Cardiff lost two of their four festive games, winning just one, and Jones was gone just five days into the window, confirming what many had envisaged to be true. Cardiff couldn't afford to maintain his contract and he wasn't keen on taking a big pay cut. He would only depart on loan for now, joining Al Jazira, but his time in South Wales had come to an end. Supporters weren't too disappointed given the prospect of signing new fan-favourite Watt on a permanent deal, but little did they know they were to be left disappointed ten days later when the deal fell through and Watt returned to Charlton.

It got worse, too. Cardiff were handed a transfer embargo, stopping them from making any permanent signings or from paying any fees due to a breach of Financial Fair Play regulations. The rules are designed to stop clubs overspending, to protect them from making big losses, and Cardiff had spent big during the previous season. That forced Vincent Tan to put £3m into the club, also turning £13m of debt into equity, putting Cardiff around £10m over the £6m allowance. The Bluebirds hierarchy were left disappointed and a little confused after thinking they were complying with the regulations, but they had to bite the bullet and accept the consequences, as did Slade, who had been looking forward to strengthening his play-off bid with new signings.

Many supporters felt the play-off bid was dead and buried from the moment the embargo was slapped upon the Bluebirds. The team needed strengthening to keep up with those above them and now it wasn't going to happen. However, Slade did do well to make a few more loan signings. Attacking midfielder Lex Immers joined from Feyenoord; a shrewd signing he would turn out to be. Young striker Kenneth Zohore signed from Vincent Tan-owned club KV Kortrijk and Welsh youngster Tom Lawrence joined on loan from Leicester City. There were departures, too, including Joe Mason to Wolves for a whopping £3m, a figure Cardiff just couldn't turn down, especially as he had flattered to deceive again in a season which really was billed as his last chance to shine. Alex Revell also left just a year after arriving. The local estate agents must have been making a fortune from the players, given the turnover of them at the club.

However, everything finally began to settle down on that front and by January, there was a feeling that the majority of the dead wood had been cleared. The dressing room was becoming a better environment as it was one without big egos, or indeed big wages. That suited Slade, whose CV had a list of lower-division clubs, none of which had the budgets to employ players with huge aspirations.

This was Slade's first experience of working with players of this level, making demands and everything else that comes with the prima donna types. He clearly didn't like it, either, shipping many out and replacing them with lads like Lee Peltier, real hard workers whose ambition above all else is to play and give everything for the shirt. Having said that, you need a good mix to get promotion and as they would find out later, Cardiff probably lacked the number of quality players needed, much due to the transfer embargo and the lack of money available to Slade in the summer transfer window.

Lex Immers, one of his signings during the January window, would turn out to be successful. And Stuart O'Keefe, whose Cardiff career looked like it would never get going, came in from the cold almost like a new signing. He was thrown in at Wolves in January and put in the performance of his life, helping Cardiff to a 3-1 win with three excellent goals, two from Craig Noone and one from Joe Ralls.

Peter Whittingham then stole the show at Huddersfield as Immers grabbed his first goal in Cardiff colours during the 3-1 win, and Slade's men were really picking up form. Then they put in their best performance of the season in a 4-1 thrashing of promotion-chasing Brighton in front of the Sky Sports cameras.

Now the Bluebirds were within four points of the play-offs. Just three games later, they were level on points with Sheffield Wednesday, who occupied the last top-six spot. O'Keefe and Immers, the two players who had transformed Cardiff since January, scored a goal each at Ashton Gate to see off Severnside rivals Bristol City, and the play-off chase was well and truly on.

Mixed form would follow but Cardiff were still in the hunt and they knew it. The club put on a number of ticket offers in an attempt to boost support for the run-in and particularly for a clash with Derby County in early April. The Rams were one of the teams the Bluebirds were chasing for a top-six spot, and more than 28,000 turned up to see O'Keefe score the winner. Slade's men were now within two points and an impressive draw away to table-toppers Burnley kept them in with a shout.

However, the wheels came off the Bluebirds' promotion chase in two disappointing trips to London. First, Fulham completed a comeback win at Craven Cottage after Immers again put Cardiff in front. Then, after a frustrating draw at home to a resilient QPR in which Cardiff dominated from start to finish, Brentford virtually finished the Bluebirds' play-off dream at Griffin Park.

An outside chance remained, however, after a home win over Bolton and with Cardiff facing play-off rivals Sheffield Wednesday away from home in the penultimate game of the season. The Bluebirds were four points off Wednesday, who were back in the last play-off spot with two games to go. But just like in 2009, Cardiff's play-off dream was to end at Hillsborough. Wednesday showed their quality and showed that they deserved to pip the Bluebirds to sixth spot with a comprehensive 3-0 win.

There was no shame in losing the race to a side with star quality in abundance with the likes of Gary Hooper, Fernando Forestieri, Barry Bannan and many more. However, Cardiff had done so well to stay in touch with the top six throughout the season that again it ended in disappointment, even if most supporters admitted that the team wasn't quite good enough to match the teams who eventually finished in the top six.

It's the hope that kills you, and we've been there many times already in this story.

A meaningless final-day draw meant Cardiff would finish the season in eighth, capping off a strange campaign as well as Russell Slade's reign. The season had started with mixed expectations but finished in disappointment. Slade had certainly won over a number of fans by taking a club that was completely broken when he arrived up to the brink of the play-offs. However, he still had many doubters, the depth of his tactical knowledge and management came up short on a number of occasions, but then again, how much better off might Cardiff have been if Slade had been allowed to strengthen in January as most clubs do?

Ultimately, Cardiff weren't consistent enough over the course of the season, managing doubles over just three of their 23 opponents. On the bright side, they still managed to come within six points of the play-offs, improving upon the previous season's position by three places. To still improve while selling players and cancelling contracts left, right and centre was some achievement. The whole club needed repairing from top to bottom and to get into the play-offs while doing all that was probably a little too much to ask.

In on-the-pitch terms, the Bluebirds lacked a striker after losing Jones, and failing to sign Watt on a longer deal was a key moment. Winger Anthony Pilkington plugged the gap, playing up top and managing nine goals in all competitions, but he was exposed as a makeshift striker too many times, not that it was any fault of his own. Immers also contributed five goals and he became something of a fans'-favourite after making such an impact after arriving on loan. Immers had this knack of arriving into the box just on time and it would see him add much-needed goals from midfield.

Matthew Connolly was the most stand-out player, however, and he was recognised with the Player of the Year awards, although the ceremony proved to be the beginning of the end for Slade.

Change of plan

ON THE day before Cardiff's final game of the season, against Birmingham, it was revealed, out of the blue, that Russell Slade was to be removed from his position as manager. Talks were set to commence, and that was known, but a decision wasn't expected before the last match and perhaps this decision wasn't expected at all.

In a move you simply don't see in the sport, Slade was switched from manager to a new 'head of football' role. A statement from CEO Ken Choo on the club's official website read, 'This season we have improved significantly. We want to build on it so we are trying to create a leaner and meaner team for next season. The club feels that it is necessary to have a change. We want to create a spark to take us to another level.'

Clearly the club felt Slade had done a good enough job to keep him around but was unheard of to do such a thing. The Bluebirds created a new role to give to the departing manager and he actually accepted it, though he wouldn't last long. Slade said at the time, 'It's going to be different, that's for sure, and I've done an awful lot of games as a manager and now that has come to an end, but I will look forward and focus and look to see what I can do to help in the process of moving the club forward. I'm looking forward to the Birmingham game and it really would be nice to go out on a high and get three points to finish the season.'

The timing of the announcement did give Slade the chance to say goodbye to supporters, and he was well received despite some opposition to him during his reign. There was a large section of fans who couldn't stand his football and they made it quite clear on occasions. However, even they could appreciate that Slade did a good job of getting the dressing room back into a healthy place, and he was given a good send-off at the Cardiff City Stadium before moving upstairs.

Speaking after his final game, Slade addressed the media and said, 'It's been a difficult week after the disappointment of not getting that vital result at Sheffield. It was always going to be tough. And then the changes that have been announced. It was nice at the end. It was nice to have that rapport and that relationship which has grown with the fans over my time here. It's not quite enough, we know that, but at least we have stability. When I came to the club, we were 17th. We managed to stop that slide, turn it around, address the financial side, reduce the wage bill.

'I'm not a bitter and twisted man. It's for the good of the club. There's nothing bigger than the club, that's the most important thing. I appreciate that, no one is bigger than the club. I will play my part. I'm pleased and proud of what my players and my staff have done. I think it's a great opportunity now. It's not going to be the club I came into. It's going to be a club that came very close to finishing in the top six, there's a great platform to build on, that is what someone is going to inherit. It's quite exciting. I did want a bit more, we all want a bit more as a manager in terms of success, but I think the perception from outside is that me and my team have done a good job here, we just missed out, but it's a tick in the box.'

Slade was a manager who split opinion among fans and even if you asked them several years on, you would still get differing views. The football his team played was often uneasy on the eye, it lacked imagination, and not only that, it wasn't successful enough that fans could look past its ugliness. Home draws against Rotherham and MK Dons come to mind as real low points, and a home defeat to Shrewsbury Town in front of around 4,000 in the FA Cup was another. Such results did little to get supporters back on board, although there were good occasions like the home games against Derby and QPR towards the end of his last season. The Cardiff City Stadium was packed out on both occasions and while a ticket offer helped, it was the first time since the Premier League days that the stadium came anywhere close to being full. Under Solskjaer, that was unimaginable.

Ultimately, Slade lost his job because he failed to reach the target of getting Cardiff into the play-offs, but it wasn't all that easy of a task. The Bluebirds had a good squad, yes, but they also had an unhappy Kenwyne Jones for the whole of December before loaning him out. Even after the work Slade had done to get rid of the bad apples, it still wasn't the happiest of dressing rooms and that was sometimes reflected on the pitch. Things were improving behind the scenes, the club continued to rebuild relationships with supporters, but there still wasn't a coherence like there had been before the rebrand took place. The bad taste continued to linger in the mouths of many fans and it's true that many weren't ready to back the club unconditionally again. Not yet. That affected Slade, as it would any manager, and in many respects, taking the job at the point he did, it was a poisoned chalice.

When the former Leyton Orient boss arrived during October 2014, he must have been walking into one of the hardest jobs in British football at the time. He must have realised that when he watched his new team lose to a winless Blackpool just before taking the job. Slade had the job of trying to sort out a poisoned club that was rotting from the inside out. He took over a chaotic dressing room during a season in which Cardiff had 37 registered first-team players. Many would go out on loan, some would be sold, but that puts into perspective the car crash scene at which Slade arrived.

To manage on-the-field affairs, to try to achieve success on the pitch while all that is going on behind the scenes, when you have a mountain of work to complete before going near the training pitch – it was an impossible job. However, he did it well. Some will disagree, but the fact is that Slade was an important chapter for Cardiff and perhaps his critics will realise that in time, although many already do acknowledge it. Nobody will claim that he was an unbridled success, far from it, and perhaps he could have achieved more during his only full season. However, if Cardiff had got their next appointment after Ole Gunnar Solskjaer wrong, this story could have had a very sad ending. Cardiff needed someone to make decisions, someone to do a real gardening job behind closed doors, and Slade did it. He was called a 'yes man' among many other names during his time in South Wales, suggesting he did whatever Vincent Tan wanted him to, but he simply did what needed to be done.

Slade is an intelligent bloke and he knew that replacing Javi Guerra and Adam Le Fondre with Alex Revell and Eoin Doyle would annoy a lot of supporters. He knew he would get stick and lose support from many. But he also knew that he had to cut the wage bill, so he did it. He made selfless decisions and became a sacrificial lamb many times during his stint. He didn't achieve huge progress during his 19 months at the club, but what he did was create a platform for success.

Before he arrived, Cardiff simply weren't capable of achieving anything. They were sooner going down than up and everything was spiralling out of control. Wages were too high, players were too unhappy and all the while an embargo remained on the club, preventing any incomings that required a fee. By the time Slade left – and this includes the help of the CEO, the chairman and others behind the scenes as well as a return to blue – the club was becoming financially sound, the squad had been cut by ten players, the fans were far more content, the team finished six points from the top six and ambition returned, so much so that it cost Slade his position.

Clearly, he had done his job. And while form and the style of play probably weren't good enough, he managed to fix large parts of a broken club, healing very deep wounds and doing a vital job that helped the club get back on to its feet. Slade wasn't exciting, he wasn't loved by fans, he wasn't loved by the media, especially not with his unimaginative press conferences, and he didn't help himself in that respect. However, he left behind a solid job that truthfully, many would have completely failed at. He steered the ship to safety and then hit the iceberg himself in many ways, and for that, he deserves credit.

Following Slade's goodbye in that final-day draw with Birmingham, Cardiff held an awards evening and it all got a little messy. CEO Ken Choo was quoted as having said during the event, 'It was not a difficult decision to move Russell to the head of football role. Our position has always been clear, that whoever is manager or head coach should at a minimum take us to the play-offs. This squad cost £28m to assemble. Vincent's position is clear, any lower than the play-offs is a failure. He is not putting £30m a year into the business to not succeed, any businessman would want to take this team into the Premier League.'

Those comments were collected by WalesOnline journalist Steve Tucker, who was called up on his conduct following the event. Choo saw the article, which was subsequently published as 'Ken Choo says Russell Slade failed as Cardiff City manager and reveals shortlist already drawn up for new boss', and responded with a statement, in which he said, 'During an informal talk with Mr Tucker during the Supporters Club dinner on Saturday evening, I referenced the fact that we, as a club, considered missing out on the top six as a failure. At no stage was I asked for a formal interview and at no point did I say that Russell Slade has been a failure for our football club. I categorically refute the article leading supporters into thinking that this is my belief. My working relationship with Russell has always been good and shall continue to be now he has taken the role of head of football. Saturday's article and Mr Tucker's conduct disappoints me greatly.'

WalesOnline responded with a statement of its own, defending the actions of Tucker, who left his role shortly after the incident. Such spats aren't a big part of this story, nor are they that uncommon, but this one is significant because it puts into perspective the attitude the club held at the time, and their irresponsibility, in many ways. Such comments were always going to hurt Slade, who left his new role within 28 days, after which the position ceased to exist.

Before Slade left for good, though, there was one final insult from the club when his assistant, Paul Trollope, was given the main job. To provide some context, there were claims from fans throughout the season that Trollope was the driving force behind Cardiff's form and it's unknown whether that influenced the decision or not, but it was never going to go down well with Slade, who had been replaced by his number two who had only previously held one manager's position, with Bristol Rovers, compared to Slade who had just taken charge of his eighth club.

It was believed that Cardiff were going to seek out someone with experience, to take them to the next step, to achieve progress, and then they went and appointed someone with no real experience of managing in the higher divisions – a gamble. Trollope was liked by the fans, however, and that will have had some bearing. He was a Welsh international as a player and he helped the team across the line as Chris Coleman's assistant when the national team qualified for Euro 2016. Trollope was building a good CV and a good reputation, there's no doubt about that. He clearly had an impact after joining the Bluebirds. However, Cardiff were supposed to be looking for someone to take them to the next level; this appointment simply didn't fit that, and it served to undermine Slade even further.

Football isn't about sentiment, and if Trollope was the right man for the job then Slade had to deal with that, but at the time there were fears from supporters that this was a risk and it wasn't what the club needed. Meanwhile other fans felt it was more of a calculated gamble with Trollope being familiar with the surroundings and already being a face the players knew. Slade was much more of a manager, watching on from the sidelines in training as many do, while Trollope and other staff took care of the coaching, so the former midfielder did have a good bond with the players. The challenge now was for him to turn into an authoritative figure, someone who would make the calls and the change from being a friendly coach to an out-and-out boss is never an easy one.

Speaking upon his appointment, Trollope said, 'We have to be ambitious and create a belief within the club. The target is the play-offs and hopefully promotion. There are areas that need addressing within the team and we will be looking to add quality and also the right people. I had no reservations, it is a good club with a good fan base. Every coach has their own philosophies and way of doing things. I have clear ideas what I want. I will bring my own style to that. Anyone who knows me will know that.'

The last point was the biggest doubt. Fans were concerned that Trollope was going to continue down the same road and after Slade's departure, they wanted something fresh, progression in the way the team played.

BBC Wales football correspondent Rob Phillips highlighted this at the time. He said, 'Trollope's appointment suggests the club want continuity, but he will have to stamp his own authority on matters to avoid the decision being seen as a continuation of the Russell Slade regime. He has an excellent reputation as a coach and Cardiff improved following his arrival. Now he will have to hit the ground running next season to placate any doubts and to achieve the Championship play-off target Slade failed to meet this season.'

Fans also saw it as a cheap option, with the club's spending in recent years aligning with that idea, but chairman Mehmet Dalman was quick to deny this to BBC Radio Wales. He said, 'It is not us taking the cheap option. It could turn out to be a very expensive option. We have [had] stability over the last 18 months. The team is not far off, let's be honest about that. Paul is absolutely able to bring in his own coaching team, it is entirely up to him how he builds that, and I will support him with club resources.

'First of all, we interviewed candidates from outside of the club as well, and some very, very good candidates actually. I was genuinely very surprised and impressed by the number of people who have shown interest. We felt that when you look at the history of the club and the disruptions and difficulties that we have had, we felt continuity was important. And the resources we are about to have we want to put into the squad, rather than anywhere else. There will be money available for Paul, absolutely.'

The first challenge for Trollope was fitting in preparations for the new season while continuing his role with Wales. And he made it quite clear that with the European Championships just a month away, he wasn't going to give up his seat on the plane. Everyone was weary that if Wales progressed through the group stage then Trollope wouldn't be home for the start of the Bluebirds' pre-season, but on the other hand, supporters were far more forgiving than usual. This was Wales's first major tournament in 58 years and in the same way that every supporter wanted to avoid missing the opportunity to be there, Trollope wanted to seize his chance, and that was understood.

The build-up to Euro 2016 and the competition itself would grip the country, the excitement was beyond explanation, and everyone wanted a part of it. For the first time in decades, international football became more interesting than Cardiff City and club football, and so there wasn't a big deal made of Trollope's decision to go to France.

It was worth it, too, when Wales defied all expectations to reach the semi-finals, where they lost to Portugal.

Trollope would indeed return late to pre-season but only a few days after the players returned from their summer time off. Wales's success and Trollope being a part of that would help him win over some supporters. Knowing that he had coached a team that was good enough to reach the last four in the European Championships turned heads. Many supporters were now ready to believe that Trollope was good enough to take Cardiff to the next level, though, not before they had digested a rare mouthful of international success for Wales, and indeed made the most of it.

Euro 2016 truly was the adventure of a lifetime for Wales and Cardiff City fans were part of it. Suddenly club football had an awful lot to live up to.

A close shave

THE HYPE surrounding Euro 2016 would continue straight into the club's pre-season with fans still in awe of what Wales had achieved in France, and rightly so. Chris Coleman and his band of heroes arrived to a fitting reception at the Cardiff City Stadium after a bus parade around the city, and new boss Paul Trollope was of course involved.

However, it was quickly down to business after that for Trollope who was already a little late joining pre-season, conducting preparations from his hotel room in France. In fact, he had already officially signed three players before returning to South Wales, making the most of the transfer embargo having been lifted. Lex Immers made his move permanent for around £2m after a fantastic loan spell. Kenneth Zohore did the same, moving from Kortrijk despite not impressing during his time on loan. Experienced Belgium-born Benin international Frederic Gounongbe also joined. Meanwhile, there were a number of players out of contract and the likes of Eoin Doyle, Ben Turner, Filip Kiss, Kenwyne Jones and Joe Lewis all departed in one form or another.

Etien Velikonja ended his South Wales nightmare by leaving at the end of his contract. The Slovenian cost more than £1m but he had only featured in three league games during his four-year stay. Trollope injected some Welsh blood with the arrival of Jazz Richards on a swap deal for Scott Malone and he added to those incomings with the signing of Emyr Huws, a bright young talent.

Bluebirds fan Ben Price says of that period, 'The signing of Jazz Richards really got the fans excited after his noteworthy performances in Wales's qualifying campaign for Euro 2016 and was seen as the first step in introducing the Wales way to Cardiff City – getting rid of Scott Malone at the same time was seen as the icing on the cake.'

The signings didn't stop there. Joe Bennett was snapped up from Aston Villa and former England international Rickie Lambert was a deadline-day capture from West Brom, costing Cardiff around £1.7m. There was a teary goodbye for David Marshall, whose seven-year stay ended with a £2.5m move to Hull City, and fan favourite Fabio joined Middlesbrough for £2m. Kagisho Dikgacoi and Federico Macheda also departed after having their contracts cancelled by mutual consent.

Trollope was a busy man during pre-season, making a number of changes, and he was clearly looking to put his own stamp on the team. He also wanted to introduce Welsh players in a bid to give the fans something to relate to on the pitch, and what better time to do it than off the back of the most successful major tournament in Welsh football history? The Bluebirds faithful welcomed the idea, given that it had been so long since Welsh blood had broken through. Declan John did well in the Premier League season, but he wasn't given a look-in during the two subsequent campaigns, and he was one of the players given a fresh opportunity under Trollope. Other than John, you'd have to go back to Aaron Ramsey, Joe Ledley, Adam Matthews, Chris Gunter and Darcy Blake to find players who had come through the youth system and nailed down a first-team spot. Trollope wanted to bring that back, and with everyone embracing their Welshness, so to speak, it was the perfect time to install such a regime.

In terms of tactics, Trollope wanted to use the 3-5-2/5-3-2 formation that had helped Wales to Euro 2016 success. New signing Richards and Declan John were deployed as the wing-backs. The formation is a modern one and it requires two very fit wing-backs to do the role of a full-back and a winger, offering support up top while ensuring the defence becomes a back five out of possession. It's a system that worked brilliantly for Wales, offering solidity in defence to bridge the gap between the talent in the squad and some of their impressive opponents, while ensuring they had numbers on the break. It would also serve Antonio Conte and Chelsea well during this particular season. The Blues completely cracked the system and they were almost unbeatable while using it, helping them to the Premier League title.

The early signs were good for Cardiff, too, who impressed during their pre-season tour in Germany, winning the Osnabruck Cup with two victories from two games. Defeats to Exeter City and Bournemouth followed but Cardiff headed into the new season feeling quite optimistic. However, such is the risk involved in appointing someone inexperienced, fans didn't quite know what to expect going into the opening day, an away clash with Birmingham.

Ben Price recalls the feeling among supporters. He says, 'The mood among City fans was a very strange one, on one hand there was a feeling of excitement; on the other hand there was a feeling that the appointment was very underwhelming. The club were looking to develop a long-terms strategy that would see "the Cardiff way" introduced throughout the club, after the less than exciting days of Russell Slade. We were looking to recreate the magic of the Welsh summer of 2016, with Cardiff playing the same system Coleman used for the Welsh team during the Euros. City fans were (in the majority) in favour of the club finally having a sense of direction, after two years of just drifting from the Premier League to mid-table Championship football.

'The club was clearly heading in the wrong direction and it was a good thing that Vincent Tan and co. recognised this. While City fans were impressed with the clear improvement in the team's performances since Trollope joined Russell Slade's backroom team, it was clear there were many doubts over his ability to be a number one. His record as a manager wasn't going to excite even the most optimistic of Cardiff City fans – if they even exist. Fans were doubtful but the feeling from the majority was that it was only fair to give him a chance. Out of all the names linked with the job, he was possibly the fans' choice, but given the low level of rumoured names that wasn't much of a compliment.'

The Bluebirds impressed at St Andrew's, dominating with Immers hitting the bar in the first half. John thrived in his new wing-back role and the performance generally looking promising. Gounongbe then missed an open goal from less than two yards out – not the start he had envisaged – and Peter Whittingham was denied in his stunning attempt from range by an equally stunning save. The game finished goalless, but in truth, Cardiff probably should have won, so no real concern was born out of the result. In fact, it says something when the main story was Richards not doing the 'Ayatollah'. He probably didn't hear the supporters' requests, perhaps he preferred to concentrate on the game, or maybe he didn't know what it was. But he received a big booing for not taking part, and that was as much to do with the fact he had come through at Swansea City as a youngster before representing them at senior level, despite actually starting his youth career at Cardiff.

The Bluebirds then put on a rather shocking display at Trollope's former club Bristol Rovers, losing in extra time to crash out of the EFL Cup in round one, and things didn't get better upon return to league competition. The Bluebirds were dismantled by QPR in their first home game, and the manner in which they were beaten ensured concern began to mount as early as three games in. That was eased by a 2-1 home win over Blackburn which saw Shane Duffy score two own goals and also get sent off. Cardiff then went and took a 2-2 draw from Fulham despite going behind, and there was a feeling of 'maybe this will get better', especially given the quality of the goals scored by Joe Ralls and Anthony Pilkington at Craven Cottage. But it didn't.

Cardiff lost their next four games, including a home defeat to old rivals Leeds United, and despite momentary respite with of a 2-1 away win over Rotherham, in which Lambert netted a brace, form continued to deteriorate. The Bluebirds then lost another two, the latter of which was an abject display on a miserable, rainy day at the Pirelli Stadium, against a Burton Albion side who were expected to go down during their first season in the Championship. The Brewers – who would go on to defy the odds and stay up – made easy work of Cardiff, and while soaking wet on the sideline, Trollope must have known that this was the end. It just wasn't working. Seven defeats in 11 games, eight in 12 including the League Cup, and just two wins in all.

Going into the international break, which no longer involved Trollope after he left his job with Wales to concentrate on his club position, Cardiff sacked their manager. Coincidentally he was the third boss at a Welsh club to lose his job in seven days, with Newport and Swansea also pulling the trigger following disastrous starts to the campaign. The season after Wales's international success had begun so badly for the Welsh clubs in the English Football League. Trollope was partly responsible for that and he paid the price.

Speaking to the League Managers Association after his sacking, he said, 'I am of course disappointed to be leaving the football club after almost two years, however I have thoroughly enjoyed my time at the club and would like to thank the players and all the staff at the Vale training complex and stadium for their hard work, commitment, friendship and support.'

Trollope left the Bluebirds in 23rd, their lowest position in 11, years, and nobody batted an eyelid. There were very few complaints, how could there be? This had been a disastrous start to the season and while there may have been arguments that he should have been given more time, there were very few. Trollope, despite his best efforts, had spectacularly failed, in a far greater way than his predecessor Russell Slade, and he had quite possibly ended any hopes of a Cardiff promotion in just 11 games. This was a season when Cardiff wanted to achieve progression, to go for promotion and instead, they would now have to battle relegation, sitting a point from safety.

It was also revealed that Vincent Tan wanted to call time on Trollope earlier, but he had been convinced to give him a couple more weeks. The decision was eventually made and almost everyone was in agreement that this just didn't work. Paul was a good coach and he had proved that throughout his career, but management is another job altogether and he just wasn't ready to take on a club like Cardiff.

Ben Price offers the supporters' view. 'Trying to implement a whole new way of playing throughout a club takes a lot of time, every fan knows that. However, fans also want results right away, the message from Trollope and the players during pre-season was that the aim was a top six finish at the very minimum. Looking back, in a league with Newcastle clear favourites to be promoted and a very strong pack behind them, Trollope was digging his own grave with these comments. However, his aims were clear: if we didn't get into the play-offs then the season has been a poor one.

'The implementation of the Wales way was started during pre-season, with Cardiff using Declan John and Fabio as wing-backs. This was a combination that got fans very excited; both were popular with the fans. Fabio was an all-out attacking full-back that loved to get forward, while local lad Declan John was a former winger converted to left-back by Malky Mackay. Neither were great defensively but, in this system,, fans felt that they could really be vital to the new "Cardiff way".

'Our excitement and Trollope's hopes were soon dealt a serious blow: newly promoted Middlesbrough signed Fabio, leaving Cardiff with a lack of attacking options on the right side of defence. Lee Peltier is a great defender, but is lacking when going forward, which is a key part of playing with wing-backs. Cardiff also lack that Gareth Bale influence – as quick as Craig Noone is, he isn't a world class player that offers that attacking threat. It seems the players quickly lost trust in Trollope's tactics and results never picked up, perhaps if Fred [Gounongbe] had scored that open goal against Birmingham then things might have been different.'

Attention quickly turned to Trollope's successor and it was instantly clear that Cardiff wanted someone more experienced, someone whose appointment brought far less risk. They didn't have to look too far, either. Before allowing any time for speculation, chairman Mehmet Dalman was meeting with wily campaigner Neil Warnock and it was common knowledge before the end of the day in which Trollope was sacked that Warnock was the man the Bluebirds wanted. He was appointed the following day.

Warnock later revealed the story of his appointment to WalesOnline: 'I was up in Scotland at the time, but agreed to come down to London to meet him over breakfast. He said straight away, "I don't want to interview you Neil, I just want to give you the job." It's nice to be wanted and even though I thought Derby would be back, I knew straight away I wanted to be Cardiff manager. We shook hands on it, hadn't even talked money at that stage, although I knew what I was worth. Mehmet went out of the room to speak to

Vincent Tan by telephone a couple of times and came back saying he wanted me to sign something.

'"Mehmet, I've shaken hands on the deal, that's good enough for me," I said. Do you know, in the past I've lost £1m after shaking hands with two different chairmen who ended up not giving me the job, so perhaps I should have insisted upon things in writing myself. But my word is my bond. Mehmet even tried to get me to sign a serviette that was on the breakfast table, but no need.'

Warnock joined just three months after leaving Rotherham United, who he had miraculously guided to safety shortly after having returned from retirement to take over the Millers. The 67-year-old signed a deal until the end of the season in South Wales and supporters were as delighted as he was. Speaking to Cardiff's official website after his appointment, the former Sheffield United boss said, 'I enjoyed it at Rotherham last year and I've got seven promotions and, I can't tell a lie, I thought I was trying to get that eighth promotion. I decided to wait – I had talks with three or four clubs from the summer onwards and it never materialised and, although I was disappointed, I'm a big believer in fate and when this cropped up, I had one phone call from Mehmet [Dalman] and it was straight away.

'I always want to feel wanted and he told me straight away I was his number one target, the club's number one target, and that goes a long way I think. I've always liked it here. I've always liked getting off the bus. Everywhere I go I get stick, but at Cardiff – I get on quite well with the Cardiff lads. I'm sure the same people are there by the bus with their autograph books. I've always had good banter with the Cardiff people. They are my kind of crowd, blood and guts and all that, which I like. If I can get it right for them I know they will get behind me and that's what keeps me going at the moment.'

Warnock was welcomed with open arms at Cardiff. Like all fans in the English leagues, the Bluebirds taunted him while he was in charge of other clubs, but he was a manager many supporters wished they could have. Warnock's wife, Sharron, discovered that when he was appointed. She said to her husband, 'Darling, you'll never believe what I've been reading, I've been on the Cardiff forums and all the fan websites. I've been reading them, and everybody likes you at Cardiff. I can't believe it, they like you. All these fans say they actually like you.'

Warnock arrived in South Wales with seven promotions to his name, which is quite the CV. His appointment created an instant belief that he would succeed.

He had to hit the ground running, though, with Cardiff in a rather horrible position, sitting in the relegation zone. Warnock signed four free agents almost instantly, bringing in winger Junior Hoilett and defender Sol Bamba – two players who waited for Warnock to find a club – along with striker Marouane Chamakh and midfielder Kieran Richardson, who also signed on very short-term deals. Instantly, Warnock was showing his clout, using his contacts and providing a spark, even when the transfer window was closed.

His first game was hotly anticipated, and it couldn't have been set up any better with Severnside rivals Bristol City coming to the Cardiff City Stadium in front of the Sky Sports cameras. More than 22,000 turned up, and they weren't disappointed as the Bluebirds immediately looked a more exciting prospect and pulled off a 2-1 win. Peter Whittingham scored a penalty in the first half and Bamba grabbed what would turn out to be the winner to install himself as a fans'-favourite on his debut. Lee Tomlin – who would later end up at Cardiff – got Bristol back into it but Cardiff saw the game out to claim a big three points.

Bamba, from minute one, showed his leadership qualities and his sheer passion. He joined just three days before this game and already he embodied everything Cardiff City are about. From there, the Bluebirds faithful probably knew they would be okay, that they were in safe hands. Warnock would remind them that the worst case could still happen but after this win, they would only drop into the relegation zone once more throughout the course of the season and in truth, from the moment Bamba rose highest to net the winner against Bristol, any relegation fears were forgotten. That sounds hasty, but it was true on this occasion. This team was already too good to be in the relegation zone on paper, and now it had a serial winner in charge, as well as being enthused by new additions like Bamba and Hoilett who had won fans over in their first game.

The Bluebirds' form didn't take off too quickly despite that win, which was followed by a home draw with Sheffield Wednesday and an away victory at Nottingham Forest. A shock defeat to Wigan, a much more expected defeat to Newcastle and a 3-1 thrashing at Aston Villa saw Cardiff return to the relegation zone for the final time during the season. And that was despite a home win over Huddersfield Town, who would go on to secure a shock promotion to the Premier League.

The Bluebirds then took an impressive home point against Brighton, another team who would secure promotion, before an eventful draw at Ipswich. It wasn't eventful in terms of the playing action, but an incident occurred which could have panned out very badly. Bamba completely lost the plot after a challenge and he had to be wrestled off the field. He was then restrained by Warnock, who he shoved off, almost sending his manager to the ground. It really was a bizarre turn of events from someone you wouldn't think was capable. Sol is quite a softly spoken, down-to-earth and genuinely lovely guy, despite being very passionate and no-nonsense on the field. This really was strange to watch.

The altercation really concerned fans, who were now wondering how a usually strict Warnock would react. Could their new favourite defender be on his way out already? Thankfully not. The two patched things up very quickly and Bamba was appalled by his own actions.

Taking the earliest opportunity to speak to the press in the following weeks, accepting full responsibility for his actions and apologising to his manager and the fans, he said, 'It was a moment of craziness, I think I can call it that. I thought it was a bad tackle – that's it's not an excuse because I shouldn't have reacted like that at all. But I'm a strong player but I always look to play the ball and with that one I didn't think it was the case.

'What happened, happened, but it shouldn't have. When people around me saw the footage they didn't understand, especially my children. I have three, the youngest being five, and they'd seen it because they were going to school with everyone talking about it. I couldn't hide from it. I was embarrassed. Friends and family said that it's not me, they didn't recognise that person out there.'

How differently things might have turned out if Warnock and Bamba hadn't worked it out, a potential turning point for sure.

Bamba's sending-off and subsequent suspension meant he wouldn't play a part in Cardiff's superb comeback victory over Wolves. The Bluebirds got a late winner in what felt like a big result for the home side, one that could propel them away from the threat of relegation, although not before they were sent crashing back down to earth first. In one of the season's stranger games, Barnsley emerged victorious at the Cardiff City Stadium with a 4-3 win. Cardiff came back from 3-1 down to draw level just one minute from time, only to lose in the fifth minute of stoppage time.

It would prove to be the end for loan keeper Ben Amos, too, who made a catalogue of errors during the defeat, leading to him being replaced after Christmas. Not everyone gets a second chance under Warnock. Brian Murphy, who had linked back up with Warnock, started on Boxing Day for a 2-2 draw against Brentford, another game which saw Cardiff let points slip – this time giving up the lead on two occasions – again despite scoring in the 89th minute. However, going into the New Year, a confidence that things would improve remained. The belief that Warnock would continue to steer the club away from the relegation zone continued, and he did just that.

The Bluebirds kicked off the new year with three straight wins. The first came against recently relegated Aston Villa thanks to a Joe Ralls strike, and the second saw the Bluebirds make it a double over Bristol City. Warnock's men went 1-0 down at Ashton Gate before scoring an equaliser from the spot with just over 15 minutes left. Then they let it slip again, going behind four minutes later, before scoring another equaliser through an unlikely headed goal from Kadeem Harris. The Bluebirds were used to conceding late goals by the time they arrived at Ashton Gate but they scored one of their own to secure a dramatic derby-day win, Anthony Pilkington adding a wonder goal from around 25 yards to take all three points, and now Cardiff were taking strides away from danger. Warnock celebrated in front of the away end and he was quickly becoming a cult figure.

They grabbed another late goal at home to Burton through youngster Rhys Healey to make it three wins on the bounce and that put them eight points clear of the drop. Cardiff made a couple of January additions with Warnock's trusty servant Greg Halford arriving from Rotherham and experienced Scottish goalkeeper Allan McGregor joining on loan. Meanwhile, Lex Immers had been released despite costing the club £2m in the summer, Chamakh and Richardson were let back into the wilderness and recent signing Emyr Huws was loaned out for the rest of the season. Stuart O'Keefe, who had shone in the previous season, was also sent on loan, and that was despite signing a new contract in the summer. The revolving door continued to turn at a rapid pace.

Meanwhile, Cardiff had uncovered a gem in Kenneth Zohore. Remember him? The Danish striker we've barely touched upon? He hasn't been mentioned because his loan spell during the 2015/16 season was pretty forgettable and even after making his move permanent, he looked pretty useless, by all accounts. However, during the home win over Wolves, he was thrown on at half-time and told to run for his life. He responded with a terrific display and never looked back.

He went on to score at Brentford in the Boxing Day draw and then it was lift-off for his career when he scored the goal of the season against Preston in a 2-0 home win. He skipped through the entire defence, starting his run in his own half, before dinking the ball over the keeper. Fans knew they had a star on their hands. Warnock did, too, and it meant Cardiff finally had a proper striker to look to, albeit an out-of-form Rickie Lambert was still around.

Warnock recalled giving Zohore what could have been his last chance to impress, telling WalesOnline, 'The first time I saw him he was playing in the reserves but stuck out on the left wing. It was a sunny day, but he was wearing gloves which I thought a bit strange. Anyway, one of the staff was telling me, "That's Immers, that's Zohore, that's someone else." I was getting to know them when suddenly Zohore knocked the ball past the full-back and raced clear. "Hello, where's that come from, I thought? This guy's got something."

'One or two were sceptical, but I tried him up front in a few practice games, picked him on the bench for the first team. We were 1-0 down against Wolves, had no pace or legs up top and couldn't see how we were going to get back into it. Their defenders had cigars out. There's a green wheelie bin by the shower area in the dressing room and at half-time Kenneth and I were standing either side of it. He was leaning on the bin with one arm, I was leaning on the other bit. I can still picture it today. "Ken," I said, "I'm going to put you on. They are telling me you're going back to Belgium. If you're rubbish this half you WILL be going back to Belgium, I can assure you of that. But I want you to go out there and work your socks off, win the headers, put yourself about, be prepared to make runs even if the ball doesn't come. Can you do that? Can you show me you have a future here? But the thing is Ken YOU have to do it, not me." He was an absolute revelation and we came back to win 2-1. Ken hasn't looked back since.'

Armed with their new weapon in Zohore, Cardiff put together a good run of form in the February, brushing off a rare home defeat to Norwich before pulling off a surprise 2-0 victory at over play-off chasing Leeds United. Then the Bluebirds stunned Derby County with a 4-3 away win. They were 2-0 down early on, only to come back and go 3-2 up thanks to Harris and Craig Noone. Derby looked to have popped the Bluebirds' balloon with an equaliser but more drama would follow. Rhys Healey won a penalty out of nothing in stoppage time, giving Ralls the chance to win it from the spot, and he made no mistake.

Next up, a thrilling 5-0 win over a doomed Rotherham side saw Zohore wow the Bluebirds' faithful once again with a brace and Cardiff were home and dry as far as Championship safety was concerned. Some even talked about reaching the play-offs, but Warnock rightly rejected such optimism straight away, saying there was too much of a mountain to climb. After the damage suffered under Trollope, it was Everest. Even after three straight wins they were 13 points from the top six and only 13 games remained.

Warnock's scepticism proved to be realism, with Cardiff only winning four of those final 13 encounters. Mind you, such form isn't uncommon for a team with nothing to play for and fans weren't exactly displeased. The Bluebirds were already planning for next season and they were more worried about what looked to be a goodbye in Peter Whittingham's final home game, a 2-0 defeat to eventual champions Newcastle United. Whittingham was replaced before full time and his emotional departure from the turf suggested he wasn't going to extend his current deal. Just one game remained after the Newcastle defeat, a long trip to Huddersfield, which turned out to be quite the day out. Warnock's men blew away the soon-to-be-promoted Terriers on their own patch, winning 3-0 thanks to a goal from Zohore and two from an unlikely source in Joe Bennett. How's that for finishing with a bang?

It was another season that had started with hope, although admittedly many fans didn't quite know what to expect. The club hierarchy expected promotion but they weren't going to get it with an inexperienced man at the helm, and that quickly became clear. Instead, they had to settle for a top-half finish, which Cardiff secured on the final day on goal difference. The Bluebirds finished six points behind where Russell Slade had left them the previous season and that perhaps gives him the last laugh, although fans didn't care about that. They now had Neil Warnock.

A season had been wasted, by all accounts, but the foundations remained for a good one next time around. Cardiff had a serial winner in charge and he had just signed a new deal to keep him in place for the following year. That news sold a lot of season tickets alone, and it's no wonder as to why.

Warnock is known for taking teams up. Cardiff were beaten to promotion by his QPR side in 2011 so they've witnessed it first-hand. They were also in the same division as his Sheffield United side who secured promotion in 2006. Cardiff were one of those long-serving Championship teams and Warnock was a long-serving Championship manager. The two had gone to battle so many times in the past and both held admired each other. It seemed like a match made in heaven and supporters knew something special could be just around the corner. Warnock also said all the right things, which helped to some degree, but it wasn't all about that. He'd said similar things at Rotherham and QPR and supporters aren't naïve. They didn't need Neil to tell them this was his type of club or anything like that, though he did for good measure. They knew this was a good fit and you could feel it instantly.

Everything just seemed to click into place for the first time since Malky Mackay took charge and it felt good for supporters, who had

had to force themselves to back Trollope, Slade and Solskjaer. None of those managers invited support naturally. Warnock did, and fans were more than happy to back him. For the first time in a long time, the Bluebirds faithful had a manager they would back to the hilt, and for the first time, the players had a man in charge they truly respected, who they would go to war for.

Cardiff City, we have lift-off.

Here's to you, Peter Whittingham

BEFORE WE embark upon another season of twists and turns, we must first pay homage to a player who left in 2017, ten years after arriving. Peter Whittingham joined in 2007 from Aston Villa for just £350,000 and it was, perhaps, the best spent money by the Bluebirds during this ten-year period – he went on to make more than 400 league appearances, scoring 85 league goals.

Cardiff might have thought they were only buying a youngster with potential to do a job in the Championship, but what they got was a loyal servant who would single-handedly win countless games with the wave of his magic wand of a left foot. He's a player fans will talk about for a very long time and like legends before him, his image will grace the Cardiff City Stadium walls for years to come. There's seldom been a player who has wowed the Bluebirds faithful as regularly and consistently as Whittingham. His technical ability went far beyond the quality of the Championship and it's a shame that he only had one opportunity to impress at Premier League level with Cardiff – after his time at Villa, of course. However, it says a lot about his character and loyalty that he stuck around for ten years, through all of the failure and chaos.

Peter is a rather shy person, he's not drawn by the big lights. In fact, he's not drawn by anything that surrounds modern football, not the press nor the flashy cars. He's old-fashioned in that sense, but the way he plays football certainly isn't. He dictated the game with his incredible passing ability, picking out passes short and long with consistent ease. He could spot a through ball without even looking and seemed to monitor every player's movement without having to check. Neil Warnock put it quite nicely; 'I remember I used to think Bobby Charlton used to cheat, because he never ran about. Later on, I realised he was that good he didn't have to, because he had a brain, Peter's the same. You can't change him. What he's got, no one else at the club has got. He's got a mind, a vision, a brain that's twice as quick as anyone else. When the ball comes to him I'm thinking, "Get rid! Get rid!" and he sees things that are impossible for anyone else to see and makes it look so cool.'

Cool indeed. Whittingham rarely looked like breaking a sweat, and that would give some supporters a stick to whack him with when he was out of form. But that was just the way he played, he could dictate the game without having to run miles. He would wait patiently for the ball and pick his moments, which he did particularly brilliantly during the play-off final season, when he amassed 20 goals. Everything he touched that season turned to gold. He struck beauties from outside the box and got a few inside, too, timing his runs to perfection, despite many of his goals being set pieces. Whittingham always took Cardiff's penalties and he rarely missed, often going down the middle, and if he didn't he would find the corner. A 'Whitts pen' became something Cardiff would hope for in games because they knew it translated to a goal.

His ability to deal with pressure helped. He was never one to look overly disappointed, or to get overjoyed, so pressure was dealt with in the same way. Cast your mind back to some of the pressure penalties, such as the play-off semi-final extra-time spot kick to level things up against Leicester or in the League Cup Final against Liverpool. He never looked concerned. That also comes from years of practice and perfecting a technique, which was displayed in his taking of free kicks. Whittingham scored many and he was known as the Championship's set-piece specialist. He could score them from outrageous angles, like in the play-off semi-final first leg against Leicester, and he could even score them on the keeper's side of the goal, finding the postage stamp in Ronaldinho-against-Seaman fashion. They were never overly powerful, they just came with a whip and a curl that goalkeepers couldn't track. They were often so well placed that two goalkeepers couldn't stop them.

Alongside the goals, his delivery from free kicks was sensational and his corners were even better. Cast your mind back to the League Cup Final against Liverpool. For the Ben Turner equaliser, Cardiff see a chance cleared off the line from the initial corner and it's a superb delivery from Whittingham. Then, to get another corner straight after with all that pressure and deliver a cross just as good, good enough to create a goal – that's world-class ability. Whittingham, overall, isn't a world-class player, that's taking it a little too far, he was a Championship player for much of his career after all. However, his set-piece ability was world-class. Very few players in the world could deliver the ball the way he could.

If you ask Cardiff fans who they would want of all the players in the world to take a corner in the 90th minute when they were 1-0 down, they would say Whittingham. Not Neymar, Messi, Ronaldo; maybe not even Beckham. He was just so reliable from set pieces, not just across one season but for ten years. That requires a phenomenal ability and a top-class attitude.

He also scored probably one of the best goals the club has ever witnessed with his effort against Barnsley in 2011. His outrageous volley to find the top corner won him the Mitre Football League Goal of the Year award that season, and there surely hasn't been a better goal than that at Cardiff, not in terms of technique and sheer ability. Another that springs to mind was a strike at Reading a year later, when he scored from around 25 yards with what was effectively a tackle. It was a 70/30 challenge, but aware that he would have the first touch, he swept it towards goal and found the top corner. Simply sensational.

Whittingham called time on his Cardiff career in 2017, moving to League 1 club Blackburn Rovers in the hope of playing more regular football than he had been offered for the following season, given that he was coming to the end of his career. He never got a real farewell, but there are hopes of a testimonial in the future, and one may already have taken place by the time this is read. If so, then he will have thoroughly deserved the thanks he got from the fans, who have been desperate to say a proper farewell to one of their favourite players in a generation. He's a player who lit up the

Cardiff City Stadium more than anybody else – Ninian Park too at times – and he goes down in the history books of this football club.

Whittingham spoke about his departure and his time at the club to BBC Sport Wales; 'The biggest regret for me personally is the fact I couldn't say goodbye to everyone surrounding the club, the fans. It's something I would've loved to have done. That's football, things don't work out I suppose, but I'm sure I'll be back there soon enough. The gaffer offered me a one-year contract and he said, "You're not going to play as much as probably you'd like." That kind of rubber stamped things for me. It's one of the hardest decisions I've ever had to make to leave Cardiff after such a long time. I loved my time there, it was amazing.

'[Leaving is] something I had to do for myself. He [Warnock] had his style and the way he wants to play. He's been in football long enough to know what works for him. As soon as he came in, people were messaging me saying, "Where are you going? What's going on?" I didn't really think I was going to fit in, but I never had any issues with him at all.'

'Oh Kev McNaughton, you are the love of my life'

THERE IS a second player without whom this story cannot exist. Kev McNaughton. Cardiff were blessed to have him, and he showed tremendous loyalty to the football club during its many low points. McNaughton was a Cardiff player for nine years, from 2006 to 2015, joining for free from Aberdeen in his homeland. Free transfers are often a gamble, you don't quite know what you're going to get at times, but this one turned out to be a masterstroke from Dave Jones. It saw a player join the club and, in a sense, he would never leave. In 2015 he moved to Wigan Athletic after a couple of loan spells during the promotion and relegation seasons, but even three years on, his name is still sung in the stands.

He has one of the best songs in football, too. For those who don't know it, it goes a little like, 'Oh Kev McNaughton, you are the love of my life, oh Kev McNaughton, I'd let you shag my wife, oh Kev McNaughton, I want silver hair too.' He's still welcomed back with open arms and he always will be. Why? Supporters take to some players, sometimes for no real rhyme or reason, but that wasn't the case with McNaughton. He was loved because from minute one, from his debut against Barnsley and his home bow against West Brom, a game in which Cardiff picked up an unexpected point, he gave 100 per cent. He continued to give everything not just for the season, not just for a couple of seasons but for all of his 288 appearances.

McNaughton was an erratic full-back who came with no 'slow down' button. He would run up and down the wing throughout the game and was rarely caught out. He was far from the finished article when he arrived, and he could have done with a slow down button at that point, but instead of slowing down, he just got better and mastered his own unique approach. He really was 100mph and that's what fans loved about him. Kev was also a superb defender. He never dangled a foot or went into challenges at half pace. This was a player who always went in with passion and determination. Small in stature, yes, but not lacking in desire, and that put him above so many others in terms of winning duels.

McNaughton had this tremendous engine and being a full-back, he was rarely substituted, but throughout his career, he never gave up, never let the lactic acid slow him down. His passion for the game and his love for Cardiff City might as well have been written on his forehead, it was that clear from the way he played. He was a real fans' favourite from the moment he walked through the doors, and his personality helped, too. Kev loved a laugh and a joke, and he was one of the big personalities of the dressing room. Even after he retired, he continued to follow the Bluebirds and continued to engage with supporters on social media. He makes no bones about being a Cardiff fan. He's a man of the people as footballers go, and that's what everyone liked about him.

Loyalty isn't a huge thing in the game these days, and that's something we've all had to get used to. But Cardiff City have been blessed to have two loyal players in Peter Whittingham and Kev McNaughton. Both stuck around through the good and the bad, they suffered with supporters in the cruellest of defeats and put a brave face on like everyone else over the course of the rebrand and the chaos that followed.

There's this fantastic image of McNaughton celebrating promotion in 2013. He stayed out on the pitch despite the invasion and he was lifted aloft by supporters. The image couldn't sum up his relationship with the fans any better. They love him, and he loves them. They enjoyed that glorious moment together and it goes a long way to highlight Kev's personality, too. Many players want to get off and celebrate with team-mates, but Kev wasn't bothered. He didn't care about health and safety and all that, he just wanted to celebrate the moment with the supporters, who had shared such pain with him over the years but had backed him to the hilt and helped him get the opportunity to experience the moment. It tells us a lot about the man Kev is that he recognised that, even on an occasion as grand as promotion, he still remembered what supporters have given to him and he repaid them by celebrating with them.

McNaughton's end at Cardiff wasn't brilliant initially. He was messed around like many other players before finally departing for good in 2015. However, he was given a proper chance to say goodbye with a testimonial in 2017. It was a fitting occasion with thousands of supporters in attendance to say goodbye to a player who embodied everything this football club is about. It was an emotional occasion which saw many former players and some current players turn out, and he scored, too, something he rarely did during his days as a Cardiff player. He scored a beauty at Hereford in the FA Cup run and besides that, only managed one league goal in nine years.

Kev wasn't about the goals, though, he was a defender through and through, and it's quite rare for one to become so popular, but this guy was so loved that any Scotsman who plays for Cardiff in the future already has a head start on his team-mates. McNaughton goes down as a true legend and he's another who will have a place at the Cardiff City Stadium, and indeed in the hearts of the Bluebirds faithful for decades to come. It was an emotional goodbye, but a fitting one and the man himself couldn't agree more.

Speaking at his testimonial, he said, 'It's unbelievable, it's just flashed by. It was great to play with the lads again, to have a catch-up, and I look forward to having a beer with them all. It was brilliant because it was good for the boys as well, guys like Earnie [Robert Earnshaw] who didn't get a chance to say goodbye as well, there's guys out there who deserved that as much as I did as well. [My time with the club] was unbelievable. From all the disappointments of nearly making it and things like that. I've had an unbelievable spell here, we've been to cup finals, I've been to Wembley four times and I didn't dream of that when I came down here.'

The Bluebirds
soar again

WE JOIN the Bluebirds at Taff's Well as we begin the final season of this roller-coaster journey. It's the first pre-season friendly and it's against Welsh League club Taff's Well. The sun is shining and there are smiles aplenty.

It wasn't known then, but the season would end in a similar setting. Before all that, however, comes a full season of ups and downs, another topsy-turvy journey through the Championship. Even before that, comes this pleasant friendly fixture against Taff's Well. The Bluebirds have helped them develop a new stand and they've also helped get the pitch in pristine condition. The fixture was also played in aid of Cancer Research and Velindre with ticket proceedings going to the respective charities.

It's something Neil Warnock and the club like to do, a way of giving back to community football, and it really helps a club like Taff's Well, who, on the day, give it a really good go against a strong Cardiff side. Of course, it's all about fitness at this stage, but Cardiff still grind through with a narrow 1-0 win. There are over 1,000 in attendance with away fans turning up in their numbers, as well as the locals who come to see their team pit their wits against a professional club.

Why do we begin the journey here? It's because the evening represents change, a real turning point in attitudes. The Cardiff players sign autographs, they pose for pictures, and Warnock does the same. He's a big believer in grass-roots football and he wants his players to immerse themselves in it, to be among the fans. Speaking after the game, he says, 'I had someone saying to me, "Do you want to get changed at [Cardiff City Stadium]?" but I said, "Do I hell?" I want to change at Taff's Well, in their dressing room, and let the players have a look at it – because they might be playing there if it wasn't for me!'

The players take the time to be with the fans and there's not an ounce of self-importance, none of that hiding from fans like a few years ago. These players are kept down to earth by Warnock, who leads by example in that respect. It's a worthwhile fitness test, yes, but it's more than that, it is seen as a chance to build bridges with the supporters who will be following this team all over the country for the next nine months. It's a fine and fitting way to kick off a new campaign.

There would be 15 departures, including nine first-team players, over the course of the summer, including on transfer-deadline day after the season had begun. The early exits included out-of-contract players like Peter Whittingham, Tom Adeyemi, Adam Le Fondre and Rickie Lambert, who was also released by mutual consent. Emyr Huws would go for a fee, as would Idriss Saadi and Craig Noone, who left on deadline day after five years at the club.

The summer was Warnock's first real opportunity to shape the team into what he wanted and he took full advantage, replacing the many outgoings with a total of eight summer signings. In typical Warnock fashion, he signed a number of out-of-contract players, five in total. Lee Camp came in from Rotherham, Neil Etheridge from Walsall, Nathaniel Mendez-Laing from Rochdale, Loic Damour from Bourg-Peronnas and Callum Paterson from Hearts, although Cardiff paid a grace fee of £400,000 for the latter as a form of compensation. Two loan signings arrived in the form of Liam Feeney and Craig Bryson and the Bluebirds spent a combined fee of £3m on Bristol City misfit Lee Tomlin and Rotherham striker Danny Ward. Their summer business was rounded off by spending £700,000 on Wigan striker Omar Bogle.

Those signings, on paper, don't exactly whet the appetite, but they were clever additions. Warnock likes to sign players who have something to prove, and that applied to most of them in one way or another. Mendez-Laing is a prime example. His behaviour off the field had been poor in the past, so much so that he dropped right down the leagues, before getting his act together to get his career back on track at Rochdale. Now Warnock was going to take a chance on him and the winger simply had to impress; it was perhaps going to be his one and only shot at Championship-level football.

So the signings themselves didn't particularly fill fans with optimism, but the feeling was that this squad was already in good shape with the likes of Sean Morrison, Junior Hoilett and Kenneth Zohore – and Cardiff had also managed to convince Bruno Ecuele Manga to stay. There was a quiet optimism around the project as a whole, and there was always going to be with Warnock in charge, given his sensational promotion record. But fans remained realistic, setting their sights on the top six, as they had done for the three previous campaigns. The bookies, however, were far less convinced and Cardiff were pitched in the bottom half.

Warnock himself noted that, and during pre-season he said, 'The bookies aren't silly, and we're supposed to be eighth from the bottom. But we've got a great bunch of supporters here that can make a big difference at home, and away from home they've been really vocal. What we want is a side that can go anywhere and win that game. Yes, you're going to have hiccups and disappointments but, in the Championship, you've got so many games you've just got to get over those disappointments, look forward and look how we can improve.'

The relaxed atmosphere throughout pre-season, which saw Cardiff travel to Cornwall and Devon, probably helped keep feet on the floor. Fans often get over excited during pre-season, but Warnock is clever at guiding optimism, he's always trying to keep people's heads level, and he did that by reiterating all the way through his preparations that Cardiff were tipped to be in the bottom half. Fans joined him in approaching the season with a relaxed attitude, a sort of 'we'll do what we can, and hopefully we will get into the top six' mindset, and with that, you don't really have anything to lose. It's a clever one to have and it's one that fits into this squad because they all have something to prove, yet they're not expected to prove it.

The plans stepped up a notch at the end of July with Cardiff beating Plymouth on the road, before losing to Shrewsbury Town, who would go on to enjoy a very good season in League 1. Cardiff then rounded off their schedule just a week before the big kick-off with a comfortable 4-0 home win over Scottish Championship club Livingstone, who would later that season secure promotion to the Scottish Premiership.

The Bluebirds kicked the season off with a trip to Burton Albion, who had miraculously stayed up the season before. The Brewers had had a magnificent run of promotions to reach the Championship and to stay there was, perhaps, an even bigger achievement again. They were no pushovers, especially under Nigel Clough, who has a long affinity there.

On the opening day they were as stern as ever against a Cardiff side who looked a little unsure of themselves, who couldn't quite get to grips with the formation, and who weren't creating the chances they should have with a creative Lee Tomlin in behind Kenneth Zohore. Come the 87th minute and it was still 0-0 with fans viewing it as a decent away point, as is any in the Championship, despite dominating. However, a football season is all about turning points and key moments, and Cardiff's in 2017/18 would be no different. For the Bluebirds, key moment number one arrived on match day one, and it came courtesy of Zohore. The striker, who by now was attracting Premier League interest, pushed the ball out of his feet on the edge of the box while dribbling across the periphery of the penalty area, and he bent a perfectly placed effort into the corner of the net. It hits the net right in front of the travelling supporters and the Bluebirds stole all three points with just three minutes left.

There's little better than a late winner in this sport, but beyond that, this was huge for this team's confidence. Starting with a bang is everything in a division that's all about putting good runs together and it gave Cardiff the perfect platform. Warnock said, 'It's a great way to start and you could see the optimism, the fans were fantastic today and kept us at it. The volume was unbelievable.'

The Bluebirds would take full advantage of that platform, too, winning their first six games. After Burton they destroyed one of the favourites in Aston Villa, now boosted by the signing of Chelsea and England legend John Terry. The win saw Warnock's men kick off their home campaign with a faultless display. The Yorkshireman was now going with a front three of Zohore, with Mendez-Laing one side and Junior Hoilett the other. And teams couldn't handle the Bluebirds' pace and directness. Villa simply crumbled and Mendez-Laing was the star of the show, scoring twice. He would also impress at Wolves the following week after another home win in midweek this time against Sheffield United.

Wolves were many people's out-and-out favourites, and with good reason. They had spent big once again in the summer, and they were equipped with former Valencia boss Nuno Espirito Santo, a man with an impressive managerial record. The Portuguese links didn't end there. Wolves were also working with super agent Jorge Mendes, agent of Cristiano Ronaldo and Jose Mourinho. Mendes was influential for Wolves as they snapped up top-class players like Ruben Neves, Diogo Jota and Helder Costa, whose ability could see them playing far beyond the Championship. However, they were no match for the Bluebirds, even in their own back yard. Cardiff turned up and really upset the apple cart from minute one.

Wolves struggled against a physical Bluebirds side who did everything they could to unsettle their hosts. It was a Warnock masterclass and it left the Wolves coaching staff, as well as the home support, furious. Wolves had the momentum after equalising in the 67th minute, but Cardiff won it when Mendez-Laing smashed home a low strike from the far side, celebrating in front of the travelling masses.

Cardiff and Wolves don't really get on as clubs. There have been a few issues between the two in the past – Cardiff fans were actually banned from Molineux at one point, so victories in the West Midlands taste all the sweeter. This one was no exception, especially with Wolves being favourites between the two sides who had started the campaign so well. This was a statement of intent and another ten-out-of-ten performance.

The Bluebirds' first loss would eventually come, but not when it was expected to. Perhaps supporters feared it was on the horizon when Fulham looked to have become the first team to topple Warnock's men before Ward popped up with an 83rd-minute header to take home a point in another key moment. This team were showing a real character, and that alone can take you a long, long way in this division. Unfortunately for Ward, he soon suffered a season-ending knee injury, but this contribution would ultimately mean a lot for his team.

The euphoria of that late equaliser at Craven Cottage quickly died down, when, the following Tuesday, Cardiff were humbled in a 3-0 thrashing at Preston – Deepdale memories continue to haunt many Bluebirds. It was their first shocking display, perhaps creating the first feeling that the wheels were going to come off. This had happened before, you see. One particular season springs to mind: the 2006/07 campaign. Cardiff were quick out of the traps, storming to the top of the league thanks to Michael Chopra's goals, but they slipped as quickly as they ascended and finished in the bottom half.

Back to that defeat at Preston, and you would expect Warnock to go to town on his players after such a poor display, but he didn't. He protected them and took the blame in some respects, saying, 'There's no excuse because the goals were terrible, but we had eight or nine lads not at their game today. The travelling we've done since Saturday – I said to them, without it being an excuse – we've travelled more than any other team in the country. We got back at 11pm after Fulham and had six hours travelling here so the preparation hasn't been so good, but I can't have it as an excuse because we were second best all night. But we don't normally have eight or nine missing like that.

'If we hadn't had been undefeated I would have made three or four changes, but we were undefeated – and you can make changes if you get beat and you get blasted. But when I looked at them in training I did think I should make changes because they seemed jaded. Hindsight's a great thing but you're a brave man to change a side that's never lost a game – but at least that's out of the way now and I can make changes when I see fit now.'

Cardiff responded with a home draw to Sheffield Wednesday and a win away to Sunderland before putting on another sensational display the following week. Live on Sky Sports, they hosted old rivals Leeds United, who were flying at the top of the table with Wolves and Cardiff behind them on goal difference. Even this early in the season, this was seen as a bit of a knockout. There was a sense that the loser would fall away while the winner could continue their excellent start, and it proved to be the case.

Cardiff put on another truly brilliant performance. Zohore scored two and Hoilett grabbed one on a night when he lit up the Cardiff City Stadium. Leeds did get one back, despite losing Liam Cooper to a sending-off in first-half stoppage time, but they just couldn't handle Cardiff's pace and power. They weren't the only team, either, and you could tell that something special might become of this team on the back of that.

The Championship is a division that adapts rather quickly to systems of play. If one team doesn't work it out, the next team tends to, especially with so many factors like fatigue given the quick turnover in games. However, very few were cracking this Cardiff team, and their 4-3-3 system – made famous by the Netherlands – with quick and powerful players in the front line, was causing all manner of problems for the opposition. By now, the Bluebirds were developing a reputation for shithousery, which, for those not fluent in the football language, means a bit of naughtiness, wasting time, making cynical fouls, leaving one in on the opponent. But we'll come on to that later as regardless of that perception, this Cardiff team were genuinely blowing teams away, especially at home, and Leeds were the latest victims as the Bluebirds stormed to the summit of the Championship with another big statement.

A mixed run of form followed with defeats to Birmingham and Bristol City, as well as an underwhelming draw at home to Millwall, although there was a big win at Middlesbrough to keep the Bluebirds ticking over which arrived thanks to an 84th-minute penalty, coolly tucked away by Joe Ralls, who had taken up the spot-kick mantle following the exit of Peter Whittingham. The Bluebirds then entered November, where, despite that Bristol defeat, they went on to win four on the bounce. The last of that sequence was a real sign of where things were going. Warnock's men started their run with a 2-0 home win over Brentford, then they travelled to Barnsley where they won with yet another late goal. This one came in the 83rd minute and it was scored by Callum Paterson, who effectively tackled the ball into the net, for one of the strangest goals you'll see, but nonetheless, it meant Cardiff secured a huge three points.

It was an important goal for Paterson, too, who hadn't kicked a ball until the end of October due to a serious knee ligament injury he picked up with Hearts. Warnock knew Paterson couldn't feature for a long while, but he decided to gamble, and the gamble paid off. After the Barnsley win, the Bluebirds picked up another three points at Forest. Ward scored a stunner to finish off the home side after Junior Hoilett had opened the scoring.

That was to prove Ward's last contribution of the season after suffering the aforementioned serious knee injury the following week, against Norwich. It was a strange old game at the Cardiff City Stadium. Warnock's men were poor in the first half and they paid the price, falling behind just before half-time. They didn't look like they could come back, and it was rather bizarre given the form they'd been on. Was fatigue catching up with them, perhaps? However, they left the Canaries stunned in the second half, scoring three times, one each from Ralls, Hoilett and Bogle, to make it four wins on the bounce. The second-half display was the complete antithesis of the first half, and that level of character is only seen in a successful side.

Warnock went to town on his players at the break. He revealed after the game, 'The lads really did me proud second half. We could have scored a few more but after an abysmal first half anything was better. The last time I said something like that at half-time, it was on YouTube. I wish I could have made five changes at half-time, but I am proud of them, good teams get through these games and that's what I said to them. I counted about five tackles in the first half when they came away with the ball and we were doing the wrong things in the wrong places. It was a difficult night and I shouldn't have to go off like that on my birthday.'

Norwich were left stunned and they were powerless as they watched Cardiff obliterate their first-half lead on the day Warnock celebrated turning 69. Cardiff were actually second in the table by this point, but this was the first time supporters realised something was really taking off. It was the first time members of the media looked at each other in the press conference room after the game and said 'this bunch are the real deal'. There was something about that the powerful nature of the second-half display that just left everyone stunned.

Confidence began to build further into December, but the Bluebirds would have to show their character again ten days later at the Madejski Stadium. The game was on Sky Sports again with the broadcasters starting to take notice, although viewers saw another poor first-half display from Warnock's men and Reading raced into a two-goal lead. Referee Stephen Martin was having a 'mare and even the commentators highlighted that, but their backing didn't save Warnock. He was sent off for his protests on the touchline and Cardiff were left without a manager and two goals behind.

It didn't faze them. Joe Bennett smashed home an 83rd-minute volley to give them hope, and they were really banging on the door by this point. Lee Tomlin had finally been brought off the bench and one minute into stoppage time he chipped a delicate ball into the box. Sol Bamba's header came back off the crossbar to Tomlin, but at an awkward height. In front of the Cardiff fans, he adjusted and managed to volley the ball towards goal. It hit the bar, hit the floor and hit the bar again before coming out, but it appeared to have crossed the line. The Bluebirds faithful were on edge as they gazed towards referee Martin, who hadn't given them a thing all night. He checked his goal-line technology watch as players surged towards him. And with an enthusiastic throw of his arm to point to the halfway line, he blew his whistle for a goal. Cardiff had rescued a point from the jaws of defeat and again they'd refused to be written off.

Tomlin came on despite feeling unsatisfied with his game time and did the job. He'd been billed as the start signing but his fitness was poor, and he had to be content with a spot on the bench for the majority of the season. Even so, he was happy to come on and do a job and that says a lot about the attitude of this squad, and the attitude of a player who has been called into question throughout his career.

Warnock revealed his delight after seeing the goal go in; 'I saw the second goal and obviously celebrated running around the little room on my own.' The travelling supporters were inevitably delighted, too, especially with a late goal coming at the Madejski, where they had experienced late drama in the past, namely that Federici goal in 2009. This was another key moment and another statement to say 'we won't be beaten'.

Ironically, however, after Bamba headed Cardiff to a narrow win over Hull next time out, the Bluebirds would endure their worst run of the season. The injuries began to pile up, including captain Sean Morrison, who had been a key player next to Bamba, and form began to drop. Concerns were raised once more by supporters who had seen their teams fall apart time and again over Christmas under Dave Jones. This was a habit in these parts.

The bad run began at Bolton in a 2-0 defeat and it continued against Fulham on Boxing Day in a 4-2 loss. Fulham were really picking up form by this point after a disappointing start, and they played Cardiff off the park in their own back yard. They were the first team to claim three points in the Welsh capital and they did so in style. Kenneth managed to get Cardiff in the game at one point with a stunning long-range goal to make it 2-1 but in truth, the home side were never in it, and Slavisa Jokanovic and his men were worthy winners. It got worse three days later when Preston completed the double over Cardiff with a stoppage-time winner in Wales, and heads were well and truly dropping by this point. Another poor display on New Year's Day at Loftus Road saw the Bluebirds let slip a lead and lose 2-1 to make it four defeats in a row.

Before this run, Cardiff hadn't even lost two on the bounce and suddenly they had been beaten four times in a row. There was no sense of panic though, it has to be said, and that, more than anything, was down to the buffer Cardiff had given themselves. Even after four straight defeats they sat just two points behind second-placed Derby, and it's all about context. This club were only aiming for the play-offs, so to be in this position at the turn of the year was no disaster, especially not when these supporters had seen what the team was capable of. They also had a man in charge they could trust to turn things around.

Another important point to mention is that most clubs in the league had turned on Cardiff by this point. Others saw them as a route-one team who wasted time, used long throw-ins and didn't play football. Opposition managers were adding fuel to the fire by the bucket-load. Brentford boss Dean Smith was one of many and after his team's defeat in November, he said, 'It's disappointing when you come to the Championship when your own players have to go

THE BLUEBIRDS SOAR AGAIN

and get the ball. From watching it, I would have wanted my money back because the ball was only in for 20 minutes. I don't blame Cardiff, but the officials have to get a hold of that.'

For a time, it seemed that for every Cardiff home win, there was a bitter opposing manager who would take a dig, however small or big, and that spread. Opposing fans would also label the Bluebirds this, that and the other, but Warnock and his team weren't interested. They knew there was an element of shithousery about their game and it was important. This was a very average squad competing for promotion with teams who had huge budgets, they had to mix things up in order to compete, and they had to master doing that in order to win.

After that torrid run the Bluebirds were given the perfect chance to bounce back against a shoddy-looking Sunderland side, at home and in front of the Sky Sports cameras. They took full advantage, winning 4-0 with a confident and thorough display. Callum Paterson, signed as a left-back but now playing as an attacking midfielder, scored two, but Joe Ralls's goal was the pick of the bunch. Ralls was finally thriving under Warnock after years of trying to prove himself. Ralls is a different player to Peter Whittingham but being in the same position, he was expected to display the magic that his team-mate did so often. He impressed at times during the 2016/17 season but faded later on in the campaign and struggled, but in Warnock, he had a manager who trusted in him. He thrived under that and really came to the fore during the 2017/18 season, making the centre midfield role his own to become a key player.

In the following game, Cardiff underwhelmed at Hillsborough in a goalless draw, despite being boosted by the loan signings of Liverpool youngster Marko Grujic and Norwich wide man Yanic Wildschut. But they soon came back to life upon their return to Yorkshire.

Before their return north, though, there was the small matter of the FA Cup fourth-round fixture at home to soon-to-be Premier League champions Manchester City. Cardiff had secured the dream draw after knocking out Mansfield at the second time of asking, and it was built up to be a huge occasion in South Wales. The world's media were in attendance as well as the 32,339 supporters, a record for a club fixture at the stadium.

The Bluebirds were hoping to shock City, who had spent the season so far blowing teams away, wowing supporters and pundits alike. Pep Guardiola's boys were a class apart from everyone in the Premier League, and Championship high-flyers Cardiff would be no exception. A fantastic atmosphere was popped like a balloon when Kevin De Bruyne scored with a clever free kick under the wall after just eight minutes. City effectively ended the tie in the 37th minute when Sterling made it two, but still there was time for controversy in the first half. Bennett lunged in on winger Leroy Sane in a desperate attempt to stop him breaking into the Cardiff penalty area, and upon doing so he injured the German. Joe's challenge was ill-timed, and horrific images later emerged of his studs placed above the ankle Sane's ankle. It would go on to dominate attention after the game for several days and weeks. Bennett was sent off in the second half, too, receiving his second yellow for another poor challenge on Brahim Diaz, and it was in fact that challenge that angered his manager.

Warnock responded with a classic line, saying, 'I've not spoken to him if I'm honest, I'm disappointed in him really. To get a yellow card was unprofessional I thought. It was a ridiculous booking so what else can you expect? He'll be training Saturday and Sunday if you want to come and watch him, 11 o'clock until 1.30, anybody's welcome!'

Warnock accused Bennett of trying to get out of a trip to Leeds the following week, and the full-back did indeed train throughout the weekend, regardless of his suspension and the absence of his team-mates. He was also subject to a plethora of abuse from Manchester City fans, as well as other supporters, for his challenge. Some horrible comments emerged on social media with people sending their worst wishes. Guardiola also called for 'protection' of his players after the game, saying the referee should have done more. However, it was clear that his players weren't blameless; they had put in some overly physical challenges during the game and indeed would do so during the coming weeks in different fixtures.

The criticism of Bennett went on for a good fortnight, but the incident hardly merited that reaction. It was a sending off and it was a bad challenge, but he would have done well to hit the target – with the target being Sane's ankle – given the pace the winger was running at. There's no doubt Joe meant to take him down, but there's no way he meant to seriously hurt Sane. However, football fans can be short-sighted in that sense and Bennett was a victim of that.

When the dust settled, and Cardiff returned to league action, they ensured there was no hangover by completing another hammering of Leeds, this time at Elland Road. Paterson, Hoilett and Morrison effectively ended the game by half-time, especially when Gaetano Berardi was sent off in first-half stoppage time. Neil Etheridge had also pulled of a monumental save early on to keep Leeds at bay and this was the start of a fantastic run for him. The unproven former Walsall keeper had been dropped for a game at QPR after a bad run, but he stormed back into the team and proved himself with marked improvements in every area, from kicking to possessing a previously absent confidence in the air. A Bamba own goal gave Leeds a thin veil of hope but Anthony Pilkington, who had become a bit-part player after failing to get a move in the summer, rounded things off to take home three more points with a stylish victory.

The Bluebirds made that trip to Elland Road boosted by several of new signings after a busy deadline day. Bolton Wanderers striker Gary Madine arrived for £5m, which would eventually rise to £6m, and two loan signings also arrived; Jamie Ward and Armand Traore both came in from Nottingham Forest, and Tomlin went the other way on loan.

Tomlin hadn't prove to be the star signing people had hoped. He simply wasn't fit enough, and community service, relating to a common assault charge dating back before he arrived in South Wales, meant he had to miss some training sessions. Tomlin wasn't as happy as others to play a role off the bench so he left without any issues or bad blood. In fact, he would stay in regular contact with Warnock between his departure and the end of the season. Youngster Declan John also left permanently for Rangers after a successful loan spell, and Lee Camp, Omar Bogle and Rhys Healey all went out on temporary moves.

Boosted by new signings and that comprehensive win over Leeds, the Bluebirds headed to The Den to face a Millwall side who were surprising many. The Den is always a difficult place to go, with one of the most hostile settings in English football. And Millwall were making it a fortress during their first season back in the Championship.

Neil Harris and his men were defying the odds to build up a play-off bid. Cardiff had passed an important test at Leeds but straight afterwards they had another big question to answer and the Sky Sports cameras were again keen to see whether they were capable of coming up with the goods. It looked as though they were when Hoilett fired in a brilliant long-range effort after just three minutes, but Millwall were dominant. Lee Gregory equalised after 40 minutes and Cardiff were on the ropes. It was the full-blooded encounter many expected it to be with two physical teams, and Madine's nose felt the brunt of that.

Millwall continued to have the better of the chances but Cardiff ended the game on top. The introduction of Kenneth Zohore and Loic Damour gave them something a little different to throw at Millwall and it appeared to work. Bamba scored with a bicycle kick in the dying moments only for referee Keith Stroud to disallow the goal and give a Cardiff free kick. It was a truly diabolical decision. There was a foul on the edge of the box, but Stroud played advantage, watched the ball all the way, and as Bamba's foot made contact he decided to blow. There was no explanation for the decision, which was also appalling, and Warnock made his feelings known, too. He exclaimed, 'I think it is appalling at this level. Sol is going to shoot and then he blows. I don't accept that. He is a really experienced referee and I feel let down. He cost us the game. We are fighting to get in the Premier League. But for the referee, it would have been three points.'

Decisions are often down to discretion and you can argue either way, but Cardiff really were robbed of the points at The Den and even Millwall boss Harris recognised that. It was a real mistake from Stroud, who hasn't always gone down well with Cardiff fans. It meant the Bluebirds were left to lick their wounds after missing out on what could have been a crucial two points.

The draw in London left Cardiff fourth, just three points behind second with a game in hand, and it was becoming a scrap at the top of the table. The Bluebirds would then put together an extraordinary run of eight straight victories, the first three of which were particularly crucial. Warnock's men made easy work of Bolton at home before scraping a 1-0 success over Middlesbrough, who were now looking strong contenders for the play-offs following the appointment of seasoned boss Tony Pulis. Captain Sean Morrison scored the winner in that one and his return was huge for the Bluebirds. He had come back ahead of that Manchester City FA Cup clash and made a huge impact, as was proven in this winning run. Morrison wasn't always a fans'-favourite and he was known as a liability for some time, especially given the price tag for which he arrived, but he shone during this season and by the end of it, you wouldn't hear a bad word spoken about him. That goes for many who proved their doubters wrong over the course of this season.

Zohore ended his goal drought with a scrappy winner at Ipswich, before grabbing another the following week. Another highly anticipated Severnside derby awaited with Bristol City in town and another war of words commenced between Warnock and Lee Johnson. The veteran boss never liked the Johnson family and his rivalry extended to Gary Johnson's son, Lee, Bristol City's boss, following in his father's footsteps. He was doing well, too, with City in sixth spot, and the derby itself flattered to deceive. Zohore scored the clincher in a tight contest which had the backdrop of a fantastic atmosphere at the Cardiff City Stadium.

Johnson then became the latest to criticise the brand of football on offer in the capital. He said, 'I got in for free, but I still wanted my money back. But that's what we expected to happen. I'm not going to chastise the players, I'm just going to use this as encouragement to say "come on, let's not settle for mediocrity".'

However, the taste was only sweeter when opposing managers came out with such comments and it didn't matter one bit how the game was won. It was another test passed, and Cardiff were back in control of second spot, four points clear of Aston Villa in fourth.

Heavy snow in April meant a trip to Brentford was postponed, so Cardiff had won two more home games, against strugglers Barnsley and Birmingham City, by the time they eventually went to Griffin Park. It would prove to be worth the wait. The rearranged evening kick-off was again broadcast on Sky Sports and supporters felt the curse of often disappointing on television looked set to continued with a poor start from Warnock's men. Neal Maupay, responsible for a horrible miss in the home fixture earlier in the season, put the Bees ahead and it should have been two shortly after.

But Cardiff hung on and it was crucial that they did. Bamba levelled the scores with the their goal of the season, looking more like a Brazilian striker than an Ivorian centre-back as he swivelled with one touch before smashing the ball home from just inside the box. From there, Cardiff were rampant and Paterson, still thriving in his midfield role, put the visitors ahead just before the break. Zohore then wrapped up the points before the hour mark to make it three goals in five games for him, and Warnock's men were home and dry. Once again that character shone through and this was another key moment, coming when the opposing side looked powerless to stop the Bluebirds, whose desire simply couldn't be matched.

Cardiff were flying, and they were ready to take their form into a tough away trip to Derby despite still struggling with a number of injuries in the camp. However, Derby's injury situation was significantly worse, training with just ten first-team players in the days beforehand. Then, on the morning of the match, came the controversy of the season. A few hours before kick-off, the game was postponed due to adverse weather conditions, although it all seemed a little strange when images of a rather snow-free Pride Park emerged on social media. Then the Cardiff team bus turned up without travel woes to tell of. Warnock spoke from inside the stadium and said, 'We got to the ground and the car park was clear, the pitch was perfect.

'Absolutely disgraceful really. All week I have listened to comments from Derby, they have all been negative, and that's before the snow came down. They have been talking about the injury situation, yesterday the manager Gary [Rowett] said they only had ten players training and if they could get away with this weekend's game, they would be fine. Things like that should be looked into. All the lads were raring to go and looking forward to it, but you can't blame Derby for wanting it off – you wouldn't want to play us at the moment.'

A statement from the Football League said that the decision to call the game off was taken 'following discussions between Derby County, Derbyshire Police, and the local Safety Advisory Group'. However, Derbyshire Police then issued their own statement, saying, 'For clarity, Derby County Football Club took the decision to postpone the match due to the weather conditions and the health and safety of people travelling to the ground. The club made this decision independently. It was not made by Derbyshire Constabulary.'

The Football League carried out an investigation into the events surrounding the postponement but, after submissions from both clubs, it found that Derby's decision was correct. The EFL did, however, remind Derby of their responsibilities about 'clearer and more effective communication around the decision making processes on the day', which it was felt would have 'assisted an already challenging situation'.

Rams boss Gary Rowett later responded to Warnock's comments by telling BBC Radio Derby, 'I know Neil is an excellent manager, but I didn't actually realise he's also a qualified health and safety inspector.' The bickering would go on for some time and it wouldn't just be limited to the two managers.

There was more football to be played and Cardiff returned to action after the international break – which Derby hopefully used to good effect to get their players fit – and they defeated strugglers Burton at home. The Bluebirds were under-par after struggling in midfield through the absence of the injured Ralls, but they still powered through with a 3-1 win with Zohore, Mendez-Laing and Paterson getting the goals.

Then came a trip to Yorkshire and yet another Sky Sports fixture as Warnock returned to Sheffield United, the club he supports and one of his former employers as a manager. The Blades had been promoted in 2016/17 and were chasing a play-off spot, having started excellently before dropping significantly away from the top two. The Bluebirds travelled to Bramall Lane on the back of an eight-game winning run which gave them a seven-point buffer plus a game in hand over Fulham in third – who were on a fantastic run of their own. The clash with Sheffield United was to be the first of three tricky games, with leaders Wolves and Aston Villa both to play in the coming weeks, so the pressure was on, somewhat, despite the huge gap.

It looked like they they would need all of that advantage when Leon Clarke put the home side ahead after 28 minutes. Warnock's men looked all over the shop as the home side pressed and pressed, but they held on. It was more of the same in the second half as the Blades continued to dominate. Clayton Donaldson hits the post and late on and suddenly something changed. Cardiff woke up and they were going for the result in an end-to-end encounter in which they were as likely to lose as net an equaliser in.

However, in the Steel City, Cardiff showed a steel-like character to equalise in stoppage time. Ecuele Manga looped a high ball into the air in the Blades' box and Cardiff won two headers, then Madine flicked it into the box with a third header to find fellow substitute Anthony Pilkington. Pilkington stole a yard on two opponents and struck a volley across his body, into the ground and into the bottom corner. It was another key moment as the Bluebirds celebrated wildly in front of the travelling support after grabbing a point they didn't deserve based on the play. Taking a late point from the jaws of defeat is a mark of successful teams and the Bluebirds were doing it time and again.

Pilkington had come in from the cold to score the goal. Cardiff tried to sell him during the summer, but he was forced to stick around as a back-up option and with hardly any league minutes under his belt, he kept his chin up and supported his team-mates. How often do you see that these days? Coming in and scoring the crucial goal was a deserved reward for a man who is the ultimate team player and an example to youngsters.

Warnock told Sky Sports after the game, 'I'd like some of those lads in the trenches with me. Look at Pilkington, He's only had ten minutes since Christmas! You have to have a lot of guts and determination for that.'

Pilkington's goal was the latest in a long line of key moments through the season, earning a crucial point to preserve Cardiff's run of 13 games unbeaten ahead of a top-two showdown with leaders Wolves.

Supporters reliving this part of the story – take a deep breath. Inhale, exhale, you can do it. Think of it as closure. Here we go.

More than 29,000 were in attendance as Wolves and their wonder-kids arrived at the Cardiff City Stadium. It was a Friday night kick-off in front of the Sky Sports cameras, of course, and this was Cardiff's last shot at the title. Six points separated the two teams with Wolves having played a game more, and just seven matches remained for Cardiff. The build-up was as big as you'd expect and Cardiff went into the encounter the more confident of the two, with Wolves having suffered something of a slide in recent weeks, although their excellent first three quarters of the season meant they sat on the edge of title glory nonetheless. They knew that a win in South Wales would pretty much wrap things up. Meanwhile Cardiff, who had been on that extraordinary run, believed they could spoil the party. They also knew they probably needed something from this game and the following one at Aston Villa if they were to keep Fulham at bay, with the Londoners just five points behind and coming like a train. Let's relive the night.

The atmosphere is electric, and it truly feels like a big game. The nerves are clearly felt by both sets of fans and it's the sort of atmosphere not seen at the Cardiff City Stadium since the play-off semi-final against Reading in 2011. Not even the play-off semi-final the year after had this sort of buzz, this sense of do-or-die.

As is often the case in these big games, the action starts slowly, but Wolves look more assured. With a classy Willy Boly in defence, they dominate posession. Boly is a wonderful, modern centre-half who sits on the halfway line and dictates play. He's also aided by a number of top-class players in front of him, who will surely make a statement in the Premier League, as they have done in the Championship.

Wolves have their moments but Cardiff, with one of the best back lines in the league, hold strong, play things safe and keep out their visitors. In fact, they have the best opportunity of the first half when Joe Bennett is played through down the left-hand side of the box, but he tries to place the ball with his left foot and puts it wide. A big chance missed.

Half-time arrives, and the goalless scoreline does nothing to ease nerves in the home or away sections. Wolves are classier on the ball – as you'd expect given their budget – but Cardiff are as pragmatic as ever, they work openings on the counter-attack through that trusty front three, and this is anyone's to win.

It remains tight, albeit Wolves have already hit the post in the second half, until the 67th minute when Wolves win a free kick. It's the best part of 25 yards out but still, with the ability this team has, it almost feels like a penalty. In big games like this, everything is magnified, even a throw-in an opportunity and if you're on the receiving end, it's not nice to watch. A free kick even less so, and Wolves have one here.

Ruben Neves will take it and he's already blasted one over, but so often the second attempt is more dangerous. The first tends to be a case of finding your range – and so it proves. The £15m midfielder steps up and loops it over the wall and into the top corner. Neil Etheridge is powerless in the Cardiff goal and Neves is off celebrating in front of the Wolves support.

It's a killer blow for Cardiff, who now have to find an equaliser against another of the league's best defences. Cardiff go all out but it creates more Wolves chances on the break and it looks to be over for a second, only for Helder Costa to miss a gilt-edged chance. Then, in the 93rd minute, after heaps of pressure and it coming to no avail, Cardiff get a lifeline. Aron Gunnarsson chips one into the box and substitute Anthony Pilkington is bundled over. No complaints from the assailant and this is it, 'we'll take a point' at this stage.

The Bluebirds have a good reputation with penalties over the years, largely thanks to Peter Whittingham. Joe Ralls had continued that, and Pilkington often stepped in when Whittingham wasn't present in the past. Pilkington had actually wins this penalty, but he's not going to take it. Substitute Gary Madine is primed and looking confident with a short run-up. The doubt begins to set in for fans with Madine yet to score in Cardiff colours since his £5m move from Bolton. He's already developing a bad reputation, despite making an impact in the dressing room, but now he has the chance to make himself a hero, in front of the Canton Stand. He steps up and puts it right in the corner, but John Ruddy in the Wolves goal has gone early, he's taken a chance and it's come off as he pushes the ball wide. The stadium falls silent while the Wolves players and fans celebrate wildly. That's it, that's the chance has gone.

Cardiff continue from the corner and something of a goal-line scramble ensues, the ball flicks up and it looks to be going in for a second, but Ruddy is there again to paw it away – this man's not going to be beaten today. From that clearance, Gunnarsson runs on to the ball out wide and flicks it into the box, over the on-rushing Ivan Cavaleiro who dives in recklessly – hang on a moment, that's another penalty! It is! The assistant referee flags furiously and Mike Dean agrees, pointing emphatically to the spot. Unbelievable. Cardiff have another chance. 'There is a God!' the supporters must feel, as Nuno Espirito Santo rages on the touchline and the Wolves players wander around in disbelief. There can be no complaints, it's as clear a foul as you could wish to see, and it was just inside the box.

We move into the sixth minute of added time and this truly is the last chance, this will be the last kick. The penalty taker will change, Warnock always insists on that, even if the first one is scored. This time it's Junior Hoilett. He's Cardiff's top scorer and the Bluebirds' faithful have full belief this one is going in, not only because Junior is an excellent technical player, but because of the law of averages, because it simply must, not even football can be that cruel, can it? Yes, it can. Ruddy goes early again but it's the wrong way; Hoilett's penalty sails towards the top corner but it's still rising, still rising and crack! The ball hits the crossbar and comes back out, it's headed across goal in one final attempt but the whistle sounds as it crosses the byline.

The Wolves players pile on top of each other, in disbelief, in elation. The Cardiff players collapse to the ground in disbelief, too, but in devastation. Sol Bamba, so often a strong leader on the pitch, produces a powerful image, slumped down, leaning on the post, exhausted and crushed. It perfectly reflects the feelings of fans, and even those of a Bluebirds persuasion in the press box are seen shaking, trying to rewrite match reports while this horrible lump builds in their throats. This is cruel, even by Cardiff's standards. To get two penalties in stoppage time is a footballing miracle; to miss both is beyond comprehension.

Warnock was of a similar belief after the game. He said, 'I thought it was a cracking game, a good advertisement, a good crowd and a world-class goal for Wolves. I'm disappointed we didn't get a point or even win. It's football I'm afraid. We just have to get on with it. We have to get on with it. We stick together when we win, and we stick together when we lose. We are disappointed today, but tomorrow is another day. We have to go again. It shows how far we've come. We've played against the so-called best team in the Championship. We've more than held our own and we have to go again in the next six games. I think the teams that we play won't look forward to playing us. I've been asked some silly questions but on TV, "How do you feel?" Fantastic! How do you think?'

Warnock was visibly a little shaken and even he, with more than 30 years in the game, hadn't seen anything like this. It wasn't just the penalty miss, either; this was also the giving up of any chance of winning the league, and Wolves celebrated like they won the title. Credit is due to them in terms of the game itself because they answered a question that needed answering. They were bullied all over the park by Cardiff in the August meeting between the two teams, and that was their big concern arriving in South Wales. However, they proved they had become far more streetwise over the course of the Championship season and in truth, they deserved to lift the trophy at the end of it, regardless of whether their budget far outweighed everyone else's.

After all, Cardiff outspent everyone during their title win in 2013, so it would hypocritical for them to come out and lament what Wolves had done.

It did all get a little hairy in the aftermath of the game, mind you. Wolves boss Nuno raced off on to the pitch after the second penalty was missed and the final whistle was blown. And it didn't go down well with Warnock. Nuno was seen on *Sky Sports* following Warnock, offering him an apology, and the Cardiff boss replied with 'fuck off, fuck off!' several times. When asked about the incident after the game, Warnock said, 'I don't give a toss what he says. I won't accept his apology. It's a great game and they've had a great win. You should shake a manager's hand after the game. I thought that showed a complete lack of class.'

He was furious, and nothing was going to change his mind on the evening. He even said he wouldn't be welcoming Nuno to his office, even if he came to say sorry, and the Portuguese was left to apologise to the press instead. He said, 'I've been in football many, many years and I have experienced everything. I don't recall being in this situation, that's why we love the game. It gives you, it takes you and this is football. This is why we love it. I have a chance to say I'm sorry and I hope Neil understands that I tried to tell him. It's very difficult to control your emotions when there are two penalties in the final minutes. The only thought I had on my mind was seeing John Ruddy. It's nothing to do with manners. I have been in football many years. I understand and I'm sorry. I will try to avoid it. Last season I was coaching in the Champions League, Champions League, Champions League. I'm very proud to manage in the Championship. Nobody can ever, ever say that I'm not a respectful person.'

It all got a little sour in the aftermath but the upshot of it was that Wolves were going to be champions. And Cardiff now had to somehow pick themselves up from the lowest of lows to face another promotion hopeful in Aston Villa the following Tuesday in order to keep Fulham off their back. Meanwhile, Bamba had picked himself up off the post and he surprisingly arrived in the press conference room to give a message of defiance; 'We have to get on with it. We stick together when we win, and we stick together when we lose. We are disappointed today, but tomorrow is another day. We have to go again.'

Outrunning the Cottagers was proving to be a real task. They were now unbeaten in 18 games and they would close the gap to two points by making it 19 the following day. It was going to be a psychological battle for Cardiff as much as anything. Form wasn't the biggest concern – this was the first defeat in 13 games and it came against the best team in the league – but the fashion in which it unfolded would inevitably leave scars. In a strange way, you can almost compare it to the 6-1 defeat to Preston towards the end of the 2008/09 season when the Bluebirds' campaign fell apart on the back of that result. There was no loss of dignity here in terms of the scoreline, but psychologically the defeat had the potential to be just as damaging, and the timing couldn't have been worse – just six games remained.

On the Tuesday, Cardiff made the short trip to the West Midlands to face Aston Villa, backed by around 3,000 supporters. Villa were still in the promotion race but defeat to Norwich the previous weekend had put a big spanner in the works and it left them seven points behind Cardiff and with a game less to play. Still, they could mix things up with a win over the Bluebirds and having not lost at home to their Welsh opponents since 1954, they could be forgiven for being in confident mood despite suffering a hammering in the Welsh capital earlier in the season.

All eyes were on the Bluebirds for another televised fixture as Warnock's men looked to bounce back from that gut-wrenching defeat and they responded well. They had the better of the chances throughout, with Mendez-Laing hitting the post, showing glimpses of returning to form after a disappointing spell, and Zohore should have scored in the second half, only to be thwarted by Sam Johnstone. The on-loan Manchester United goalkeeper put on the display of his life to frustrate Cardiff and it would prove oh so important.

After dominating for large spells, Villa seemed to realise they weren't made of glass and they bravely went for it in the latter stages. Cardiff held out well until the 85th minute, when they were left powerless. A poorly cleared corner found its way out to Jack Grealish on the edge of the box. The controversial youngster hit a world-class first-time volley to find the net with the help of the upright just five minutes from time. The roof was lifted off Villa Park and the travelling fans were left with that lump in their throats once again.

It had to be Grealish, too, a player much maligned by Championship supporters. He broke through as a youngster only to be thrown out of the Villa first-team setup through bad behaviour and attitude. However, credit where it's due, he got his act together and came back in with a different, more professional approach. Still, he's very much disliked by opposition fans due to his shithousery, which he has an abundance. Diving around, attempting to get opposing players booked and so on. He's nicknamed Joey Essex because of his modern haircut, rolled-down socks, shaven legs and so on. But you've got to give it to him, he's a very talented player and he showed that against Cardiff. He's just one of those players you'd love if he was on your team, but you despise him if he's not, and there are plenty of those around.

So, another wonder goal sent fans home thinking that once again their team was going to completely bottle promotion, and this time in the most spectacular fashion. Fulham did their bit that night, scraping through with a 1-0 win over Reading despite looking under par, and suddenly it all began to look doubtful. Cardiff were faltering and despite still having control of their own destiny with a game in hand still to play, Fulham were very much the form team and every pundit worth their salt was tipping them to take second place. But this is the Championship, nothing's straightforward, and if you think that's the last unexpected turn of this story, think again.

The following Saturday Cardiff travelled to Norwich for a must-win game and they played before Fulham, a chance to pile the pressure on, but they headed east with a lingering doubt and the devastation of two cruel defeats still chilling their bones. Having said that, the team had a character that goes beyond what you would usually expect, and they had shown that throughout the season. While you couldn't help but doubt them, they were always capable of proving you wrong. They did just that at Carrow Road. Norwich dominated for large spells, but Cardiff held strong, much to the thanks in large part to the woodwork and goalkeeper Etheridge. Then Zohore came on for Madine and changed everything with a marvellous display of skill.

Four minutes from time, Gunnarsson's long throw caused trouble and the second phase saw Zohore force a save from Angus Gunn with a header. The ball was palmed wide and Zohore turned towards goal right on the byline, looked up, assessed his options, and tried the unthinkable. The big Dane saw Gunn take a step to his right in anticipation of a cross and he acted quickly, slotting the ball inside the near post from the tightest of angles. Carrow Road was left stunned as the Bluebirds stole a huge and vital three points out of nothing, the result being rubber stamped by a stunning long-range volley from Hoilett.

That feelgood factor was back and all eyes turned to Fulham, who hosted London rivals Brentford in the evening kick-off. At that time of year and in the thick of a promotion race, you are supporting every one of Fulham's rivals as if they are your own team. The Bees dominated and were wrongly denied a stonewall penalty. Fulham took advantage with just 20 minutes left when loan striker Aleksandar Mitrovic scored again – since arriving from Newcastle United he had been pulling the Cottagers over the line at a rapid pace.

Everything seemed to be going for Fulham, and Cardiff fans just couldn't shake that feeling until in the 94th minute when the ball was headed across the Fulham box to an unmarked Maupay. He missed an open goal at Cardiff earlier in the season but wasn't missing this one, sending the Brentford fans – and indeed every Cardiff supporter watching up and down the country – berserk. Now it was Fulham's turn to feel the heartbreak and they they had to pick themselves up. Game changer.

Cardiff had returned to second ahead of another pivotal weekend which saw Fulham take on Millwall, a game in which everyone was expecting a slip-up. Millwall were in fine form as they closed in on the play-offs, but Fulham – looking relentless with the help of young talent Ryan Sessegnon – made a clear statement of intent that Friday night. They dismantled Millwall with a 3-0 win at The New Den so it was over to Cardiff, who knew they had to win at home to Nottingham Forest in front of the cameras 24 hours later to stay second. They did. Sean Morrison scored the opener but Liam Bridcutt put a spanner in the works. Still, however, Cardiff found a way.

Their character shone through, and Gunnarsson grabbed the winner with a smart close-range effort 16 minutes from time. He emerged from the crowded box with his Viking-like Icelandic expression; bald, bearded and full of passion. Gunnarsson had missed a large chunk of the season through injury, and he had come back with a vital contribution. His look of defiance in the celebration showed he refused to be beaten by injury and Cardiff refused to be caught by Fulham. It felt the tide had turned, and then came that rearranged trip to Derby County.

Snowgate continued to linger on despite the EFL closing its investigation. When the teams were supposed to meet, Derby had just ten fit players in training and now they were back in form with a full team, so the postponement had worked out perfectly for them.

That aside, the controversy surrounding this fixture was added to by the emergence of a video on social media which showed Cardiff captain Sean Morrison launching a foul-mouthed tirade at several Derby players. In the video he called one former Rams man 'an insecure c***' as well as insulting his manhood. He also called out defender Richard Keogh, saying he was 'shit at football' and needless to say, after the video was leaked and posted on Twitter, it completely blew up. Most national media outlets covered the story and the video was everywhere.

The footage was shocking upon first viewing, but the context was later revealed by Warnock: 'While I don't condone the language and it leaves a lot to be desired, our lads have videos of them as well. After the game, our lads were in an airport, having a drink in a social place, and both parties were there. Bradley Johnson with [Anthony] Pilkington who had played at Norwich, [Alex] Pearce and Morrison who had played at Reading, and it was just a lot of banter between themselves. When you first hear about that, you think "oh no", but when you see the videos our lads have got – which we're not prepared to release – it's just banter really and a lot of hot air, it just makes it more mouth-watering when we play them in a couple of weeks.

'[Morrison] was apologetic, he said, "These things are said between pals, we've known each other for many years." I've seen the [video] they sent us – there'd be more headlines in that if we let that go out! I'm not on social media, I don't even know how to switch one on! I don't understand it, but it was in good banter and it was two weeks ago. I don't want us to get our own back … let's move on.'

Derby manager Gary Rowett went on to call the video 'distasteful' and the spat between the two clubs continued, especially when Rowett said in the build-up that Warnock was 'a bit panto'. By the time the two teams met on 24 April, the stakes, you could say, were pretty high. And not only because both teams needed three points.

Cardiff fans attended the game in good spirits, dressing as snowmen and bringing shovels to mock the postponement decision, and the atmosphere inside Pride Park was sensational. The game itself was an open affair, in front of the Sky Sports cameras again, and Derby should have gone in front early on, but it was instead the visitors who took the lead when Paterson scored a stunning first-time volley. That took Cardiff into the break with a safe-looking advantage following an excellent first-half display, but things would take a turn for the worse in the second half and the Bluebirds capitulated in spectacular fashion.

It all began in the 69th minute when Cameron Jerome took advantage of some shocking defending to level the scores. Then Warnock threw on winger Yanic Wildschut in a bid to get back on top, but in reality, the Dutchman's only contribution was going to be a catastrophic error of judgement. Deep in his own box, Wildschut tried to turn away from Andre Wisdom instead of clearing the ball, and lost possession. Wisdom crossed and the next touch came from Championship top scorer Matej Vydra, who smashed the ball home.

Derby had all the momentum and Cardiff had well and truly caved in by this point. There was even time for a third when Jerome took advantage of Morrisson's untimely slip and Derby were home and dry. Jerome is one of those players who always seems to score past the Bluebirds. It would have been quite ironic, too, for a man who played a big part in starting this adventure with his transfer to Birmingham City raising £3m, to have gone and ended it by condemning Cardiff to another slip-up just two games before the end of the season.

In reality, this was no disaster for Cardiff because it was their game in hand so even losing meant they stayed second, but it was a huge chance missed and it gave Fulham confidence. They were licking their lips again, still on that unbelievable unbeaten run.

Just two games remained with Cardiff holding a one-point advantage. The Bluebirds travelled to a resurgent bottom-half Hull City before facing a Reading team battling for their lives. Fulham hosted an already-relegated Sunderland before travelling to a Birmingham team also deep in relegation trouble. Prior to this season no team had ever missed out on automatic promotion with 91 points, but that unprecedented scenario would have been on had Cardiff and Fulha,m both won their last two fixtures.

Fulham played Sunderland the day before Cardiff faced Hull, so again they had the opportunity to pile on the pressure. This time every Bluebird was a Sunderland fan for the night, backing former Wales manager Chris Coleman. It was a black cat named Trixie who was believed to be the lucky charm during Cardiff's only FA Cup win in 1927, and they were hoping the Black Cats of Sunderland could prove to be the omen at Craven Cottage. Unbelievably, that looked to be the case when Joel Asoro put Sunderland ahead in the first half, but Lucas Piazon levelled just before the break after Sunderland were denied a clear penalty. There was a sense of inevitability about a Fulham win by half-time, although Jokanovic's men didn't find their winner until 14 minutes from time when an offside-looking Mitrovic headed home and they returned to second spot.

The Bluebirds arrived at the KCOM Stadium probably feeling a little sorry for themselves, but the Derby defeat wasn't as damaging as it appeared on paper. Yes, after all that had been said, it was a sucker punch of sorts to lose, but Cardiff were beaten due to their own silly mistakes and they knew what they had to do to put it right. It wasn't two missed penalties or a Jack Grealish screamer, this time they could learn from it and that makes a defeat far more acceptable. They had to learn their lessons and move on quickly, especially with this huge game against Hull coming just four days later, where they knew they simply had to win. Anything less than a win would have handed Fulham control, and that simply couldn't happen.

Fulham were now 23 league games unbeaten – half a season – and if they were in the driving seat going into the final game they were winning, as far as Cardiff were concerned. Nothing less than a win would do at Hull. A Championship season is full of ups and downs but the beauty of it is that when you suffer a setback, you have a chance to make up for it just around the corner. However, the time for all that was gone. Cardiff could not slip up at Hull, and they did not.

Hull started well but Cardiff withstood the pressure and looked as solid as ever at the back with Bamba and Morrison leading by example, in a game which would be all about doing just that. Morrison's big performance really started in the 32nd minute when he climbed a yard higher than even the goalkeeper to head home Ralls's perfect corner. He was filled with desire and determination to bounce back from a defeat that he will have felt more than anyone else. Morrison was singled out throughout the Derby game on the back of that video, and he left the pitch looking defiant but hurt after the result.

Speaking of hurt, Gunnarsson had left the pitch at the KCOM with a season-ending injury that would put his World Cup with Iceland in jeopardy. It was a hammer blow to the Cardiff midfield. Despite that, Cardiff came close with two more decent attempts before the game meandered towards a nervy finale. The visitors braced themselves for a Hull onslaught and the fans prepared for the longest ten minutes of their lives.

Hull won a corner with ten minutes left, which was cleared out to Mendez-Laing, whose progress was like a bolt from the blue. He had been on for the entirety of the game, but he found an inner energy and second wind as he flew past his marker, taking big touches as he raced into the Hull half.

After reaching the corner of the box he looked up to find Morrison in space. The captain, in the opposition penalty area with ten minutes to go, in open play! Morrison took a touch, faced the goal, and feinted to shoot, but instead kept control in a clumsy fashion. Then he wrapped a long left leg around the ball and it flew into the far corner of the net. Cue bedlam in the away end, and cue one of the biggest roars you'll hear from a travelling support as Morrison slid on his knees in front of his fans. He should never have been in the opposition box from open play, but thank God he was.

This was a captain leading by example, proving his point and helping his club put one foot in the Premier League. Warnock spoke of Morrison's goal and his team's character after the final whistle. And in stark contrast to the aftermath of the Wolves game just a few weeks previously, he was predictably in a good mood. He said, 'When you watch the goal, I find it incredible, he's actually in his own six-yard box when he sets off. And he carries on, and I'm thinking, "What's he doing?" It's incredible. I don't know why but he must have realised it was on. It's as big a game as I've had in my career probably.

'Everybody keeps expecting us to fall away don't they? Decisions are going left, right and centre for Fulham at the minute, with penalties and things like that. It's hard. A lot of teams might be demoralised. I woke up up at 4am thinking of Keith Stroud, who didn't give us two points at Millwall. So, I don't know what the other lads are thinking about. I know I say it a lot, but they're just a great bunch of lads. I know we're limited, and we're not everyone's cup of tea, but we keep going and we're like a rash. They just don't know when they're beat. They get knockdowns and decisions and they get on with it. It's great to be the manager. I thought the fans today, the last time I heard the national anthem of Wales like that was when I went to watch Wales play Australia at rugby. My hair stood up. I thought they were brilliant.'

For weeks and months Cardiff and Fulham fans had been doing the maths. On the final day of the Championship season it was simple. If Cardiff matched or bettered Fulham's result they would be promoted, but if the Cottagers bettered the Bluebirds, they would be going back to the Premier League. Cardiff faced Reading at home in front of a sell-out record league crowd for the stadium; the Royals could still go down, albeit there was a very slim chance. Fulham travelled to Birmingham at a sold-out St Andrew's where the Blues could also be relegated, though two teams below them would have to better their result for that scenario to play out.

On paper it was Cardiff with the better of the final fixtures, but Fulham were unbeaten in 23 and they had been backed all season thanks to their flashy, modern brand of football. They had caught the eye of many, to the point that pundits and neutrals were saying that they deserved to be promoted, and all the while Cardiff were embracing their own mindset. They had thrived with the underdog tag all season and they would continue to do so until the end, even if the ball was firmly in their court.

As with that dramatic night at Wolves, let's re-live things as they happened.

It's a stunning day in the Welsh capital and the stadium fills up at an unprecedented pace. More than 32,000 are in attendance for the game, and many of those are in the ground and waiting an hour before kick-off, perhaps through nerves or perhaps wanting to drink in every moment of what could be such a memorable day. It has the feel of a special occasion and it was always going to help that the game is played on a Sunday before a bank holiday, which is not always the case.

It's fantastic to see the Cardiff City Stadium full, including the new stand, which usually only happens for international fixtures. It may be a rare sight, but the noise generated by supporters when this ground is full is sensational. It's aesthetically pleasing, too.

We've talked a lot about the greatness of Ninian Park, and the atmosphere there will always be unique. But nine years into the life of this new stadium – and while it will never be Ninian Park – it feels like home for Cardiff fans. Perhaps it helps that there have been so many ups and downs, so many emotions. It's helped this stadium age rapidly in terms of history and growing an attachment to the people who sit inside it. It's become a fitting successor to Ninian Park, and even more so when the upper tier is full, like it is today for this huge occasion when Cardiff have a chance to etch another memory in the young history of their home ground.

It's a nervy occasion but the build-up is relaxed. The pre-match press conference has attracted national media from up and down the country – a stark difference to the four or five who turn up during the bulk of the season – and that represents a victory in itself. So much of the national media have taken every possible swipe at Cardiff during the season and in the past. Throughout the season, so many have backed Fulham and they've been proven wrong time and time again. Now they have been to Cardiff's press conference instead of Fulham's, now Cardiff are in firm control and there's a sense of getting the last laugh about that, especially for Warnock, who is often portrayed as a bad guy in English football and one of the 'old guard' standing in the way of progression.

Regardless of all the running around the mood remains relaxed in the Cardiff camp. There are no hotels, nothing changes, the players sleep in their own beds before the game and the training schedule is no more intense. Before the game, Warnock reveals, 'You can't change anything. We've already sorted things out because for a game like this, you get ridiculous things to do with tickets and families and I made sure that was all put to bed by Tuesday. There's no reason for anyone to look after people, which they do, it's automatic promotion. We have a job to do and we have to prepare as normal. We're doing it like we have been doing it. If they're not nervous, there's something wrong. I talked about my own preparation for matches and three or four hours before a game, I can't even smell food, let alone eat it and I'm sure the players will be in a similar situation.'

Everything remains as it is; it's a sensible move from the experienced boss who's been through this before and that certainly helps. There's nothing like experience in a position like this, and Warnock is an advantage for Cardiff over Fulham.

Kick-off seems to come around all too quickly as a sweltering heat promises to make things difficult for both teams. Cardiff start well and Hoilett comes close, bending an effort just around the far post. The atmosphere is electric but it's not quite as intense an occasion as you would imagine. The Bluebirds' faithful are making a right racket, armed with their new 'Allez, allez' song, pinched from Liverpool, who themselves pinched it from Italy. The Cardiff version goes, 'We're the famous Cardiff City, we come from Sloper Road, and when they talk about the Welsh Cup, we won it fucking loads, we beat Real Madrid, we won the FA Cup, and still they don't believe us, the Blues are going up! Allez, allez, allez, allez, allez, allez, allez allez, allez!'

If you're a Bluebird and you're not singing that in your head, you may be superhuman, but either way, hopefully it's taking you back to 6 May, when it became the theme song of that final day.

Supporters continue to sing and Cardiff continue to dominate when the first flash of news filters through that Lukas Jutkiewicz has put Birmingham ahead against Fulham in front of a raucous St Andrew's crowd, a goal celebrated just as loudly around 100 miles down the road.

The Bluebirds, buoyed by the news, continue their search for a goal but Reading are in no mood to concede, putting bodies on the line to deny Zohore. Still, Cardiff need a goal, Fulham have proved themselves capable of completing a comeback over the course of the season and you simply can't leave it to chance.

Then just before half-time comes another cheer from supporters, but this one is more doubtful. With more than 32,000 people in the stadium and almost everyone following scores elsewhere, the signal is jammed and the club wi-fi isn't much better. The refresh option on everyone's phone and laptop gets a hammering as fans clamour to verify what might be. Then, there it is, Harlee Dean has doubled Birmingham's lead. Cue more celebrations as half-time arrives and the Bluebirds head in knowing they may not have to do their job after all. Warnock later confesses, 'I was really pleased at half-time to find out it was 2-0 [at Birmingham], I think I kissed the guy who told me!'

Birmingham's two-goal lead helps relax things even further and nerves are far less of a factor in the second half. Having said that, this is Cardiff City, who are capable of anything– the most amazing comebacks and the most spectacular capitulations. The more cynical fans wanted a goal, and who could blame them? But that is still proving elusive with Reading refusing to go down without giving everything. Results are also going their way, but they aren't going to leave it to chance and still they rebuff everything thrown at them.

Then, in the 84th minute a concerned groan sounds around the stadium as Tom Cairney grabs one back for Fulham. Still, Jokanovic's men will need to win if the score in South Wales remains the same. However logic doesn't come into it when you've been through all these ups and downs, all those surreal moments that make you a Cardiff City fan.

Still, the supporters pick themselves up to back the team, and in the 89th minute emerges such a roar that if you are been sitting with your eyes closed when you hear it, you would think Cardiff have scored. They haven't. Che Adams has made it 3-1 to Birmingham with a minute of normal time remaining, securing his team's safety and ending Fulham's chances of making the top two.

The party atmosphere at the Cardiff City Stadium goes up another notch and fans can't contain themselves. Even an early pitch invasion follows, but the game isn't finished. After fans eventually depart again, they stand waiting for it to become official. Reading are safe, and they know it. Cardiff are up, and they know it. Even referee Robert Madley becomes more interested in planning his departure than the game itself as Reading pass the ball pointlessly around their back four without a Cardiff player in sight. Then comes the inevitable rush of joy as Madley calls his fellow officials off the pitch while the game continues, followed by an army of supporters and the final whistle, which is met by a deafening roar.

Cardiff City were back in the Premier League and this time, it was in blue. The Bluebirds had secured promotion with a goalless draw just like they did five years previously but this time, they had defied all the odds to do it. They beat Fulham, who were everyone's favourites to go up. Fulham, the pretty team, the modern team, the 'proper' team who had put together a run of over half a season unbeaten. Beaten by Cardiff, the underdogs, the team who were supposedly 'boring', 'route one', 'old fashioned', led by a 'football dinosaur'. They'd even done it with more points than when they won the league in 2013, outlining the scale of this monumental season for such an unfancied team.

This was an achievement of epic proportions and they was fittingly celebrated with a traditional pitch invasion, with pyrotechnics thanks to a stroke of genius from the club, who in anticipation of promotion, set up fireworks to go off above the stadium roof. They were a lovely addition to an emotional scene which saw everyone on the pitch embrace the moment. They couldn't even get the fans off to do the presentation of the Championship runners-up trophy, they didn't even try. The team emerged, with Gunnarsson on crutches, to lift the trophy and to end what felt like a marathon of a promotion bid. Warnock lapped up his deserved praise from supporters and Vincent Tan celebrated behind him donning in his blue shirt, happy and welcomed by supporters.

Warnock announced his pride after the celebrations finally subsided: 'The fans are proud to be Bluebirds again. Everyone wants to support the club now and that's a lovely thing. I know we're not easy on the eye, but what can you ask as a manager? You can only work with what you've got and I'm really proud that I've got a team who have ruffles a few feathers. It's not quite sunk in yet. I daren't have a drink, I would be drunk in five minutes. I've not seen a crowd like that. Before the game, during and after. It's great for Wales as well, it's good to put a team like us back in.'

This was a club transformed, enjoying its day in the light, and my goodness do these supporters deserve it after all the ups and downs, trials and tribulations – some even beyond football.

Players then celebrated on the pitch with their families and the echoes of those celebrations, the smiles of joy etched on the faces of supporters as they applauded their heroes, will live long in the memory. This historic achievement had finally been done in the right way and you could see the difference.

Cardiff City are back in the Premier League and this time, they're in blue. Most importantly, this time they are united.

'Told you we'd be back'

IN 2014, teenage fan Owain Harries held aloft a sign which read 'we'll be back' and four years later, he was again pictured at the Cardiff City Stadium but this time with a new sign; this time it read 'told you we'd be back.' It says something about supporters, that they retained an everlasting optimism, even when Cardiff were relegated in 2014, when everything pointed down, when the club became toxic. Many still believed they'd have their moment back in the Premier League. You can't overestimate the importance of that belief. It's what keeps a club alive, it's what makes football worth it.

Football is nothing without its fans, without the energy, the passion, the love they feel for their club. Owain, like many others, had belief that relegation wasn't the end, and his feeling wasn't misplaced. For many clubs it can be, and the decline can continue, but Cardiff survived and just four years later they returned. It's rather impressive when you think about it, too. To go back up only four years later given the messy situation the club found itself in is one hell of an achievement. Some clubs don't return in ten years under good circumstances, let alone managing to turn everything around and then get promoted.

It's a statement of defiance, and living proof that Cardiff City Football Club has a character and a strength that goes beyond the norm. The rebrand might have buckled many clubs, as might the constant financial strain and all those near misses of going under. Relegation was another bitter pill to swallow and in years gone by, it's managed to almost wipe out some clubs. Blackburn Rovers, Portsmouth, Sunderland and Blackpool are all proof that relegation from the Premier League can leave you on your knees.

This football club has been through so many difficult challenges and faced so many curve balls that, at times, it seemed unimaginable to bounce back. However, bounce back it did and the final day draw against Reading, achieving promotion to the Premier League in blue for the first time, with more than 30,000 happy faces, was the culmination of so much hard work. Not just by Neil Warnock, Joe Ralls, or Callum Paterson. Nor Vincent Tan, Ken Choo, Mehmet Dalman nor even Russell Slade. There have been so many contributions to this journey, and the end result is something to be proud of. It's also a just reward for a club that kept fighting.

And especially so for Tan, who at one stage, was the most hated man in South Wales. When he was sitting in the directors' box at Anfield with those leather gloves, having turned the club red and ready to sack the supporters' favourite manager, with a smile across his face, you couldn't have found a more despised figure. Fast forward just four years and he's wearing a blue shirt, smiling, being applauded by many fans. He is not forgiven by everyone, don't make that mistake. But the majority will, at least, eventually forgive him. After all, if he wasn't around, this club may not have survived to see the day of another promotion, let alone one to the Premier League. In reality, it would have survived, it could have survived, but without all the ups and instead with plenty of downs. With Tan's financial support, it's been allowed to thrive, supporters have been given memories to last a lifetime, and that's what football is about.

'I have been here nine years. It was back in 2009 that I first put money in,' said Tan after promotion. 'I must admit I made a mistake early on changing the colour, but I removed the mistake. There will be no more tinkering with the colours. I feel the club is united again, everybody is pulling in the same direction. The board, the team, the fans, the media. We need everyone to be positive because there is lots to be positive about. I can understand how the fans feel. But I reverted back to blue. I want to say thank you very much to them for continuing to support the club. There are good positive feelings, and you need that to be successful. Together, hopefully, we can make this club bigger, stronger, better, greater.'

You can't overestimate the damage the rebrand did and the hurt it caused so many supporters, but equally, you have to hold your hands up when someone admits their mistake. Tan has done that, and he has built many bridges by doing so. For many, it will take a lot longer to forgive, but Tan will also be aware of that. He knows that by offering the club stability and a chance to compete at the top level, he will earn the sort of trust Warnock has from the fans.

Warnock's part in this promotion is simply undeniable. He managed to build a squad of misfits with something to prove and in 46 games they made their point. Players like Neil Etheridge, who was released by Fulham earlier in his career. He slept on his friend's sofa, played as a number-three goalkeeper and worked his way back up the ladder until one day, he denied Fulham automatic promotion as Cardiff's number one. There are so many wonderful stories like that from this promotion, and that's because this team is made up of ordinary people. There is a person behind every name and number in this dressing room.

And think back to Taff's Well, where we started this season's journey. You could see how down to earth these players were and that level-headedness took them all the way, as did their ability to stay calm in order to score late goals, to steal results. And their ability to not get carried away after a ridiculous run of 13 games unbeaten, for example. Warnock helped by never going all out for automatic promotion in public. That allowed Cardiff to avoid the sort of pressure placed on rivals Aston Villa and Fulham. It allowed them to remain the underdogs.

WalesOnline digital sport writer Dom Booth, who covered Cardiff throughout the season, believes that was one of the many keys to their success. He says, 'The "underdogs" tag absolutely played into Cardiff's hands. It suited them to the ground. Warnock, the fans and particularly players like Sean Morrison, Nathaniel Mendez-Laing, Junior Hoilett Sol Bamba, Joe Ralls and Neil Etheridge – all of whom had been written off at times in their careers, and who felt revitalised by Warnock's siege mentality. "Prove them wrong" was the mantra, and Cardiff did just that. The wins against Aston Villa, Wolves and Leeds United – all bigger clubs than Cardiff – were proof of a team that loved being backed into a corner. It was when they were most dangerous. I certainly see parallels with Claudio Ranieri's [2015/16 Premier

League champions] Leicester City. Cardiff spoiled the big boys' party and did it with a smile on their faces.'

A smile on their face indeed, and you'll seldom see a group as relaxed and as happy as this one, even in the height of a promotion race. Leaders like Bamba, Gunnarsson and Morrison kept everyone ticking over and they kept everyone's feet on the ground. Warnock revealed before the final run-in, 'If anyone's feet left the ground, it wouldn't get as far as me, I wouldn't know about it. Those lads would sort that out and that's what you need. You need leaders, men about the place, people to stand up and be counted, and I'm sure I've not mentioned some like Connolly. You don't need anything else. I've had seven promotions and I look back at them and they all have characters, leaders, people who take responsibility.

'This group may be the best I've ever had, and I don't know how far they can go because we've only just started on the journey. I don't know if we can get where we want to be, but it won't be for the lack of trying and we're enjoying the moment.'

They did get there in the end and in magnificent fashion. They surpassed 2013 their title-winning points tally of 2012/13 by three to finish second, beating a Fulham team who went half a season unbeaten. Fulham had been backed by every pundit, playing next-generation football that so many want to see in the Premier League, and they still went on to win promotion through the play-offs.

The Cottagers' brand of football was the antithesis of Cardiff's in truth. Warnock's men are direct, they play for throw-ins and they play long balls when they need to; there's also shithousery in abundance, perhaps more than any other Championship team. But to say that alone would be doing them a serious injustice. This team are far from boring or ugly. In fact, it's the most entertaining football many of the Bluebirds faithful have seen since the days of Dave Jones. Even Malky Mackay, for all his success, didn't employ an entertaining style.

Warnock's side is full of pace, and effectively plays with three up top, home or away. That's not boring or negative and neither was the football. This team completely overpowered so many good Championship outfits with pace, power and skill. They put balls in the box. With lightning-quick wingers, they took on opponents one-to-one and with Kenneth Zohore up top, they turned defences inside out. The simplistic view may be that they wasted time and conceded lots of niggly fouls, but you've got to look beyond that. Bluebirds fans won't need to, they've seen it all season, but that's just it. This narrative of Cardiff being a horrible team to watch comes from sections of the media that only took notice later in the season, when they had to do whatever they could to get results. The amount of televised games in the second half of the season is completely disproportionate to the first half, and so many neutrals didn't see the fast-paced football Cardiff produced earlier in the campaign, infused with a freedom.

Dom Booth agrees, and he too says there's far more to this team than the ugliness singled out by many. 'It's easy to say that Cardiff City had a unique team spirit and work ethic, but they genuinely seemed to just run harder and further than any other side in the Championship. They were fearless in defence and frighteningly fast in attack, and many teams were beaten before a ball was kicked, such was the Bluebirds' imposing nature. Other more cultured sides thought they had the beating of Cardiff but came unstuck because they simply couldn't match them for power and presence, despite enjoying more possession. At times, it was a delight to watch them dismantle more experienced, more talented outfits. You have to credit Neil Warnock and his staff for developing that team spirit and that insatiable appetite to work harder.'

That is another side to this team. That work ethic that has taken them so far, setting them apart from so many rivals. They have the desire to go the extra yard. It's leaders like Bamba with his desperate outstretched leg denying the opponents a chance, or Morrison climbing yards above everyone else to win a header. It's true that the team doesn't possess the ability of Tom Cairney and Ryan Sessegnon of Fulham, they don't have players like Ruben Neves and Diogo Jota of Wolves, so they make up for it in sheer desire. They will go to war for each other, and that comes from the team spirit in the dressing room.

Even Warnock admits he's never had a dressing room like this one, in which the whole group are friends. They all get on and they all do things together outside of football. Even their families are friends and that makes a difference, too. It's a wonderful scenario and a perfect working environment. A far cry from the toxicity of years past. This is a close-knit group and it shows on the pitch. It's a cliché to say no one gets left behind but it's also true for this team. They win as a group and they lose as one, too, as Bamba confirms; 'We stick together when we win, when we lose it's the same.'

This season, they have won. They have struck the jackpot and after all the trials and tribulations of the Championship campaign, seeing them distraught following that Wolves game, it was fitting to see so many smiles on their faces after securing promotion. They celebrated in style on the day, and then the following week in the city centre. The club held an open-top bus parade from the stadium to just in front of Cardiff Castle, and thousands turned up to congratulate their team. It felt like the whole city was in attendance to create a sea of blue.

Each of the players and coaching staff was welcomed to the stage. Warnock took to the microphone and entertained the crowd with his much-loved fist pumps, before reflecting on a memorable season. He said, 'I think everybody's singing from the same hymn sheet, from Vincent right down to the cleaners. When you see a turnout like today, I feel really proud as a manager it turned out like this. You can't put a price on everybody together. I did it at Sheffield, took me seven years there – whereas it's took me 18 months here. That's what makes it almost a miracle, really.'

It's a team welded with togetherness and that's been the message from minute one. 'City As One' reads the club's official hashtag and these are often empty messages, but this time it fits. Especially seeing thousands of people turning up with smiles on their face to celebrate this promotion. This time it's embraced by everyone, from the supporters in the stands to the players on the pitch. This is a united club achieving something special.

This is Cardiff City returning to the fore in the right way. It's a club that has made so many mistakes, a club with a reputation of bottling it, of behaving badly off the field, of being run like a circus. But no more. Now it returns to the Premier League professionally run, with fans backing the club in the right way and having achieved promotion against all the odds. There were stumbles but no falls, and they have crossed the line with a smile on their face, achieving what nobody expected them to achieve and become a Premier League club once again. The Bluebirds are up.

The Warnock way

THERE ARE moments in time that can change everything. Think of it as the butterfly effect. Whether something occurs or not can severely alter the course of history, it can alter what happens to someone or something. In this case, we're talking about Cardiff City. The something that changes everything in this scenario is Neil Warnock answering the phone to Mehmet Dalman, and then agreeing to become the club's next manager. That changes the course of the Bluebirds' future.

Why does it have such a profound effect? It's because Cardiff found themselves drifting towards the edge of a waterfall. They needed a stable rock, something to hold on to and keep them safe while they tried to advance away from the drop.

There are strange parallels to a waterfall in this story. First come the choppy waters, the rapids which we know as the rebrand, the relegation and the transfer embargo. Then all of a sudden, it all goes calm, you think you're okay, that you're safe and then before you see any warning signs, you're heading towards a big drop and which relates to Paul Trollope's reign. Starting with optimism, with hopes of progress, and then a steep fall which took Cardiff to their lowest ebb in 11 years. At that point, Cardiff needed a very specific manager in charge and Neil Warnock was that man. They found themselves in a position where one more bad decision could have cost them everything, but they got it right. No more messing about, no more cheap options.

'I'm a big believer in fate,' admits Warnock, and it applies more than ever to this situation. This feels like fate, like Cardiff got the right man, at the right time, and it paid off.

We've talked about Dave Jones, Malky Mackay, Russell Slade and everyone else, but the effect Warnock would have perhaps outweighed the lot. That might seem unfair to Jones, who started this adventure, for example, but you won't find many in the blue half of South Wales who disagree. The scale of this job and the time frame in which Warnock has done it are simply remarkable.

The manner in which he has gone about it means he has gone down in Cardiff City folklore forever, as Dom Booth alludes to: 'You cannot overstate the job he has done. His experience of seven previous promotions, his rapport with the fans, charisma, expertise dealing with the media and, like I said, that team spirit he managed to harness were all crucial. Cardiff were a team without one star player. Warnock was the star of the show and he deserved all the plaudits that inevitably came his way. Football in South Wales has rarely seen such a charismatic cult figure and that counts for a lot at a club like Cardiff City.'

This is a man who had seven promotions to his name before arriving and he's now got a record-breaking eighth. That was his motivation in all this, but whether he actually expected to get it, deep down, only he could tell you. There's no doubt that he believed in his team from minute one, but it would have been a tough ask to predict this; second place above all those big spending teams. It's something out of the ordinary, especially where Cardiff came from. To go from 23rd in the Championship to finishing second at the end of the following season, it's almost unheard of. Rome wasn't built in a day, nor did Warnock fix Cardiff in a day, but it didn't take him much longer. That's what has stunned people the most. Few doubted Warnock's ability and the moment he arrived at the club, a belief was founded that this man would give Cardiff a chance of going up. However, nobody expected it to be this quickly and certainly not without the agony of the play-offs.

So how did he do it? When Warnock arrived, he walked into a 'fragmented club', dysfunctional from top to bottom with relationships between colleagues frosty throughout. Task number one. He spotted that early on, and while it had nothing to do with the first team, he still made it his business. Bad apples were sent on their way to give everyone in the club, wherever they worked, the chance to create the best working environment. Warnock wanted everyone pulling in the same direction, and that wasn't going to happen if there were people who didn't get on behind the scenes. 'I went around all the departments, asked them about any problems they had,' said Warnock. 'I know it's not my business, but I made it my business because I wanted to get everyone together and that was the best way of doing it. When I say fragmented, I just think every department looked after themselves, really. They're together now with a group of players we've got. The players intertwine with the staff we've got. All the departments were pulling in different directions. They all needed telling, "If we can all pull in the same direction, we've got a chance."'

It's also something that Booth observed; 'As is the case with every managerial appointment, results are the single most important thing and Warnock got them early in his tenure. Opening with a hard-fought win over then high-flying rivals Bristol City was the perfect start, and stabilising Cardiff so they finished 2016/17 in mid-table proved to all Bluebirds that he was the man for the job. After taking over a "fragmented" club as he put it, Warnock took it upon himself to bring everyone together and get people behind the team first and foremost. The rest would follow, and the relationship between fans and board has healed a huge amount since the rebrand.

'I always thought Warnock relished the challenge, after what he'd done saving Rotherham, whereas Paul Trollope had been uncertain and tentative in the job. Outsiders rightly thought Warnock was being over-ambitious targeting promotion in 2017/18 but again, it captured the imagination of fans. He then brought a real swell of good feeling and with it momentum and confidence, which just went on and on. And best of all he did it on a shoestring.'

Then it's a case of getting the fans on side. He's got a head start here because many fans already wanted him at the club for a number of years. However, he still says what they want to hear, and it sets the tone nicely. Upon arrival he said, 'I've always liked it here. Everywhere I go I get stick, but I've always had good banter with the Cardiff people. They're my type of crowd – blood and guts and all that, which I like – and I know that if I can get it right for them, they'll get behind me.'

Get behind him they did, and in their numbers from minute one. That win over Bristol City was a springboard, the perfect start for a new regime which everyone would buy into. Everyone had to. The Warnock way just doesn't work unless everyone is on board, you can't get promoted with an under-strength squad unless everyone is pulling in the same direction. That's the key to it all.

Fans bought into it whole-heartedly. They trusted him from the off and that says a lot in itself. The fanbase was hurt by so many bad decisions, mis-represented by Malky Mackay, let down by Vincent Tan and still they were willing to pour their trust into one man. It says something about Warnock and his charisma that he's able to command that trust, and he does it excellently. He mesmerises the media with his open and frank approach in press conferences and everything is just so natural. You could say it's down to 30-odd years of managerial experience but it's far more than that. This is just him; what you get in press conferences is what you get in real life. What you see is what you get and that's often the Yorkshire way, as it is in Wales. There is a similarity between the two attitudes to life, there's no doubt about that.

There's also an element of Warnock being shaped by life experiences. We're all shaped by what we go through, the challenges we face and how we experience different pressures. The Warnock family hasn't had it easy with Neil's wife, Sharron, suffering from breast cancer and lymphoedema. It's what got him back into the game following retirement. He revealed, 'She had breast cancer developed late last year [2015] and I was getting under her feet a little bit at home. One day the nurse was there doing her chemotherapy and she was joking with her about it. Rotherham rang and offered me the job, so I told them I couldn't take it. But she told me she wanted me to take it.'

From there he pulled off a miracle to keep Rotherham in the Championship and then with his wife's blessing, he decided to give the record-breaking eighth promotion a crack with Cardiff. He added, 'Sharon knew I really wanted to go for this eighth promotion. She's in a really good place now and she said, "I want you to go and do your best." I wouldn't have done this if she hadn't said that, but that's the sort of woman she is.'

Neil is a family man as well as well as a football man and there's been a noticeable mellowing of the crazy character we've grown used to seeing down the years.

There's a realisation that it's football and there is always a chance to do better. Sometimes there are more important things in life, and losing a game isn't the end of the world. It can feel like it sometimes, some games more than others, for fans, players and managers alike. And sometimes it takes a significant event in life to make you realise that football is not as important as family. That's the case for Warnock, who has been through this tough experience with his wife, and he can only speak for himself, but it seems to have given him a different outlook. He's still a winner, that's never going to change, but life is bigger than all this and that outlook allows him to connect with his players, to take the pressure off.

The family side of Warnock is also reflected in his clubs. At Cardiff you now have a fantastic feeling inside the club, from the groundsman to the players, and that's not just down to success. That is, above all the football, the real Warnock way. Uniting a club, getting everyone pulling in the same direction, working together and creating something special as one. That's completely overlooked by the football purists who want modern football, the clipboard coaches, and it's often their downfall. It's also overlooked by fans who don't like Warnock's football, but it won't be by Bluebirds. They would have put up with almost anything on the pitch in exchange for what Warnock has done behind the scenes. For it to become the community's Cardiff City and for smiles to return, for the doors to supporters to reopen. The Premier League is a grand old reward, but it's not the only way Cardiff have won under Warnock.

The big victory under the 69-year-old, however, is of course promotion to the Premier League and the big jackpot of around £200m that comes with it. The footballing side of this promotion really is a miracle. However, it can be explained simply by looking at that killer team spirit Cardiff possessed during the season, their willingness to go to war for each other, and that comes from the manager. Players must be willing to do anything to win for their manager and if they're not, it becomes quickly apparent. Warnock does that by building his squad based on honesty. If he doesn't like the look of a player, then he will tell them in no uncertain terms. That may sound harsh to us non-footballing folk, but as a footballer you appreciate it. Footballers are so often messed around by clubs and managers that when someone tells them straight up that you're not in that person's plans, it's a breath of fresh air. It means they have been unsuccessful in proving themself but at least they know where they are.

Anthony Pilkington was one of the men told he would be sold during the summer of 2017, but with reasonably large wages, there were no takers. Still, he got his head down and pitched in where he could, even if opportunities were few and far between. He was still happy to play for Warnock and that's because the boss was honest with him. It's also because he wasn't excluded by his team-mates. In this group, nobody gets left behind, no matter how small or big their contribution is. Even Pilkington, who featured in just eight league games from a possible 46, was swept up in celebration when he scores at Sheffield, was still a huge part of the promotion festivities, and even hosted a barbecue for his team-mates after they crossed the line. Even Lee Tomlin, who seemingly didn't quite fit in, continued to text Warnock until the end of the season, wishing his team-mates luck throughout. It truly is a rare case of having no bad apples, no disruptions to a perfect dressing room.

This group is like a family, and clearly, that's worth something. Evidently, it can even outweigh millions of pounds' worth of talent. That's how Warnock gets around the money-spinning, but even he admitted the special atmosphere among the squad is something he hasn't seen before. He said, 'We keep getting kicked in the teeth and we keep bouncing back up, and that's surprising a lot of people. It doesn't surprise me though, because of the quality of the dressing room – it's as good as I've ever had.'

The team spirit is built on characters and there are several leaders among the group, several captains who all want to be part of the club. That was proven when Sean Morrison and Joe Bennett had the chance to join Sheffield Wednesday and Fulham respectively in 2017. Both were offered improved contracts by the interested clubs, and both would have been allowed to leave. Neither did. Both felt 'something special' was going to happen at Cardiff and they wanted to help make that come true. It only further epitomises the spirit in that dressing room, and why these players are also so loved by supporters.

Beyond the flawless team spirit, Warnock is a man-motivator better than any other and he knows how to get the best out of his players. Step forward Kenneth Zohore as prime example number one. A once-hopeless player who looked as though he would never be good enough for League 1 football, let alone the Championship. Then Warnock arrived, throws him on at home to Wolves at half-time and told him he had 45 minutes to save his Cardiff career. Zohore shines and never looks back, completely changing his outlook on the game and transforming from a lazy striker to one who does more miles than most of his striking colleagues in the league.

Fast forward a few months and Cardiff City are turning down offers of more than £10m for Zohore from Premier League club Brighton. Now he's a Premier League player anyway, but with the Bluebirds, and having starred in that superb front three. And he still hasn't got carried away, admitting Warnock may have saved his career. He revealed, 'He has been very good to me, he is the reason I am where I am today. He's been pushing me, telling me I can do things I didn't know I could, and you can see that now. I ran 10km the other day – I've never done that before in my life.'

Zohore isn't the only one, either, with Joe Ralls having his biggest opportunity since joining the club as a youngster under Warnock. He's been in, out or used as a utility by most, but Warnock has given him a prolonged run in the Bluebirds' midfield and he's flourished. Ralls has now proven himself as a solid player and fans are now disappointed if he's not present. Some turnaround in 12 months.

We've already mentioned it, but everyone has something to prove, and that's been so healthy in this race for promotion. There has been no pressure – why would there be? Nathaniel Mendez-Laing was playing in League 1 during the previous season, as was Neil Etheridge, and they've already come further than they expected. Now they are Premier League players. They've been managed to perfection by Warnock, kept on the ground by the leaders in the squad, and it has paid off perfectly.

Warnock now has that record-breaking eighth promotion, which would surely rank as his greatest. He revealed, 'Given the state of this club when I came in, and what had gone on, this has to be the best job I've ever done in my life in football. This is the best achievement – if you only knew what I have to deal with off the field.'

His work was also recognised when he was voted EFL Championship Manager of the Year by his fellow managers, even outdoing Nuno Espirito Santo, who he eventually made up with following Wolves' title win.

Cardiff owe a great deal to Warnock for this promotion and not a single fan would deny that. He's shaped the club to his own liking and it happens to be the same shape that the supporters adore. This club has become more united than even before the rebrand and it's certainly closer to its fans. Warnock has done things his way, as he always does. He, like no Cardiff manager before him, has got Tan doing what he wants, instead of the other way around. Tan wouldn't dare tell Warnock what to do, but that's no insult to the owner. It's out of pure respect. Tan is Warnock's boss, he will always have the final say, but he fully trusts his manager. It's a perfect working relationship. They listen to each other and work out the best path. Tan is a business man, he's no football expert, and it's the opposite for Warnock. On paper, you would think it could never work, but it does and that's based on trust. Doing good by each other and achieving results. Whether that will continue in the Premier League, we will see. However, it's worked so far and it's a breath of fresh air.

Warnock now takes Cardiff into the Premier League and there's no better man to do it. He's won the supporters' trust and become a cult hero in these parts, for his work on and off the field.

Warnock has been a revolutionary for the club. He has been a catalyst for change for the sake of the football club he manages, and you can't overstate the importance of that. Whether you believe in fate like Warnock or not, you just have to admit, Cardiff and he are a match made in heaven, and the proof is in promotion.

What the future holds

IF THERE'S one thing you have learned from this up-and-down, topsy-turvy, roller-coaster adventure, it is that Cardiff City Football Club is completely unpredictable. So it seems crazy to predict what the future holds. However, perhaps that is the biggest silver lining of the lot. Perhaps that, Premier League aside, is the true happy ending to this story.

From when we began back in 2008, and even way before that, there was no security. Everything balanced on a knife edge. It could be glory or it could be disaster, and that was the life of the Bluebirds for so long. Now, for the first time in a very long time, the future feels more predictable. Now, more than ever, supporters will feel reassured that this club can handle whatever is thrown at it. Perhaps that's through surviving the worst, perhaps is through mastering the consequences of failure. However, now, it feels like Cardiff are in a safe place. Things can change very quickly in football, and you're never far away from the edge of a cliff, but still it feels like the worst won't happen.

The Premier League now awaits Cardiff for the second time and this time it feels right. The challenge that awaits Neil Warnock and his men is gigantic, and it would be yet another miracle if they stayed up with the smallest budget in the league. Still, there remains a belief that they can do it. Even if they don't, so what? They didn't expect to be here in the first place, as Warnock has already alluded to. He told the club's official website, 'Which Cardiff fans thought we would be looking forward to having the fixture list for the Premier League season? I don't think anybody would have thought that. By all means you can look at it with a bit of trepidation, but I don't see it like that. It's a bonus season so let's enjoy it. With the fans like we showed at the end of the season and the noise they make down here, there's no reason why we don't fill this place and get the right results so I'm really looking forward to it.'

So much work has been ploughed into this project in recent years from so many people, and the culmination of that work is that the club has been significantly repaired, so much so that it's now going beyond what it once was. Now it feels much closer to the supporters than it was even ten years ago, even before all the chaos in recent years. Success inevitably helps, but this has become the community's club again and that goes beyond the city of Cardiff. It involves people in the Valleys, the Vale of Glamorgan, Newport and many who travel to games from afar to see their beloved Bluebirds. This club needs to belong to those people for them to feel a sense of community, and it now feels that way.

It now feels as though the supporters have a big say. They feel like their support matters and that is crucial. It has to count for something. These fans pay thousands of pounds out of their hard-earned money, and that cannot be discounted. Supporters are by far the most important part of this sport we all love. They're exploited so much these days and are a tragic casualty of the money-dominated world we live in. Hopefully, clubs will start to see their value. The supporters are what set football apart from any other sport, and they must be rewarded for their never-ending loyalty. Cardiff have taken significant strides in doing that in recent years and they are reaping the rewards. Their supporters have played a huge part in this promotion and now, it seems, the club and its fans are eager to share the experience of the Premier League together.

Even Vincent Tan is in a better place than ever with fans, and that relationship simply had to be improved for the sake of the club. It appeared as though the two had gone down a road upon which they could never return, but against all odds things have improved rapidly. If there is something we have learned in football in the last 20 years or so, it's that it never ends well when supporters and their owner don't get on. Prime examples include Blackpool and Coventry City. It is now more important than ever, with all the money in the game and how it can dictate a football club's very existence, that fans and owner need to appreciate the part they both play.

There doesn't have to be a love for each other, which is quite rare these days – to have a revered owner who is one of the fans. However, there needs to be a common goal, a desire for the club to succeed, and that seems to be happening for the first time in a long while. Fans and Tan seem to be willing to understand each other now, and that can only benefit the football club in the future.

WalesOnline digital sports writer Ian Mitchelmore offers insight. He says, 'It's understandable why the relationship between Tan and supporters became so toxic, with the rebrand alienating so many fans. But following the club's promotion back into the Premier League, Tan was quick to admit the change of kit colour was a mistake, and crucially, one he wouldn't make again. While he is clearly doing his best to build bridges, Neil Warnock has unquestionably played a major part in how many fans now see Tan.

'The Yorkshireman has galvanised the club from top to bottom, and by all accounts has a terrific relationship with the men at the top, be it with Tan, Mehmet Dalman or Ken Choo. Warnock clearly appreciated the faith the owners showed in him when he was named as Paul Trollope's successor in October 2016, and he's rewarded them with a stunning promotion, and one that was achieved against all odds. But he's done so with – not only the fanbase and his players – the backing of those in the boardroom.

'There's been a greater trust in the manager from those at the top, because they know they have a man at the helm who is capable of getting the club to where they want to be. Whatever success comes on the pitch, under Warnock or even further into the future, some supporters will never forgive Tan for the mistakes he made. But it seems time has once again proven to be a healer, and with Tan showing he isn't too stubborn to hold his hands up and concede his regrets over the rebrand, you feel that fans are willing to move on and hopefully keep the club united from top to bottom to help ensure the current period of success continues for as long as possible.'

In terms of finances, 'the work required to maintain the club's financial viability remains great,' according to Cardiff City Supporters' Trust chair Keith Morgan. However, the promotion to the Premier League will have significantly helped that. It's estimated a place in the top flight is worth a minimum of £100m, and the Bluebirds will benefit from that this season. If they can stay there they will continue to benefit significantly from the highly lucrative television deals the Premier League possesses. So, in short, the finances are in an okay place. There are no dangerous debts surrounding the club like in previous years. And while there's significant work to be done, there has been progress.

The Bluebirds are not in a position to spend big. They will have to plot their moves carefully, ensuring the players they sign possess sell-on value in case of a relegation back to the Championship. Keith Morgan believes Cardiff should look to follow the model of Burnley. The Clarets spent around 60 per cent of their budget on wages in their first season back in the Premier League, allowing them to make a profit despite relegation. They then went on to gain an immediate promotion back, finishing seventh in their most recent season at the top level. Failure to go up could have caused Cardiff some problems, there's no doubt about that, with significant losses in recent years and with parachute payments coming to an end. However, elevation will now provide a timely boost. From here, it's just about learning from the mistakes of the past and treading carefully to plan for the future, and not just for their first season back in the top flight.

On the pitch, the Bluebirds have a great challenge on their hands to survive in the Premier League. They're not going to spend as much as many, or perhaps any, of their rivals, and they already have a limited squad, on paper. However, this group has already proved so many people wrong. They have defied the odds to secure promotion and their desire to succeed will not end there.

Warnock wants to preserve that unique, golden team spirit going into next season, and quite frankly he will have to for the Bluebirds to stand a chance. They simply don't possess the spending power to give themselves a huge chance in terms of quality. So they must look to do it through sheer desire, as they did in 2017/18. They'll have glimpses of quality through the squad and the early pre-season signing of Josh Murphy, for example, will help add to that. But for the main part, Warnock will need to concentrate on keeping together that fantastic team spirit. They will have to want it more than the teams they play and quite often in football, that can be enough.

It was probably enough this season in what was a poor Premier League campaign on the whole. West Brom, Stoke City and Swansea City were relegated – meaning there'll be no Premier League derby with the big rivals in 2018/19 – and the standard as a whole was poor, Manchester City aside.

That will surely change and Cardiff will have to pull out all the stops to survive. However, as Warnock says, this will be a bonus season for the Bluebirds, and with that underdog mentality, they can go a long way. Journalist Dom Booth gives his verdict on Cardiff's chances in the Premier League. He says, 'You could say promotion has come too soon for this group of players as individuals. But not for Warnock or his brand of man management: he wants another crack at the Premier League after a series of disappointments in the top flight with various clubs, and will feel he can succeed at Cardiff. No doubt the Yorkshireman holds the key to the future and if he can continue in the Premier League where he left off in the Championship, Cardiff are genuine contenders to stay up – and most fans (in the Welsh capital) would agree.

'Whatever happens, Warnock needs to stay around because he's come to define the club and in truth they'd be lost without him. I also believe lessons have been learned in the boardroom from the disaster that was 2013/14, Malky Mackay, Ole Gunnar Solskjaer and all the rest of it. Cardiff won't spend a ridiculous amount, they won't change the philosophy that's served them well and they'll continue to play the part of underdogs backed into a corner. Personally, I think whatever happens in the Premier League, the club will be in a better place than it was two or three years ago.'

They should certainly do better than their last venture to the top flight, when they finished bottom and were relegated without much of a fight. Even if they do go down, you will see this squad battle tooth and nail until the death, and that's all supporters can ask. They just want to see passion and desire and that's why this squad and management team fits so well. They do passion and desire better than most and the fans adore it. 'You've just got to enjoy it,' as Warnock so often says, and these supporters certainly will.

Whatever the future holds, whatever it throws at this football club, fans and everyone else involved can take comfort in knowing that it can't be any worse than before. This club has been through them mill and experienced everything from the incredible to the inconceivable. They've survived all that and it has given them a sort of protection, a thicker skin.

However, it now feels like the worst is in the past. It now feels as though their time to shine in the light has arrived. They have been here before, but not in the right way, there were far too many barriers preventing supporters from enjoying and embracing the fruits of their team's labour. Now, in blue and armed with a togetherness that this football club has cultivated, they can enjoy it. The Bluebirds can embrace it, and they deserve to.

It has been a chaotic decade, but important lessons have been learned. There's no predicting what the future holds but it now feels that not only are Cardiff ready for success, but they are ready to deal with failure. That's the silver lining from all these trials and tribulations, all these ups and downs. It means a bright future may be awaiting the Bluebirds as they embark upon their return to the promised land.

Bibliography

FA Cup final: Cardiff manager Dave Jones disappointed after
defeat to Portsmouth – By Jim White (*The Telegraphy*)
https://www.telegraph.co.uk/sport/columnists/jimwhite/2300830/
FA-Cup-final-Cardiff-manager-Dave-Jones-disappointed-after-
defeat-to-Portsmouth.html
Dave Jones: 'I'd rather have been accused of murder' – By Nick
Szczepanik (*The Independent*)
https://www.independent.co.uk/news/people/profiles/dave-jones-
id-rather-have-been-accused-of-murder-2376297.html
Sheff Wed 1-0 Cardiff (BBC)
http://news.bbc.co.uk/sport1/hi/football/eng_div_1/8015132.stm
Blackpool seal Premier League place after enthralling win over
Cardiff – By Jamie Jackson (*The Guardian*)
https://www.theguardian.com/football/2010/may/22/blackpool-
cardiff-play-off-championship
The day Cardiff City hearts were broken by Blackpool...The
story of the Bluebirds' 2010 play-off final horror told by
those who were there – By Gareth Rodgers (WalesOnline)
https://www.walesonline.co.uk/sport/football/football-news/day-
cardiff-city-hearts-were-9265123
Cardiff City captain Mark Hudson aims to put play-off pain
out of his mind against Ian Holloway's Crystal Palace – By
Graham Clutton (*The Telegraph*)
https://www.telegraph.co.uk/sport/football/teams/cardiff-
city/9765261/Cardiff-City-captain-Mark-Hudson-aims-to-put-

play-off-pain-out-of-his-mind-against-Ian-Holloways-Crystal-Palace.html

Michael Chopra: What really happened at Cardiff City (WalesOnline)

https://www.walesonline.co.uk/sport/football/football-news/michael-chopra-what-really-happened-1829990

The end of a reign of terror – By Mike Sullivan and Alex Peake (*The Sun*)

https://www.thesun.co.uk/archives/news/452934/the-end-of-a-reign-of-terror/

Michael Chopra: I left Cardiff City to pay off my gambling debts (WalesOnline)

https://www.walesonline.co.uk/sport/football/football-news/michael-chopra-left-cardiff-city-6351360

Jon Parkin's Cardiff City revelations: Chopra and Bothroyd got away with murder... and Malky Mackay 'treated me like rubbish' – By Steve Tucker (WalesOnline – Original interview by Built On Sloper Road podcast)

https://www.walesonline.co.uk/sport/football/football-news/jon-parkins-cardiff-city-revelations-9597869

Cardiff City 0 Reading 3; agg 0-3: match report – By Graham Clutton (*The Telegraph*)

https://www.telegraph.co.uk/sport/football/competitions/championship/8518889/Cardiff-City-0-Reading-3-agg-0-3-match-report.html

The Anthony Gerrard Cardiff City interview: My tearful, ferocious row with Malky Mackay on morning of Carling Cup final – By Jon Doel (WalesOnline – Original interview by Built On Sloper Road podcast)

https://www.walesonline.co.uk/sport/football/football-news/anthony-gerrard-cardiff-city-interview-9673175

Former Cardiff City striker Jon Parkin lifts the lid on his clash with Craig Bellamy and Malky Mackay's 'hatred' of him – By Jamie Kemble (WalesOnline)

https://www.walesonline.co.uk/sport/football/football-news/
former-cardiff-city-striker-jon-14347583
**Malky Mackay proud of Cardiff despite Carling Cup final loss
(BBC)**
https://www.bbc.co.uk/sport/football/17174391
**Johnson, Scott, *Cardiff City: Rebranded* (Sussex: Pitch
Publishing, 2016)**
**Cardiff City's promotion to the Premier League after 0-0 draw
with Charlton sparks jubilation and relief – By Graham
Clutton (*The Telegraph*)**
https://www.telegraph.co.uk/sport/football/teams/cardiff-
city/9999886/Cardiff-Citys-promotion-to-the-Premier-
League-after-0-0-draw-with-Charlton-sparks-jubilation-and-
relief.html
**'We've finally done it' – Cardiff celebrate promotion to Premier
League – By Stuart James (*The Guardian*)**
https://www.theguardian.com/football/2013/apr/17/cardiff-
celebrate-promotion-premier-league
**Cardiff owner Vincent Tan: Malky Mackay was LUCKY to get
job and I'll leave if the fans p*** me off – By Paul Gorst (The
Irish Mirror)**
https://www.irishmirror.ie/sport/soccer/soccer-news/cardiff-
owner-vincent-tan-malky-3191210
Mackay: I won't quit Cardiff (*The Express*)
https://www.express.co.uk/sport/football/449951/Mackay-I-won-t-
quit-Cardiff
**'Worst moment' of Ole Gunnar Solskjaer's career as Cardiff
City go down – By Agence France-Presse (*The National*)**
https://www.thenational.ae/sport/worst-moment-of-ole-
gunnar-solskjaer-s-career-as-cardiff-city-go-down-
1.248754?videoId=5606786929001
**The Mark Hudson farewell interview: Cardiff City's promotion-
winning skipper issues an explosive parting shot – By Steve
Tucker (WalesOnline)**

https://www.walesonline.co.uk/sport/football/football-news/
cardiff-citys-departing-captain-mark-7727793

Danny Gabbidon's fascinating insight into what life at Cardiff
City is really like – By Steve Tucker (WalesOnline)
https://www.walesonline.co.uk/sport/football/football-news/
danny-gabbidons-fascinating-insight-what-11005435

Ole Gunnar Solskjaer believes the pain of relegation can help
Cardiff City to bounce back to the Premier League – By
Jonathan Liew (*The Telegraph*)
https://www.telegraph.co.uk/sport/football/teams/cardiff-
city/11020152/Ole-Gunnar-Solskjaer-believes-the-pain-of-
relegation-can-help-Cardiff-City-to-bounce-back-to-the-
Premier-League.html

4 heroic Cardiff City captains tell Vincent Tan why he should
return their beloved club's kit to blue and white – By Terry
Phillips (WalesOnline)
https://www.walesonline.co.uk/sport/football/football-news/
cardiff-city-captains-tell-vincent-7092244

Defiant Cardiff City owner Vincent Tan says club will remain
red as he dismisses fans' protest plans – By Jon Doel
(WalesOnline)
https://www.walesonline.co.uk/sport/football/football-news/
defiant-cardiff-city-owner-vincent-8345293

Watch: The moment Cardiff City announced they were
returning to blue ... and fans' emotional reactions – Simon
Gaskell (WalesOnline)
https://www.walesonline.co.uk/sport/football/football-news/
watch-moment-cardiff-city-announced-8414982

Cardiff City settle historic Langston debt as club reaches
out of court agreement – By Steve Tucker and Sion Barry
(WalesOnline)
https://www.walesonline.co.uk/sport/football/football-news/
cardiff-city-settle-historic-langston-10819251

Cardiff City's new crest: What ex-player, diehard fan and our football writers make of new Bluebirds' badge – By Simon Gaskell (WalesOnline)
https://www.walesonline.co.uk/sport/football/football-news/cardiff-citys-new-crest-what-8800591

Cardiff City 'not shopping at Harrods now' – Russell Slade – By Rob Phillips (BBC)
https://www.bbc.co.uk/sport/football/30947794

Emotional Russell Slade speaks out after losing Cardiff City manager's job: 'It's been difficult but I'm not bitter and twisted' – By Steve Tucker (WalesOnline)
https://www.walesonline.co.uk/sport/football/football-news/emotional-russell-slade-speaks-out-11299471

Cardiff City move manager Russell Slade to new role (BBC)
https://www.bbc.co.uk/sport/football/36231307

Ken Choo says Russell Slade failed as Cardiff City manager and reveals shortlist already drawn up for new boss – By Steve Tucker (WalesOnline)
https://www.walesonline.co.uk/sport/football/football-news/ken-choo-says-russell-slade-11300291

CEO And Media Exchange Blows In 'Failure' Row – (Cardiff City Mad)
http://www.cardiffcity-mad.co.uk/news/tmnw/ceo_and_media_exchange_blows_in_failure_row_887330/index.shtml

Cardiff name Paul Trollope as new manager to replace Russell Slade – By PA (*The Guardian*)
https://www.theguardian.com/football/2016/may/18/paul-trollope-cardiff-new-manager

Cardiff City: Mehmet Dalman denies coach Paul Trollope is 'cheap option' (BBC)
https://www.bbc.co.uk/sport/football/36325609

Cardiff City sack Paul Trollope as head coach (BBC)
https://www.bbc.co.uk/sport/football/37552009

NEIL WARNOCK APPOINTED AS NEW CITY MANAGER (Cardiff City FC)
https://www.cardiffcityfc.co.uk/news/2016/october/neil-warnock-appointed-as-new-city-manager/

Neil Warnock's first interview as Cardiff City manager: 'Bluebirds fans are my type of crowd' – By Dominic Booth (WalesOnline)
https://www.walesonline.co.uk/sport/football/football-news/neil-warnocks-first-interview-cardiff-11983126

Neil Warnock on his wife's cancer treatment and why he has come out of retirement for a SEVENTH time to take charge of Cardiff: 'Sharon's ill – but she wanted me out from under her feet!' – by Riath Al-Samarrai (*Daily Mail*)
http://www.dailymail.co.uk/sport/football/article-4010732/Neil-Warnock-wife-s-cancer-treatment-come-retirement-SEVENTH-time-charge-Cardiff-Sharon-s-ill-wanted-feet.html

When Blakey met Neil Warnock: 60 compelling minutes with the Cardiff City boss as he opens up on everything – By Nathan Blake, Paul Abbandonato, Dom Booth (WalesOnline)
https://www.walesonline.co.uk/sport/football/football-news/blakey-met-neil-warnock-60-14455549

Peter Whittingham: Blackburn midfielder regrets no Cardiff City fans farewell (BBC)
https://www.bbc.co.uk/sport/football/40737849

Report – Burton Albion 0-1 Cardiff City (BBC)
https://www.bbc.co.uk/sport/football/40760771

Derby vs Cardiff postponement fallout continues as police distance themselves from decision and Rams issue new statement – By Mike Walters and Alex Richards (*The Mirror*)
https://www.mirror.co.uk/sport/football/news/derby-vs-cardiff-postponement-fallout-12215080

Gary Rowett: 'I did not realise Warnock was a health and safety inspector' (BBC)
https://www.bbc.co.uk/sport/football/43554505

Everything Neil Warnock said after Cardiff City moved
back ahead of Fulham with victory over Hull – By Ian
Mitchelmore (WalesOnline)
https://www.walesonline.co.uk/sport/football/football-news/
cardiff-city-hull-neil-warnock-14590336

The Vincent Tan Premier League interview: Cardiff City
owner outlines Bluebirds' plans for the top flight – By Paul
Abbandonato (WalesOnline)
https://www.walesonline.co.uk/sport/football/vincent-tan-
premier-league-interview-14623591

New Cardiff boss Neil Warnock credits his wife's selflessness
for his return to management – By Colin Mafham (*The
Express*)
https://www.express.co.uk/sport/football/719028/Cardiff-City-
Sharon-Warnock-debt-of-gratitude-Neil-Warnock-Premier-
League-promotion

Kenneth Zohore: 'Neil Warnock is why I am where I am today'
(BBC)
https://www.bbc.co.uk/sport/football/43421224

Neil Warnock: Cardiff promotion my greatest achievement
(Sky Sports)
http://www.skysports.com/football/news/11704/11361941/neil-
warnock-cardiff-promotion-my-greatest-achievement